ADMINISTRATIVE THEORY AND
PUBLIC ADMINISTRATION

Politics

Editor

PROFESSOR W. A. ROBSON
B.SC(ECON), PH.D, LL.M
*Professor Emeritus of Public Administration
in the University of London*

ADMINISTRATIVE THEORY
AND PUBLIC
ADMINISTRATION

R. J. S. Baker

Head of the Unit for Management in
Public Services, Sheffield Polytechnic

HUTCHINSON UNIVERSITY LIBRARY

LONDON

HUTCHINSON & CO (*Publishers*) **LTD**
3 Fitzroy Square, London W1

London Melbourne Sydney Auckland
Wellington Johannesburg Cape Town
and agencies throughout the world

First published 1972

*This book has been set in Times type, printed in Great Britain
on smooth wove paper by Anchor Press, and
bound by Wm. Brendon, both of Tiptree, Essex*

ISBN 0 09 110680 x (cased)
0 09 110681 8 (paper)

CONTENTS

Acknowledgments   7

Preface   9

Introduction: Public administration in its context   11

PART ONE: GENERAL THEORIES OF ORGANISATION   19

1 Classical organisation theory   21

2 'Human relations' and related theories   41

3 Organic and systems theories   64

PART TWO: THE NATURE OF PUBLIC
ADMINISTRATION IN BRITAIN   79

4 Authority, environment and function   81

5 Tasks (I): Control, decision-making and coordination   92

6 Tasks (II): Personnel management and general planning   112

7 Processes   128

8 Forms and structures of Government Departments   141

9 Forms and structures of some other public bodies   165

Conclusions: Towards a theory of public administration   185

Select reading list   197

Index   203

ACKNOWLEDGMENTS

Acknowledgments are due to the following for the use of copyright material; Oxford University Press, from *Government and Parliament* by Herbert Morrison and *From Max Weber*, Eds. Hans Gerth and C. Wright Mills; The Clarendon Press, from *Industrial Organisation: Theory and Practice* by Joan Woodward and *The Higher Civil Service of Great Britain* by A. H. Hanson; Fontana Paperbacks, from *Governing Britain* by A. H. Hanson and Malcolm Waller; University of Illinois Press, from *The Symbolic Uses of Politics* by Murray Edelman; Methuen and Company Ltd, from *The Administrative Process in Britain* by R. G. S. Brown, and *The Art of the Soluble* by P. B. Medawar; Tavistock Publications Ltd, from *The Management of Innovation* by T. Burns and G. M. Stalker; Chapman and Hall Ltd and Basic Books, Inc., Publishers, New York, from *The Art of Judgement* by Sir Geoffrey Vickers; Curtis Brown Ltd, from *Eros and Civilisation* by H. Marcuse; Elspeth Cochrane, from *A Sort of Traitors* by Nigel Balchin; Victor Gollancz Ltd, from *Decision in Government* by Jeremy Bray; George Allen and Unwin Ltd and the University of Toronto Press, from *Nationalised Industry and Public Ownership* by W. A. Robson; *The Guardian*, from an article by the City Editor, 31 March 1970; Gerald Duckworth & Co Ltd, from *The Living Brain* by W. Grey Walter.

PREFACE

This book originated with Professor Robson's invitation and encouragement to write it and I wish first to thank him warmly for this and for the immense amount of trouble he has taken in offering comment and criticism during the various stages when it was taking shape.

Some of the key ideas in the book were first developed in my article on 'Organisation Theory and the Public Sector' in the *Journal of Management Studies* of February 1969. I was, and remain, most grateful to the *Journal*'s editor, Professor Tom Lupton of the Manchester Business School, for his advice and help in developing these ideas into their first publishable form.

My next thanks would have been to the Post Office Headquarters, where I was an Assistant Secretary (1951 to 1971), for agreeing to its publication. As, however, I have now left their employment for an academic post, such agreement is no longer necessary; but I am grateful that it was given so readily (on the normal understanding that I wrote in a personal capacity only). I also owe more than I can say to them as a great collection of friends and colleagues and as a dynamic and changing working environment within which I have, over the past thirty-four years, learnt the larger part of what I know about public administration.

It will probably be some time before a comprehensive work on the theory of contemporary British public administration and its processes can be written. The present book is only a series of brief exploratory surveys over a few parts of the vast field. Yet it does claim to raise some important questions about the relevance of general administrative theories to concrete administrative situations. Although it cites American as well as British theoretical literature, and two major works from France and Germany, its factual evidence is confined to Britain. Nevertheless, I venture to hope that, as I have thus made its limitations explicit, some readers overseas may find it of interest, at least for comparison and contrast. There are, moreover, a good many countries which share some of the characteristics of the British administrative environment, and others which have somewhat similar institutions in very different environments.

I cannot name nor even remember all the people from whom I derived the information and ideas which have found their way into these pages; but in addition to Professor Robson I would like to thank Professor J. F. Morris of the Manchester Business School, Professor Maurice Kogan of Brunel University, Sir William Harris, Judge Jean Graham Hall, Dr N. F. Coghill, Mr M. B. Brodie of the Administrative Staff College and my son, Mr Peter F. Baker, for specific advice, information and criticism. Naturally, however, no one but myself can bear any responsibility for opinions which I have expressed nor for the accuracy or adequacy of any of my information.

I am grateful to my wife and family for much tolerance and stimulation, and specifically to my daughters, Isobel and Alison, for practical help in the preparation of the script.

London　　　　　　　　　　　　　　　　R. J. S. BAKER
September 1971

INTRODUCTION

PUBLIC ADMINISTRATION IN ITS CONTEXT

Public administration—why it is important

Administration, particularly public administration and public administrators, are not, it must be admitted, generally loved. Yet
administration is a job which one can love doing. It can be fun. To
say this is not to be cynical or to refer to the occasional warped
personality who can enjoy getting other people into tangles. The
real fun is in untangling tangles, reconciling the irreconcilable, getting
useful and worthwhile things done, and getting people to cooperate.
But this is how, at best, it feels from the inside. To those outside it,
whether they are manual workers in some big industry or public
service, or scientists in a research institution, doctors in a hospital,
'the Administration' can often be just 'They', the impersonal, in-
comprehensible, intangible obstacle to everything one wants to get
or to do. Because it deals with things that are large and multifarious
and complicated, it can easily become a mystery. Then the final
stage is for it to become a bogus science, and barriers go up in
people's minds, and they feel that it is impossible to understand, or
that they do not want to understand it. Yet if it is a necessary human
activity it should be humane and reasonable. If it is to serve large
numbers of people it can and must be made acceptable to large
numbers of people. It should *involve* them.

Data mainly British

Although this is a book of theory rather than comprehensive description we must develop our theory with a body of factual material.
We will take this material largely from Britain, indeed the greater
part from contemporary Britain, set against its history in the last two
or three generations. We shall also pay some attention to its earlier

history and draw occasional comparisons with other countries,
simply to emphasise the limitations of our evidence. It is hoped this
book may be of some interest or value to readers overseas, but this is
only possible if it is clearly understood what its limitations are.

Definition of 'public'

Let us begin by some definition of our terms. By 'public' we mean
first any category of British organisation which was publicly owned
in 1971. We can extend this definition to include any institutions or
agencies which are run, or directly or indirectly owned or primarily
financed, by central or local government, with some slight extensions
covering some other forms of ownership by or in the name of the
whole community. We then find in this category all government
departments, the administrative organisation of the courts of law,
local authorities and other publicly owned corporations, notably
those set up to run the nationalised industries, and other concerns
of national or regional scope. The public corporations include some
which are almost Government Departments like the Forestry Commission, and some which are very far removed from the normal
governmental structure, such as the Arts Council. To keep our
subject manageable, rather than within strict logic, we exclude the
armed forces, colleges and schools as well as Universities. We also
exclude purely or largely voluntary or sectional bodies, however
venerable, like the churches. There are, however, a group of joint
or mixed consultative and advisory bodies such as the National
Economic Development Council, the University Grants Committee
and other boards, commissions and committees whose work is essentially a public function, even though some of their members are
nominated to represent sectional or independent interests. We cannot describe or discuss every category of public institution individually; but this is the general scope of our study.

The meaning of 'administration'

The word 'administration' is much more difficult to define than
'public'. It is really beyond the scope of any dictionary to give the
full flavour of its meaning in its various contemporary contexts. It
is certainly not quite synonymous with 'management', although one
might get this impression from plodding through the New Oxford
Dictionary's meticulous histories of these two words since the end of
the Middle Ages. The derivation of 'manage' from any other language does not seem entirely clear, although it has an echo of
'ménage'—suggesting a household or any physical collection of
things, people and/or animals, which can be subject to some sort of
rudimentary control. 'Administration' has a Latin parent adminis-

trare which can mean 'assist' as well as 'direct'. 'Administer' in various contexts seems to have affinities with 'minister', which can mean 'serve' or 'servant'. Some of the early meanings of both 'manage' and 'administer' can be summarised as 'looking after things' or 'taking charge of' and one simple modern definition of both would be 'getting things done'. Yet 'administration' has a rather more subtle and more extended series of meanings. It is more usually found in the public sector than the private and, in general, carries an implication, not of ultimate sovereign control, but of directing and coordinating things on behalf of other people or authorities. It is often connected with some notion of service.

Distinction from management

The term 'management' usually carries a rather different flavour. There are a variety of 'styles of management', some very sophisticated and some even 'permissive'; but as most commonly used, 'management' carries rather more than a suggestion of authoritarianism. A great deal of the more popular use of the word tends to reflect the authoritarian management theories of the last generation which we shall describe in Chapter 1. Management can sometimes be referred to in an almost mystical sense as an abstraction—'the prerogatives of management' and so on—and this can get mixed up with the notions of the 'managerial revolution'. On the other hand good management, in the sense of a practical process of getting things done efficiently, is a common need of both the public and the private sectors and indeed all types of organisation. Yet in coordinating complex situations where there is no one single criterion of efficiency, 'administration' is probably a more appropriate word than 'management'. It is also slightly more all-embracing, in that it includes a lot of preparatory and supportive work for higher-level decision-making, and various things which we shall describe below as the 'Secretarial process'.*

Distinction from policy

To clarify further the meaning of 'administration' we need to consider its distinction, not only from 'management', but from policy in the political sense. Certainly administrative theory can be distinguished from political theory, as a part to be distinguished from a whole. The distinction is not hard and fast nor easy to draw. *Politics* is concerned, throughout the sphere of Government, with the whole business of deciding what to do and getting it done. *Policy* is decision as to what to do: *administration* is getting it done. Yet, as we shall see, administration is also concerned with serving and assisting the

* See pp. 128–30.

policy-making process. Administration is concerned with forms and structures, functions, tasks and processes in public affairs. These are means not ends, although they can greatly influence ends. Hence they form part of the larger subject of political theory or the theory of Government. Moreover all this is a distinction of functions, and there is often an intermingling in the allocation of functions between persons. Political people, Government Ministers, M.P.s, and councillors, are not continuously occupied in making policy. They all have to do a lot of things which are more properly described as administration. Moreover, their officials are sometimes much involved in policy-making, Hence it is not strictly true to say that politics is what politicians do and administration is what officials do. Politics is what politicians do as a distinct group of persons and are particularly there for: administration is what officials as such are primarily there for and what is mainly done by them.

Yet it is essential to emphasise the fundamental distinction between administration and policy, despite the ways in which the functions and the people who perform them are intermingled in contemporary Britain. If the distinction is not clearly maintained, the literature of political theory will not be able to deal adequately with certain moral and philosophical questions, which are outside the sphere of administrative theory, but with which political theory ought to be essentially concerned. The utter inadequacy and fallacy of a purely administrative view of Government—'Whate'er is best administered is best'—has been demonstrated with terrifying clarity in such institutions as Hitler's gas-chambers, which may well have been almost perfect organisations from the purely administrative point of view. This is the logical conclusion of the kind of thinking which would hand over essentially political decisions to 'independent' experts.

The importance of theory

One could theorise a lot about what 'theory' means, but we will not do so here. We will simply make a brief comment starting with the linguistic derivation of the word and its meaning as first used in English—'a viewing'*—taking a general look at a subject. It has the implication of the way something is looked at from a height, so that one sees the whole essential pattern, just as an aerial photograph enables one to distinguish underlying patterns in a landscape. In the natural sciences, according to Sir Peter Medawar, F.R.S. (a Nobel Prizewinner in medicine), an idea, a hypothesis, or a theory must precede rather than follow factual investigation. (In this he differs from some earlier writers who have philosophised about scientific

* Greek θεωρία (theoria)—a looking at, viewing, contemplation.

method.) He says a hypothesis must be a guide for the investigation and a means to enable it to make sense. It must, however, be abandoned or revised if not supported by the results of investigation. He quotes the physiologist, Claude Bernard:

A hypothesis is . . . the obligatory starting point of all experimental reasoning. Without it no investigation would be possible and one would learn nothing: one could only pile up barren observations. To experiment without a preconceived idea is to wander aimlessly. . . .
    When propounding a general theory in science the one thing one can be sure of is that in the strict sense such theories are mistaken. They are only partial and provisional truths which are necessary . . . to carry the investigation forward; they represent the current state of our understanding and are bound to be modified by the growth of science.

Medawar argues from his own experience, and observation of other scientists, that this is how in fact scientists do work, despite the fact that published scientific papers have to be written the other way round, describing investigation of facts first and the theory that explains them afterwards. Hence 'they not merely conceal but actively misrepresent the reasoning that goes into the work they describe'.[1]*

    The foregoing perhaps provides some of the justification for starting a study of public administration, even though it cannot be a science, with some general theory first and some facts afterwards. The facts cannot be fitted entirely into any general organisation theory. So it seems justifiable for the author to add some sketch of a framework of ideas of his own within which to arrange these facts—a framework beginning with environment and functions and leading on to tasks, processes, forms and structures. Yet it must be a very provisional sketch, even at its conclusion, something which other writers must modify and improve on.

Its academic status

The subject of public administration is at the moment rather sparsely provided with any kind of theory of its own, old or new. It still has a somewhat uncertain status in Britain, both as an academic discipline and as a basis for practical action. In the Universities it often tends to be a poor relation of the general theory of Government, artificially separated by faculty boundaries from the general theory of organisation and management, and too heavily concentrated on institutional structures. As a basis of training in the public services it tends to be an uncoordinated patchwork of mere descriptions of institutions and bits of often undigested doctrine of business management, some of it

* Superior figures in the text refer to end-of-chapter notes.

outdated. There are notable exceptions, but far too few. Public administration theory ought essentially to be a branch not only of political theory, but of general organisation theory. Yet most of the best thinking and research in organisation theory in Britain has been concentrated not only on the private sector but on manufacturing industry—which accounts for the work of under nine million out of the twenty-five million in the whole of the working population, while well over three million are in central and local Government and public utilities.[2] American organisation theory on the whole is much more all-embracing, but it has limited value for public administration in Britain and any other country whose political and social basis differs from the American model.

Plan of the book: varieties of organisation theory

The first part of this book will attempt to draw out the highlights of some of the most important work on the theory of organisation as a whole, mentioning particularly that which seems most relevant to the public sector. We shall start in Chapter 1 with some writers who have contributed directly or indirectly to what has in recent years come to be generally defined as the 'classical' school of organisation theory. This school is basically concerned with order and authority, rationality and legality, and with mechanisms. Then in Chapters 2 and 3 we shall refer to a selection of the many writers who, in the past four decades, have claimed to look at organisations organically, as things flexible, living and of many dimensions. Many of these writers are psychologists or sociologists. They have been concerned with organisations as collections of people. Others look at organisations, either biologically or mathematically or engineering-wise, as 'systems'. The approaches of all these various writers are much more flexible and subtle than the 'classical' models suggested. The two types of approach, the classical and the various others, have sometimes been described as 'mechanistic' and 'organic', although we shall suggest the distinction is not so sharp and simple as these words imply. We shall also suggest that both approaches are necessary for a full understanding of organisations. They have much in common with the recurring and complementary themes of order and freedom which run through the history of political thought.

Varieties of public administration

We will then go on to describe, again with highlights only, some important features of British public administration today. We will not start, as some descriptions do, with a catalogue of institutions and their structures and then go on to describe what they do and how they do it. We will go the other way round, looking first at the environment and functions of Government and other public bodies as they have developed historically in Britain, then the main types of administrative tasks which these functions involve, and then look closer at some of the more detailed processes. Only after completing this selective review will we attempt to look at institutional forms and structures.

As we go through these various aspects of public administration we shall find two series of features which echo the two types of organisation theory we have referred to. First are the elements of order, legality, authority, responsibility, direction and control, the making and enforcement of laws and rules and the elaboration of organisation structures. Secondly, we shall find elements in the nature of public administration, and its functions, tasks, processes and forms, which have a different character—flexible, subtle, multi-dimensional. We will find public administrators ordering, controlling, directing, adjudicating and defining; but we will also find them conciliating, negotiating, compromising and persuading. Moreover we will find public organisations where all authority and initiative does not flow in one direction from one or a few individuals at the top, but whose dynamic forces are widely diffused. This picture will, we hope, gradually emerge in Part Two as we sketch in the various details with only occasional specific reference to the general theories in Part One. Only in the concluding chapter of this book will we draw the threads together and try to suggest a model of free and flexible institutions operating within an outer framework of order. We shall find another guiding theme in the contrast between the 'optimising' and 'balancing' functions of administration as expounded by Sir Geoffrey Vickers.*

Administration not a science

Nowhere will we claim the title 'science' for the study of public administration. Science, properly so called, must surely always include not only the formulation of systematic hypotheses, but also linking them up with and testing them by controlled experiment and/or measured observation—experiments or observations which can be independently replicated and tested. All this is accepted as axiomatic in the natural sciences and no doubt in large areas of the social sciences. The subject matter of public administration, however, is in constant flux, sometimes observable only from within, sometimes only from a distance. It never stands still to allow replicated and controlled experiments and the amount of measured observation that can be carried out is limited. Theory is needed to make sense of what would otherwise be chaos; but much of it must necessarily be

* See pp. 69–72.

based on somewhat abstract reasoning, although allied with practical, but never comprehensive, observation and experience.

Relevance to larger issues

Despite these limitations public administration is a subject of the greatest importance. Perhaps one of the most important problems humanity now faces is whether the huge and elaborate organisations on which modern society appears to depend—governments, public corporations and multi-national privately owned corporations—can be made tolerable for human beings to live with. There seem to be various kinds of pessimists who would answer this question in the negative. Certainly many sensitive people looking at our vast public and private bureaucracies and technocracies seem to be so horrified by their size, rigidity and oppressiveness that they retreat into historical escapism or purely negative anarchism or nihilism. Those who would attempt a more constructive approach have a vast range of subjects to consider—technological, economic, political, cultural, psychological. But one of the things to be looked at most carefully is administration itself, its purposes, forms and processes. They may not prove to be so complicated or so frustrating if looked at steadily and without panic.

1. P. B. Medawar, F.R.S., in an essay on 'Hypothesis and Imagination' in *The Art of the Soluble*, pp. 151, 153. Methuen, 1967.
2. Central Statistical Office, June 1970. *Monthly Digest of Statistics*, pp. 7, 16–17, paras 14 and 15.

PART ONE
General Theories of Organisation

I

CLASSICAL ORGANISATION THEORY

Roman origins

Organisation theory proper is virtually a creation of the twentieth century. The organisation of people for work in large numbers is an activity at least as old, not only as the Pyramids, but as Stonehenge; but that was the kind of organisation which, as far as we know, could proceed without theory. For about two and a half millennia there has been political theory—about the nature of states, their purposes and their relations with their members and with each other, but not much, until fairly recent times, about their administration. Certainly our basic concepts of authority, responsibility and delegation are historically Roman and etymologically Latin. The Romans were probably the first people to have a system of imperial authority which was not only delegated through a hierarchy, but articulately and rationally expressed in a legal system. The reason for this was that, with certain Greek exceptions, Rome probably had the first very widely extended system of government authority exercised by, or in the name of, a deliberative legislature, the Senate. Hence the various forms and levels of authority had to be spelt out legally and explicitly delegated. Roman administrative concepts have been carried into European thought and the practice of nearly all succeeding centuries, and the law of Rome influenced first that of the medieval Church and then that of most modern European states.

The Roman legal and governmental tradition is embodied, not only in the law of most Continental countries, but also in their highly legalistic administration, and indeed their business methods. Roman Government, Roman law and Roman ecclesiastical tradition have also left many important traces in Britain and America, where it is still common, even in private business, to talk and think in terms of 'hierarchies', 'jurisdictions' and so on. However, in the English-speaking world the Roman tradition has been mingled with older, as well as later, ideas. From this mingling has emerged the tradition of the English common law—the concept of law subsisting in the customs of a people rather than the commands of a ruler, the concept of the adaptation of rules to changing conditions, the concept of independent authorities, the concept of the 'reasonable man' and so on. In view of this division of western governmental and legal tradition into two streams, the Anglo-American and the Continental, it is not surprising that we shall find the formal rigid school of 'classical' organisational theory originating with Fayol in France and Weber in Germany, and the modifications in the direction of flexibility, subtlety and adaptability mainly coming from Britain and the USA.

Political theorists, at least from the seventeenth century onwards, wrote much about the nature, rights, duties and mutual relationships of the main component elements of states, such as monarchy, legislature and judiciary, but little about their internal management. Nor did any organisation theory emerge from the private sector until under a century ago. Until the late seventeenth century there were few large organisations outside the Churches, the Universities and the State (including the armed forces). The earliest kinds of large-scale private enterprise were commercial rather than manufacturing, and really large-scale manufacturing industry, when it did grow up—generally in the early nineteenth century and after—seems to have been content, for a long time, to follow fairly simple commercial or military models. There could be, at first, a merely physical concentration of many sub-contractors into one building, or simple military-style regimentation. The management of individual factories seems to have developed variously and empirically from these foundations, throughout most of the nineteenth century, with little if any theory.[1] So, apparently, did the somewhat larger organisations of central government in that century—Customs, the Post Office and so on. The large privately owned industrial organisation extending over many localities, and then over more than one nation, is a creation of the late nineteenth and early twentieth centuries, and only when its substantial growth began to produce substantial problems of organisation did people begin to produce theories about it. Even then, such theory was seldom applied to the public sector. Some people (most of them in Britain and on the continent of Europe) perhaps thought so well of the internal management of their public bodies that they believed they could continue to be guided by their own internal rules and traditions, and had nothing to learn from the private sector. Other people (most of them probably in the USA) perhaps thought so badly of their public bodies that they would regard them as irredeemably inefficient, perhaps even irredeemably corrupt, and looked to the private sector as the only field for the application of 'scientific' principles and social progress.

The twentieth century

Thus 'classical' organisation theory, in the first four or five decades of the twentieth century in Europe and America, although based on very general abstractions, was applied largely to the private sector, especially to manufacturing industry. It is classical in the sense that it attempts to propound simple principles of general application and also in the sense that certain styles of architecture and literature are termed 'classical'—having characteristics of formality, symmetry and rigidity. Like classical physics, it has not been rendered wholly obsolete merely because it is now seen to have limitations, or because more dimensions of thought and more complex ideas have been developed since. It still contains concepts of basic value, even though there is dispute about their application and though they have to be used with more subtlety than their authors implied. Its principal exponents had three types of background—industrial, academic and military.

Fayol, founder of administrative theory: administrative order

Henri Fayol (1841–1925) had a long and successful career as a general manager in French mining and engineering. His classic *Administration Industrielle et Générale*,[2] based on a contribution to a professional mining industry conference in 1908, was published in Paris in 1916. Its belated English translations (1929 and 1949) have tended to obscure its subtlety and wide application. Fayol makes clear that his purpose is to define '*administration*' (which means something a little wider than either 'management' or 'administration' as often understood in English) as an important professional function in its own right, something which can and indeed must be taught. It should also be a subject for research and experiment. He does not equate it with '*gouvernement*' but he regards it as a predominantly important element in the government of any sort of affairs, 'large or small, industrial, commercial, political, religious or other'. In the operation of any enterprise, he says there are six 'functions'. Apart from '*administration*', his five other functions need not detain us here: '*operations . . . techniques . . . commerciales, financières . . . de securité . . . de comptabilité*'. The rest of the book deals with the administrative function. This is concerned with the 'coordination' and 'harmonising' of all other activities, 'setting up the general programme of activities and creating the social structure'.[3]

The argument continues in a lofty, magisterial, almost Napoleonic vein. Fayol regards administration as a high intellectual and moral function. At a later point the essential personal qualities of the *chef*, or of administrative capacity in the abstract, are ambitiously defined —intellectual, moral and physical qualities, broad-mindedness (*culture générale: notions diverses*).[4]

Although Fayol's tone of thinking is generally authoritarian, and in places rigid, it is not purely authoritarian in its initial definition of the administrative function. Administration is said to be not an exclusive privilege, nor the concern of one chief or group of top managers, but is rather one which involves a relationship between the head and the other members who together make up the whole social structure of the enterprise.[5] He also stresses that responsibility must go with authority. The higher one goes up, says Fayol, in the level of supervision and management in any enterprise, and the larger the enterprise, the more an individual is occupied with the administrative function and the less with the other five 'operational' functions mentioned above, particularly the technical function.

The five elements of administration

Having distinguished the administrative function from the other five, he goes on to subdivide it into his five classic elements—foresight, organisation, command, coordination and control. He attaches great importance to the first. The English version at some points translates '*prévoyance*' as 'planning'; but he makes it clear it includes not only planning, but forecasting and foresight as to future events and the environment of the organisation, and looking far ahead and deeply to ultimate objectives. He quotes the aphorism '*gouverner c'est prevoir*', which means more than just that planning is a predominant function of all management. He goes on to be quite specific and discusses one-year and ten-year forecasts and plans. In this he was far ahead of his time—and of our time. We are still so often content with five-year planning which is not really long-term planning at all, when it includes projects which may take longer than that to come to first fruition. It is significant that Fayol started in mining, where long-term planning is often physically almost unavoidable. He has a section on '*prévoyance nationale*', which he says is rarely of a long-term character. He puts his finger on the reason —'*l'instabilité ministérielle*'.[6]

In explaining his four other elements of administration he defines 'organisation' as providing both the material and social organisation. Social organisation includes both personal leadership and organisation structure. 'Command' and 'coordination' involve both knowledge and will. '*Control*' he uses in the French sense of watch, monitor, check, audit and obtain feedback. He also lays down a number of 'general principles' of administration, not so clearly separate as his five 'elements'. Indeed some of them overlap, but most of them provide facets of his main themes of order, logic, clarity and simplicity. The full list is: Division of labour, authority, discipline, unity of command, unity of direction, subordination of particular to general interests, remuneration, centralisation, hierarchy, order, equity, stability of personnel, unity of personnel, initiative.

The value of simple clarity

It is easy, and to some extent justifiable, to smile at Fayol's apparent love of rigidity, bureaucracy and authoritarianism. He endows both his principles of division of labour and of centralisation with the attributes of laws of nature, and at a superficial reading his remarks about unity of command, authority and responsibility, hierarchies and stability may seem just platitudes and truisms. So do most kinds of safety regulations—till an accident occurs. The difference is that muddle and confusion in large organisations occur very much more frequently than physical accidents, and when they do the remedy is usually the application of some very simple principle, not necessarily Fayol's, but something of the kind. Personal experience suggests that some of the most useful things a senior manager in any large concern does involve cutting through very complex tangles by applying very simple principles. For instance a man should only receive his orders on one subject from one chief (Fayol's own explanation of his principle of 'unity of command'). Self-evident? Principles like Fayol's are in fact so far from self-evident that, as we shall see later, they are not only often violated but sometimes rightly violated. They are too simple to cover all kinds of complex situation. Yet how many managers, struggling with complex interlocking committees and co-ordinating meetings, long for the simplicity and sense of Fayol's principles—such as unity of command, 'subordination of the particular to the general interest' and 'no authority without responsibility'.

The nature of organisation structures

It is indeed in his enunciation of simple lucid principles that Fayol's chief value lies, but also his weakness. When we seek his ideas as to the essential nature and *structure* of organisations, as distinct from their functions, we find he has some very simple ideas indeed—so over-simple as to come within the category later to be criticised as 'mechanistic' in contrast to 'organic'.* Fayol does indeed explicitly cite not only mechanical, but also botanical and zoological analogies

* See below, p. 65.

for the structure of what he calls the *corps social* of an enterprise, yet in fact he is not being at all as subtle as this three-fold analogy would suggest. Whether he cites a series of wheels and cogs in a machine (with nothing about control mechanisms) or branches in a tree, or cells of the nervous system in a human body, he is all the time referring to a very simple straight-line diagram with authority and power all emanating from a central point. The only concession to biological thinking is when he points out that whereas in a machine energy is lost in the course of transmission, there should be no such loss in a human organisation as the individuals forming its parts can themselves generate further energy on their own initiative. But the analogy is not pursued. It is simply assumed that such initiative will automatically extend, or at least perpetuate, the power of the all-powerful chief at the apex of the pyramid. Where the principle of centralisation is discussed its extent is reckoned to be limited largely by the degree of personal force, intelligence, experience, and quickness of thought of the chief, although it might also depend on the capacities of his subordinates. At one point it is stated that the question of centralisation or decentralisation is merely a matter of size, degree and balance, but the specific disadvantages of centralisation are never discussed. 'Hierarchy' is made a very important principle and the rigidity of Fayol's thinking is shown by his regarding it as a great simplification to allow two managers in parallel positions in a hierarchy to communicate direct and not through their respective chiefs— *provided they keep their chiefs immediately informed of what they agree*(!).

Fayol on Government

Although Fayol's whole working experience was in private industry, after his retirement he turned his attention to the public sector. In a paper on 'The Administrative Theory of the State',[7] he seemed almost to equate Government with administrative, and to take little account of political factors, saying that a Prime Minister must above all things be a good administrator, and only specifying oratory as the quality required in Government over and above those qualities required in business. However (with typical foresight), he pin-pointed the forward planning function as vital, and criticised the Prime Ministerial office in contemporary France as lacking a proper secretariat and its own advisory services. He suggested a Government needed a 'Council of Improvement'.* In another paper he drew analogies and contrasts between a state and a business.[8] While he recognised that the State had some additional and different functions,

* Compare the ideas about planning and research of the Haldane Committee discussed in Chapter 6 below, pp. 120–1.

the two sorts of organisations were in his view basically similar, the State being larger and more complex, but not of a different nature. Hence similar administrative principles and practices should apply. His approach was very similar to that being made just at the same time by the Haldane Committee* in England, for instance, in his recommendation for reducing the number of Cabinet Ministers.

Fayol, prophet of Post Office reform

The conclusion of his year's examination of the French Posts, Telegraph and Telephone Department was that 'the State is unfit to run an industrial enterprise well'[9] because it violated his basic principles, such as strength and stability of top management, responsibility and long-term planning. Ministers were incompetent, frequently changing, and they encouraged political interference with day-to-day management. Officials lacked authority or adequate rewards for achievement. Nevertheless, he recognised that the State could not disinterest itself from the postal and telecommunications services. It should, however, limit itself to giving general policy directions, exercising overall control, especially of charges, and subsidising necessary but unremunerative services. Subject to this, the P.T.T. should be handed over to private enterprise by means of a State concession limited to a term of years.†

An immediate start should be made with telephones. Meanwhile posts, telegraphs and other public services should be reformed by measures (not very fully specified) to stabilise and improve top management, restrict political interference and establish long-term planning.[10] Here again Fayol was half a century ahead of his time, and foreshadows some of the reforms currently being introduced in the British and French Post Offices. He did not hit upon the device of the public corporation, but he sketched part of the essential outlines of the specification on which it was designed.

Fayol's creative authoritarianism

To sum up, in this and his earlier work, Fayol was a kind of Napoleon of industrial and general organisation theory—immensely creative in opening up clear straight lines through hitherto not easily penetrable jungles; and hence, like Napoleon, stimulating the creativity of others. Yet he was also the originator of ideas which were to become later, in the hands of lesser men, of narrower outlook than himself, instruments of restriction, frustration and indeed downright oppression.

* See below, pp. 120–1 and 160–4.
† *A l'Etat la haute direction et controle: a l'industrie privée, dans la plus large mesure possible, l'exploitation.'*

Taylor—management as a science

In the voluminous writings[11] of the American, F. W. Taylor (1856–
1917), there are only a few key ideas which contributed substantially
to organisation theory. His greatest contribution was probably his
basic claim that management should be treated as a science. In this
he went too far. As we have argued in the last chapter, management
and administration can seldom be studied and tested by the rigorous
standards of the true sciences. Taylor, however, with a somewhat
more detailed, pragmatic approach than Fayol, did management a
great service by insisting it was worthy of systematic study, as a discipline in its own right. As a graduate mechanical engineer who had
worked as a labourer, foreman and chief engineer of a steel works,
he could make his claim persuasively. His examples, such as the
manual conveyance of quantities of pig-iron, were sufficiently related
to practical experiment and measurement to give him some claim to
the term 'scientific'—certainly more scientific than many later writers
who have used the term 'scientific management' and more indeed
than Fayol. This basic novelty of approach is far more important
than any of his specific proposals. Moreover, writing in English and
from the vantage point of expanding American industrialism, he had
a much wider audience than Fayol.

Functional management

His belief in detailed, systematic study of every function, indeed of
almost every minute manual motion, led him on to the much more
questionable notion of 'functional foremanship'—a series of functional specialists all concurrently supervising different parts or aspects of the activities of the same group of individuals. This proposition, at least in its original context of the shop floor, has not been
taken up on any large scale, but it may have influenced the division
of the headquarters and lower formations of large organisations into
specialist or functional departments. He analysed the various qualifications required of a foreman into technical, planning, disciplinary
and inspectorial categories, but with further subdivisions (nine in all)
and concluded that no one man at this level could combine all these
qualities. If he did possess them all he should be works manager (a
revealing definition of Taylor's ideas of the nature and quality of
higher management). Hence the functions must be divided.

All planning and clerical work, indeed 'all possible brain work',
should be removed from the shop floor and centred in the planning
and layout department. The remainder of the foreman's work should
be divided between (1) 'gang bosses'; (2) 'speed bosses'; (3) 'inspectors'; and (4) 'repairs bosses'. This 'functional management' he con-

trasted with the normal type of unitary control which he called 'the military type of organisation'[12] and he said his system involved each man receiving orders and help from eight different bosses. Fayol knew of and had some admiration for Taylor and quoted his work; but was puzzled at how Taylor's system could work in contradiction to his own principle of unity of command. He supposed Taylor somehow managed a reconciliation, but he thought it dangerous to let the idea spread that his own basic principle could be violated with impunity.[13] Burns and Stalker comment that Fayol and Taylor's 'discrepant views about the necessity for unified command and functional specialisation still survive actively in the dilemma of the line and staff organisational structure'.[14]

Taylor's philosophy

Taylor is one of the founding fathers of work study and organisation and methods and similar activities; but these are somewhat peripheral to organisation or administrative theory. They are just some of the subsidiary technologies of organisation, like typewriting, telephones and computers. In a more far-reaching way 'Taylorism' has been, and still is, extremely influential, and extremely misleading, in its mechanistic, authoritarian doctrines of control and motivation. Taylor was not, however, concerned solely with the interests of management and argued at length that the adoption of his principles would produce great benefits for all grades of workers—but mainly cash benefits. Work itself was to be subdivided, narrowly specialised and precisely prescribed and directed from above. Motivation was to be primarily financial, but as the activities of management as well as workers were to be self-evidently rational, Taylor hoped that rational explanation would ensure wholehearted cooperation between management and workers. He was well aware of systematic restriction of output by workers, but believed it was simply due to lack of understanding which could be removed by logical argument. Argument on this subject has indeed been proceeding ever since Taylor started to write and no doubt a lot of progress has been made. But it does not yet seem to be concluded!

Management by exception

One of Taylor's ideas was more subtle, 'the exception principle'. Reports going up to higher managers should be streamlined so that they need only look at the exceptions, cases better or worse than the average. Information about the normal should be eliminated or drastically summarised at lower levels. This was one of Taylor's few recognitions of delegation, in contrast to his normal emphasis on firm centralised control and the concentration of intellectual work in higher management and among specialists. The modern concept of 'management by exception' is more subtle still and a very important element in making the control of very large organisations by delegation possible at all.

Development and spread of classical theory

Many writers in the thirties, forties and later have developed and popularised classical management doctrine. Outstanding examples in the USA are Luther Gulick (born 1892), a former director of the New York Institute of Public Administration with much practical experience of public administration, and James Mooney (1884–1957), a Vice-President of General Motors. Gulick collaborated with European writers[15] in developing Fayol's analysis of management functions. He made an over-simple distinction between 'doing' ('line') and 'thinking and planning' ('staff'). Mooney[16] sought to universalise organisation theory with historical analogies from Moses onwards, nearly all from authoritarian régimes. 'Organisation', he said, 'is the form of every human organisation for the attainment of a common purpose.' (He seemed to assume that every organisation has only one purpose and that everyone agrees what it is, which is more than could be said of most Government Departments.)

Colonel Urwick—theorist, consultant and propagandist

In Britain, the outstanding exponent, developer and propagandist of classical theory, and also of various other ideas about management, was Colonel Urwick (born 1891). His academic education was in history and his formative experience in the Army in World War I. His style of thought and writing is highly military. He explored and developed the ideas of Fayol and others. He has written numerous books and articles, founded and directed an important firm of management consultants, and travelled widely constantly stressing that management is an important scientific profession in which a high level of efficiency can be developed by thorough training and careful attention to sound principles.

He expounds[17] his 'principles of administration', as 'investigation, forecasting, planning, organisation, coordination, order, command and control' and the 'scalar' process (hierarchy), assignment and integration of functions, leadership, delegation, functional definition. In making this analysis he consciously followed and developed Fayol's and also cited Taylor, Mooney, Follet[18] and many others. In discussing organisations as social groups, he writes, 'the correct analogy must be the analogy with the living organism—the biological parallel—but men and women are still as yet unaccustomed to thinking scientifically about themselves and one another. For this reason the mechanistic parallel can be very helpful in discussing organisation. Another name for it is the engineering approach'—and his exposition of how organisations of human beings work suffers accordingly. His reluctance to use the biological analogy is strange, as it was already a very old one when Paul of Tarsus used it in the first century A.D.[19] Nevertheless Urwick is a practical, humane and broad-minded man who has done much to encourage thinking deeper and wider than his own.

The main value of classical theory

What specific ideas of practical value emerged from what may seem to be the abstractions of the 'scientific' or 'classical' management school? The first was simply the identification of management, organisation or administration as a distinct function to be studied and practised in its own right. To surround it with high-flown semi-philosophic language, to call it 'science', was an exaggeration necessary for emphasis. The practical achievement was to make men think and apply themselves to the problem of management and organisation and to give those who did so some feeling of pride and self-respect.

Secondly, some clearer thinking was introduced concerning authority, responsibility and delegation, and an emphasis on the definition of clear lines of command and subdivisions of functions—and hence responsibilities. All this, simple and boring in cold print, comprises the essential difference between an organisation that works and chaos.

The exhortations which were heeded least, until quite recently, were those to plan ahead; but planning is so much a function in which the public sector ought to give a lead that we must leave its consideration till a later chapter. We must, however, discuss two particular notions of the Classical School which have never been clarified sufficiently to give them the true status of principles, but which have probably caused as much confusion as clarification. These are 'line-and-staff' and 'span of control'.

The 'line-and-staff' muddle: The military analogy*

In a paper in 1933[20] Urwick devoted considerable space to explaining the special meaning of 'Staff' in military organisation and the special position of the military 'Services'; but did not carry through the analogy sufficiently fully into the civilian sphere. The armed forces

---

* The brief references to military organisation which follow are based on World War II experiences. I am advised that they are accurate for that period, although not entirely so for today but that this does not invalidate the conclusions which I draw and the general argument which follows in this chapter.

have traditionally been accustomed to the idea, not only of a hierarchy of commanders of higher and lower formations (from Army Group to Corporal's section), but also, within each higher Commander's Headquarters, of 'staff officers' authorised to act on the Commander's behalf and transmit his orders, for instance:

123 Independent Brigade will move from A to B at 1200 hrs. on . . .
Signed C. D. Major
for Lieut-General
Commander 4 Corps

The Corps Commander will have approved a general plan. He may or may not have gone into details. The latter will in any case have been worked out by staff officers of varying ranks. A staff officer, in this instance a Major, signs the order, knowing it is in the terms required to fulfil the General's wishes. The Brigadier of 123 Brigade complies with the order knowing it carries the proper authority. But not all officers at Corps Headquarters have this authority—not for instance the Deputy Director, Supplies and Transport, or the Deputy Director, Medical Services (both Brigadiers). They are 'Heads of Services' with authority limited to their own special spheres and their own specialist personnel.

The confusion of terms

When analogous arrangements are made in privately owned industry, it is usual to call the general managers (at various levels in the hierarchy), 'line managers' and their specialist advisers 'staff'—a term which itself confuses the military analogy. The confusion is increased because civilian industry is not much accustomed (as Urwick points out) to employ deputy managers to whom as much authority is delegated as to military staff officers. Hence, in some organisations, 'line management' may effectively mean only the individuals at the head of separate units—all their supporting assistant managers, advisers and specialists being categorised as 'staff'. In other organisations there are 'line departments' and 'staff departments'. For instance, the production department might be called 'line' and the personnel and accounting and finance departments 'staff'. But in other organisations again, such departments might have considerable executive authority delegated to them by the board of directors or the chief executive. What about the marketing department—especially in a company in whose business marketing is as important a function as production? One definition of a line department is one whose functions contribute directly to the profitability, or other objectives, of the organisation. But this may not only vary from one organisation to another but sometimes may be a matter of opinion.[21]

No management theory has yet provided a sufficiently clear guide as to what the line and staff principle should mean in civilian organisation. Seldom is the principle worked out in practice in as logical and thorough a way as it is in the armed forces. The basic fallacy is one of authoritarian outlook—the idea that only one individual, group or organ of management, can exercise independent initiative and authority, while everyone else must only advise and obey. In really large and complex organisations such ideas are simply out of touch with reality.

The 'Span of Control' fallacy: Graicunas

The 'Span of Control' doctrine is even more confusing and misleading. It has been preached by Urwick and many others, originally as a practical principle concerning the numbers of subordinates any individual can effectively control. Although it may in a sense be as old as any kind of hierarchical organisation—perhaps including that of ancient Egypt—it is supposed to have been first specifically enunciated by General Sir Ian Hamilton who wrote 'The average human brain finds its effective scope in handling from three to six other brains'.[22] Various figures have indeed been proposed and it has generally been admitted that the supervising of 'routine functions' (whatever that may mean) is an exception. Obviously much must depend on the nature of the work to be 'supervised'—from the Prime Minister or President with his Cabinet Ministers to an Assistant Inspector of postmen in a sorting office. And what about headmasters, sales managers, nursing sisters and so on? As a practical warning that the spread of each man's direct responsibility needs careful consideration, it may be useful. Elevated into a mathematical principle it is nonsense. The responsibility for so elevating it rests mainly with V. A. Graicunas, a French management consultant who produced the formula of 'five or most probably four' by a calculation of the total number of subordinates at all levels and the maximum possible number of links between them individually.[23] This assumed that the superior manager's difficulty in exercising control arises from his need to maintain contact, not merely with all his own immediate subordinates, but apparently with all their subordinates, and with the mutual relationships of all these people. The basic fallacy is the authoritarian assumption that the top manager needs to be concerned with every bit of the necessary range of relationships below him. A further fallacy is to ignore the simple fact that in large organisations the more things are simplified by narrowing the span of control, the more they are complicated by increasing the number of layers in the hierarchy. There is indeed a fundamental unsolved

A.T.A.P.A.—B

problem of maintaining, not detailed control, but a fair degree of communication, within any very large organisation. The span of control theory makes only a very limited contribution to the solution of this problem.

Bureaucracy

'Bureaucracy' is a word we should come to terms with in seeking to understand the theory of large scale organisations, but it is hard to do so because its meaning is still not universally agreed. Albrow's recent careful historical analysis seems to conclude that it can mean anything or nothing, but that the term is nevertheless 'useful in identifying a range of related problems'.[24] A well-known modern writer on management, Rosemary Stewart,[25] claims to use it as she says 'not disparagingly but with the technical meaning given to it by sociologists for a method of organisation that has certain characteristics'. *The New Oxford Dictionary* defines it as 'Government by bureaux: usually officialism—government officials collectively', but it is more specific about 'Bureaucrat'—'an official who endeavours to concentrate administrative power in a bureau'. The article on 'Bureaucracy' in the *Encyclopaedia Britannica* (1967) says 'among certain scholars it is . . . used in a completely respectable and even laudatory sense to designate the institution of a permanent professional corps of officials'. Nevertheless it goes on to admit 'that it has not been accepted as an objective scientific description' and that almost whenever used in the press of Britain or USA, or in Parliament or Congress, it is derogatory. It says 'Bureaucracy is the pathology of large organisations'. Certainly in origin and derivation it appears derogatory. It seems first to have been used in Britain in the mid-nineteenth century by J. S. Mill, Carlyle, Charles Kingsley and others to designate forms and methods of government which they regarded as objectionable and which, they alleged, prevailed in France, Germany, Ireland or elsewhere outside their contemporary Britain.

The derivation is from the French *bureau*—office—and the Greek κρατος (kratos)—strength, power, dominion, sovereignty, rule, mastery. Hence the best definition would seem to be a state of affairs where power is exercised by officials or people in offices—probably where such people are supposed to carry out the wishes of another group with sovereign power (for instance, a democratically elected governing body), but in fact usurp that sovereign power themselves. In other words bureaucracy can mean rule *by* officials, just as democracy means rule by the people and aristocracy rule by the 'best' people. On the other hand it could mean merely rule *through* rather than *by* officials. Or again it could mean rule by, or through, an office system rather than officials as groups of individual human beings—a method of rule where the system itself, the machine, had taken over from the human beings—rule by offices rather than officers. Even here there could be a distinction. Such a bureaucratic system could be envisaged as a complete Frankenstein monster, beyond human control, or it could be merely something like an automatic pilot—a machine set to reflect, and faithfully and automatically carry out, the wishes of the sovereign body. People who use the word bureaucracy often fail to distinguish between these various possible meanings and implications.

Max Weber: personal background

This last criticism can even be said of Max Weber (1864–1920), author of the original sociological writing on the subject.[26] To understand why this should be so we must consider his personality and environment. He was the archetype of the introvert intellectual, fascinated and horrified by power in general and bureaucracy in particular. Yet he was a man of intense penetration, encyclopaedic learning and profound sense of historical perspective. He has probably contributed as much as anyone in modern times both to the understanding and the misunderstanding of the exercise of power in large organisations. Weber's family and social background was Prussian, legal, political, and academic. A delicate, precocious child, he had a brilliant academic career, somewhat violently counterbalanced by membership of a duelling fraternity (which he seems to have liked) and rigorous military training (which he detested). Most of the rest of his life was spent at Universities, interspersed with severe mental breakdowns and extensive travel in America and elsewhere. Politically he was ambivalent, believing in a German national world mission and the 'herrenvolk', but bitterly criticising Bismarck and Kaiser William II and their régimes. In 1918 he had a somewhat ludicrous discussion with General Ludendorf, in which he ended by virtually agreeing with him on a form of 'democracy' in which the leader, once elected, was to act as virtual dictator with power to say to the people 'Now shut up and obey me' (Weber's words, as translated by Gerth and Mills).[27]

Weber's concept of rational bureaucracy

He characterised bureaucracy as a most advanced and profoundly rational form of human organisation which had emerged in different complete or incomplete forms at various stages of history to replace régimes based on personal status, favour and preference. In its full form it was dependent on a money economy, in contrast with feudalism, ancient empires and other kinds of régime where office was rewarded with property, rights and privileges, and customary benefits in kind. It usually accompanied any form of modern capitalism and any mass democracy; but it was specifically connected with large technological developments, such as the water systems of ancient Egypt and modern postal, telegraph and railway systems. There were bureaucracies not only in Government but in mass political parties and in large commercial and industrial companies. There could be bureaucracies in régimes of either the Right or of the Left. The characteristics of bureaucracy were:

fixed . . . jurisdictional areas . . . regular activities . . . distributed in a fixed way as official duties . . . authority . . . distributed in a stable way and . . . strictly delimited by rules . . . a firmly ordered system of super- and subordination . . . management based . . . upon written documents ('the files'). . . . The body of officials . . . along with the respective appara- tus of material implements and the files make up a 'bureau' . . . Office management . . . usually presupposes thorough and expert training . . . follows general rules which are more or less stable, more or less exhaustive . . . knowledge of these rules represents a special technical learning . . . it involves jurisprudence. . . . The theory of modern public administration . . . assumes that authority to order certain matters—which has been legally granted to public authorities—does not entitle the bureau to regulate the matter by commands given for each case, but only to regulate the matter abstractly . . . in extreme contrast with the regulation of all relationships . . . through individual privileges and bestowals of favour. . . . [Again, he writes] Modern loyalty is devoted to impersonal and functional purposes. Behind these, of course, usually stand ideas of culture-values. These are the *erzatz* for the earthly or supra-mundane personal master- ideas such as 'state', 'church', 'community', 'party' or 'enterprise'.

The official has a position of social esteem 'guaranteed by prescrip- tive rules of rank order . . .' and 'the guild-like closure of officialdom'. Officials are appointed on the basis of academic qualifications, usu- ally for life, on the basis of 'universal accessibility of office' 'the bureaucrat is chained to his activity'. Though he has an advantage over a 'dilettante' monarch or Minister owing to his expert know- ledge, he is nevertheless in a weak position because of the numbers in the hierarchy below him always ready to take his place and his economic dependence on one type of employment (unless he belongs to the propertied classes). Any determined political régime, even an invading foreign power, will find a bureaucracy a loyal and pliant tool once it can get control of it from the top. Hence 'recruitment of officials from among the propertyless strata increases the power of the rulers'.

Weber's legal philosophy
Weber stresses the importance of personal knowledge and group

attitudes reinforced by a passion for secrecy in a general body of officials—'The discipline of officialdom refers to the attitude-set of the official for precise obedience with his habitual activity . . . compliance has been conditioned into the officials . . . and . . . into the governed'. He makes a good deal of the importance of Roman law as an 'advanced' rational system accompanying the development of bureaucratic régimes, contrasting it favourably with the empiricism of English and American common law. He attributes the survival of the latter merely to the vested interests of the legal profession and seems totally unaware of any advantages claimed for it on grounds of flexibility and adaptability to changing social, economic or political conditions. Nor does he appreciate the arguments for the lack of separation of public and private law in the Anglo-Saxon systems.

Weber's love-hate of bureaucracy

Coming back to the importance and power of the trained expert bureaucrat—something which he seems to regard as inevitable without apparently welcoming it—he has a flash of prophetic vision of Fultonian technocracy: 'Behind all the present discussions of the foundations of the educational system the struggle of the "specialist" type of man against the older type of "cultivated" man is hidden at some decisive point. This fight is determined by the irresistibly expanding bureaucratisation of all public and private relations of authority and by the ever-increasing importance of expert and specialised knowledge. The fight intrudes into all intimate cultural questions.' In the last resort, it would seem he would come down against bureaucracy, without seeing any possibility of removing it, nor any alternative. 'Democracy as such is opposed to the rule of bureaucracy in spite and perhaps because of its unavoidable yet unintended promotion of bureaucratisation.'

It is easy, and to some extent justifiable, to say that Weber's picture of bureaucracy was neurotic and distorted—the product of a sick man in a sick society—and that even if things were really like that in William II's Germany, in most other times and places they were quite different. Certainly Weber's picture, if not distorted, is highly abstract. It may not even be scientific, as he does not quote his evidence on the internal working of any bureaucratic system. Nevertheless he has a profound sense of history and grasp of historical social developments which is lacking in all the writers whom we have so far cited, except, in a more amateurish way, in Mooney. His outline of bureaucracy as a system of rationally ordered communal activity, based on set patterns of behaviour and distribution of work, is of profound importance for all subsequent study of organisations. So also is his indirectly giving a foundation of some academic res-

pectability (despite his last quoted criticisms), to many forms of
organisation which emerged after his death—and of which he would
not have presumably approved. These included various kinds of
brash and arrogant managerialism and other régimes more profoundly oppressive of the human spirit.

The managerial revolution

The intellectual foundations of the classical and authoritarian school
were laid before World War I and its popular exposition was developed between the wars. New types of thinking about organisations
began to develop in the early thirties and a little earlier. But the
classical-authoritarian school is not dead. It is still the stock-in-trade
of much everyday talk among practical managers. It still has elements
of genuine enduring value,[28] both theoretical and practical, and its
development and exposition in literature, journalism, management
consultancy and management training have continued through the
thirties, forties, and fifties, and even today. In 1941 its intellectual
base was somewhat widened by James Burnham and it has since en-
joyed some revival as a kind of backlash against the human relations
school. Burnham, an American partly educated at Oxford, was not
primarily a writer on management processes or organisation theory
but a publicist concerned with political and social issues. In *The
Managerial Revolution* (1941) he extols managers as an independent
and powerful, indeed potentially dominant, social and economic
class whose power is to supersede both that of capitalism and of the
working class. The comment has been made that *The Managerial
Revolution* may be regarded as a vulgarisation of Max Weber, and in
defence of that it could have been said, to be sure, that if ever a man
needed a little vulgarisation it was Max Weber, and 'What Burnham
in fact had concocted was a sort of opium for the managerial middle
classes'.[29] Certainly, in implanting an idea and coining a phrase, he
has added enormously to the managers' myth—the belief in the
social, political, and economic necessity of oligarchic, rational, authoritarian direction of the affairs of organisations in particular, and
of society in general. Somewhat similar arguments are put forward
by such writers as Alex Rubner in *The Ensnared Shareholder*[30] although he deprecates the real or imagined shift of power which
Burnham welcomes. Both, however, are making a too superficial
analysis of economic, social and political forces. In the same way
there is a superficiality in contemporary arguments that political
power has passed out of the hands of Parliament and Ministers (and
hence the electorate) to the Civil Service. Ultimate directive power is
not to be measured by the multiplicity of management activities.
Burnham is like a civilian visitor to an army unit who hears the

Sergeant-Major shouting most of the orders and thinks the Commanding Officer must be a mere figurehead. Shareholders, politicians and indeed the parliamentary electorate may keep very quiet and indeed look quite stupid when they are tolerably content with the way things are being managed; but they can and do bring about the ruin of boards of directors and Governments if they become convinced that they are not serving their essential interests.[31]

1. See Sidney Pollard, 1965. *The Genesis of Modern Management: A Study of the Industrial Revolution in Britain.* Arnold; Penguin, 1968.
2. Dunod, Paris, 1962 edition. '*Extrait du Bulletin de la Societé de l'Industrie Minérale (3e livraison de 1916)*' '*le developpement de la Conference que j'ai faite au Cinquantenaire de la Société de l'Industrie Minérale, a Saint-Etienne en 1908*'. First English translation by J. A. Crowbrough, 1929, International Management Institute, Geneva; second by Constance Storrs as *General and Industrial Management*, 1949. Pitman.
See the very valuable article expounding Fayol's basic ideas and exposing the misunderstandings of him arising from the English translations: M. B. Brodie, Autumn 1962, 'Henri Fayol: Administration Industrielle et Génèrale', *Public Administration.* Also the same author's *Fayol on Administration*, 1967, Lyon. Grant and Greer.
3. *Chargée de dresser le programme general d'action de l'enterprise, de constitituer le corps social, de co-ordonner les efforts, d'harmonizer les actes,* ibid., p. 4.
4. ibid., pp. 6, 34.
5. *C'est une function qui se repartit, commes les autres functions essentielles, entre la tête et les membres du corps social,* ibid., p. 5.
6. ibid., p. 5.
7. Luther Gulick and L. Urwick (Eds), 1937. *Papers on the Science of Administration*, pp. 101–14. Institute of Public Administration, Columbia University, New York. This book was written in 1923.
8. Henri Fayol, 1918. 'L'Industrialization de L'Etat'. A lecture delivered and published as Annexe to *L'Incapacité d'Etat: Les P.T.T.*, 1921. Dunod, Paris.
9. op. cit., p. 8, *L'Etat est incapable de bien gérer une entreprise industrielle.*
10. ibid., pp. 79–85.
11. *Shop Management*, 1903, *Principles of Scientific Management*, 1911, with his Testimony to the Special House Committee of Congress, 1912, were republished in one volume as *Scientific Management* by Harper in 1947.
12. ibid., *Shop Management,* pp. 96–100.
13. Fayol, op. cit., pp. 80–6.
14. Tom Burns and G. M. Stalker, 1961. *The Management of Innovation*, p. 106. Tavistock and Social Science Paperbacks. Also, see below, pp. 64–6.

15. Notably Luther Gulick and L. Urwick (Eds), 1937. *Papers on the Science of Administration*. Columbia University, New York.

16. James J. Mooney, 1939. *The Principles of Organisation*. Harper Bros., New York. Revised ed., 1947, p. 1. Also, James J. Mooney and A. C. Reilly, 1951. *Onward Industry*. Harper, New York.

17. *The Elements of Administration*. Pitman, 1943; 2nd ed., 1947.

18. ibid., p. 35. For Follet, see pp. 43–4 below.

19. 1 Cor. xii. 12–31.

20. L. Urwick, 'Organisation as a Technical Problem' (Paper for the British Association, 1933). Republished in *Papers on the Science of Administration* (Eds. L. Gulick and L. Urwick), Institute of Public Administration, New York, 1937.

21. An example of the confusion generated by the 'line and staff' doctrine is J. R. Nelson's article 'The Changing Attitude of the National Coal Board to "line and staff".' *Journal of Management Studies,* vol 3, no 1, February 1966.

22. *The Soul and Body of an Army*, p. 229, 1921. Arnold.

23. Graicunas' paper in Gulick and Urwick, op. cit.

24. Martin Albrow, 1970. *Bureaucracy*, p. 125. Macmillan.

25. *The Reality of Management*, 1963. Heinemann.

26. The material in this section is taken largely from *From Max Weber: Essays in Sociology*, trans. and Eds. H. H. Gerth and C. Wright Mills, London 1948, in particular the biographical introduction, pp. 3–44, and the section on 'Bureaucracy', pp. 196–244. This is a translation of a section of Weber's *Wirtschaft und Gesellschaft*, part III, ch. 6, pp. 650–78. The whole work has also been translated by A. M. Henderson and T. Parsons and published as *The Theory of Social and Economic Organisation*, 1947. Glencoe, Illinois.

27. Gerth and Mills, op. cit., pp. 41–2. The quotations and summaries which follow are taken from pp. 196–244.

28. See the valuable general exposition of this theme by Charles Peron: *Organizational Analysis: A Sociological View*. Wadsworth, Belmont, California; English edition by Tavistock, 1970. E. F. L. Brecht is still a much quoted and influential example of the classical school in Britain (see Reading List).

29. C. R. Sisson; 1959. *The Spirit of British Administration*, pp. 127, 128. Faber.

30. Macmillan, 1965. (Pelican—Penguin books edition, 1966); notably p. 82, where he calls company directors 'disguised civil servants'.

31. For a concise summary of arguments for and against managerialism see John Childs, 1969. *The Business Enterprise in Modern Industrial Society*, pp. 34–51. Collier–Macmillan.

2

'HUMAN RELATIONS' AND RELATED THEORIES

The changing theoretical background

There are various kinds of organisation theory outside the broad description of 'classical'. We can only consider some of those most relevant to organisation within the public sector. We cannot be strictly chronological. Different lines of thought overlap in time. New theory may often take a couple of generations or more to filter into normal practice. The classical management thinking described in the last chapter is still dominant among many practising managers today. Yet its key ideas were expounded in the first two decades of this century. It is hard to date the origins of the various new kinds of organisation theory. These new ideas are sometimes categorised as the 'Human Relations' and the 'Systems' schools, with the implication that the former is employee-centred, psychological, and either soft or paternalistic or both, while the latter is scientific and mathematical. There are strands of thinking which may justify all these epithets but they are too intertwined to disentangle completely. Moreover none of the phrases quoted really get to the root of the matter or deal with the basic change in outlook which has been developing over the years. It is concerned essentially with subtlety and complexity—with the number of dimensions and aspects which can be attributed to organisations. This new outlook is something which embraces the more enduring and vital elements in both the so-called 'Human Relations' school and the so-called 'Systems' school. Burns and Stalker,[1] whom we discuss in the next chapter, distinguish between classical and non-classical forms of management structure as 'mechanistic' and 'organic'. These phrases suggest a shift, not only from engineering to biological analogies, but a fundamental change to different and more subtle and complex ways of thinking. The earlier thinkers about organisations used not only engineering analogies, but rather simple ones, as if they had in mind rather old-fashioned simple machines. The newer thinkers whom we shall now discuss, not only used biological analogies, but took them from contemporary biology which made them represent organisations as akin to very complex organisms. Indeed the newer thinkers about organisation and management have been at least indirectly, and some of them very directly, influenced by all kinds of new thinking and, indeed, new philosophy, in the natural sciences generally.

A. N. Whitehead: new 'climates of opinion'

Despite their complexity, new scientific philosophies have gradually percolated down so that they now, in some degree, affect thinking, not only of people in many academic disciplines, but also indirectly the thinking of the intelligent man in the street. Certainly they have affected the thinking of organisation theorists. It would not be appropriate in a book of this scope, even if the author were competent, to attempt even the merest summary of the new scientific thinking of the second quarter of the twentieth century; but we cannot consider changes in organisation theory intelligently without at least being aware that more general changes in philosophy have been taking place. Indeed, we must mention one outstanding philosopher in particular, Alfred North Whitehead, if only because of his direct personal influence on certain organisation theorists whom we must shortly mention. Whitehead was a mathematical philosopher who developed his philosophy at Cambridge and then at Harvard in the twenties and early thirties. He was personally interested in the work of Mayo and Barnard whom we shall mention, and indeed, of his own son, T. N. Whitehead, whose writing on organisations is also important. A. N. Whitehead is recognised as an important influence on contemporary sociology. Dorothy Emet,[2] writing in the *International Encyclopedia of Social Sciences*, sums up the aspects of Whitehead's views which are most relevant to sociology by saying that he 'saw the Universe as a pluralistic society of societies, never static but always in process, and human societies as signal illustrations of this wider view'. Members of each society in his view derived their qualities from their relationships with one another and these relationships defined the dominant social order. Yet there was also the possibility of transition to new types of order. A. N. Whitehead's relevance to organisation theory derives from his concepts of organisms. 'Science', he wrote, 'is taking on a new aspect which is neither purely physical nor purely biological. It is becoming the study of organisms', and again, 'The concept of an organism includes, therefore, the concept of the interaction of organisms'.[3] His ideas are very difficult for the layman to absorb, but their influence has certainly been in the direction of making contemporary thought about organisms and hence about organisations, more subtle, more fluid and more relativist.

Few people, even at Harvard, can be expected to have read Whitehead's philosophy and fewer still to have understood more than a fraction of its meaning, though this fraction is worth all the obvious thoughts of a hundred more comprehensible authors. But the important point is that Whitehead (along with others) was creating a climate of opinion (a now trite phrase he himself probably first coined) in which older ideas would find it hard to persist unchanged and in which new ideas could flourish. These new ideas concerned not only the natural sciences and philosophy, but also the social sciences and human institutions. Like his contemporary Keynes he was preparing the ground for the release of practical men, who would never hear of him, from the slavery of the defunct theorist.

Mary Parker Follet: leadership and the complexity of structures

Another Harvard character who contributed fundamentally in the twenties and thirties to the new ways of thinking about organisation was Mary Parker Follet. She has sometimes been classed[4] as 'classical' because she tended to propound general principles for all types or organisation, but there is nothing classical in her ideas about diffused leadership, 'power not as inhering in one person but as the combined capacities of a group', 'total inter-relatedness' and so on.[5] She gives some reflection of Whitehead, whom she quotes with approval on 'the interplay of diverse values' and 'emergent values'.[6] These somewhat abstract notions, however, had for her plenty of specific practical applications, and she developed them as much from discussions with people in business and industry in America and Britain as from her wide reading in history and the natural and social sciences. She first wrote as an academic political scientist and later became concerned with industrial and general management through an interest in vocational guidance and industrial arbitration and conciliation. The theoretical side of her approach to organisations and management seems to have been based chiefly on current new thinking in biology and psychology. She was interested in contemporary biologists' attempts to treat organisms as wholes and not merely to analyse parts, by the 'Gestalt' school of psychology, and the idea of total situations, 'reciprocal activity'.[7] She looked at organisations as complete wholes with closely inter-related elements, at decisions and orders not as the sole motivating forces coming from top management, but as elements in a complex chain or pattern of events and circumstances, as determined very often by 'the law of the situation' rather than by individuals. Much of this arose from her interest in industrial relations and conciliation but its implications went further. She understood how what may appear to be a manager's personal decisions may in fact be largely determined by the advice and information he receives, the circumstances and environment within which he is working and the means available to him to get his orders carried out. She contributed greatly to the study of organisations as complex organisms, rather than simple mechanisms with the driving force all coming from one point and going in one direction. Always, however, she hints and suggests, and seldom spells out in detail. Not all her readers would see where her thoughts should lead them. Nevertheless her writing is seminal, and indeed prophetic.

Elton Mayo: human relations

Mary Follet was the forerunner of the 'Human Relations School' of organisation theory. Its 'father' is Elton Mayo, an Australian who spent most of his working life at the Harvard Business School. His *Human Problems of an Industrial Civilization*, published there in 1933, described the famous Hawthorne researches (1927–33) which, among other things, demonstrated how measured productivity in manual work increased with the interest workers felt was being taken in them. He suggested that the most important factors in industrial productivity were not the monetary incentives, precise supervision and material environment on which F. W. Taylor relied, but the psychological relations of workers with each other and with the management. Hence industrial and other organisations were regarded primarily as systems of interdependent human beings and management thinking was focussed on 'informal organisation', groupings of people independent of the formal management structure, 'belongingness' and welfare in general. Over-simplified and taken to extremes, as Mayo's thinking, like that of all great innovators, often was, the result could be a sentimental concentration on the members of an organisation to the neglect of its work and purposes, and a general softness and lack of direction. Mayo has also been criticised, for instance, by Whyte in *The Organisation Man*, as encouraging a paternalistic domination of the private lives, and even the private thoughts, of individuals by their employers.[8]

The background of sociology, biology and psychology

None of these weaknesses, however, obscures the innovating and creative value of Mayo's best work, nor the subtlety and variety both of its foundations and its implications. It did not originate from researches in one American factory nor in purely psychological ideas. He cites first, various other people's researches into the physiological aspects of industrial fatigue, and then his own research in two very different American industrial environments. He then goes on to discuss their complex and subtle implications in the light of sociological theory, principally Durkheim's. His analogies, notably those concerning the balance of a living organism (homeostasis), often come from biology, and although his main line of thinking is psychological, he accords little value to Freud.

He describes the researches started during World War I in Britain by the Health of Munition Workers Committee and continued afterwards by C. S. Myers, founder of the National Institute of Industrial Psychology, and other researches at Harvard and elsewhere on industrial fatigue and monotony as influences on productivity. He develops the conclusion that fatigue and monotony cannot be studied as single, simple factors, either physiological or psychological, but only as parts of total complex situations with many inter-related factors. Physiological fatigue is the result of physiological unbalance, which experiments showed came much more slowly in men (of any age) who had ever been trained as athletes. In other words fatigue develops when adaptation by the individual to his work and environment fails. Similarly fatigue and monotony had less serious effects on productivity in a well-balanced, well-integrated community where informal groups worked well together, where individuals were encouraged by the interest of their managers and by sympathetic, systematic personal 'counselling' (carried to extraordinary lengths at Hawthorne). Mayo constantly emphasises the concepts of balance, 'the steady state', and homeostasis, in the individual organism and the group—and by contrast the rootlessness, discontent and atrophy of effort and vitality in individuals alienated from their work, their working environment and their colleagues and managers.

Durkheim's concept of 'anomie'

Having worked to this conclusion through analysis of research results, he makes an opposite approach to it from the point of view of the theories of sociologists and psychologists—above all Durkheim, but also Hallbwachs his interpreter and critic and Piaget the child psychologist. Durkheim, a generation earlier, had made fundamental studies of society; of religion as the symbolically cohesive force in primitive and other societies, of the division of labour as an emerging characteristic of advanced societies, and of suicide as an index of the sickness and disintegration of societies. Durkheim, an Alsatian Jew, had a broader, more humane, international and balanced view of society than the somewhat neurotic and nationalist Weber. What most interested Mayo in Durkheim's work was his concept of *anomie*, which he translated as 'planlessness in living'.[9] It is in some ways akin to, but not the same as, alienation, and means much more than its literal translation 'lawlessness'. 'Rootlessness' might be better. The phenomenon of *anomie* concerned Mayo as existing especially in Chicago, but in many other places, although probably more in USA than in Europe. The concept is of fundamental importance for any consideration of the cohesive factors in a society or organisation. Durkheim's term implies the importance of an external framework of law as well as an internal, homeostatic balancing mechanism—two concepts to which we shall return. Mayo attributed the blame for modern *anomie* partly to modern technology and partly to the classical economists and other nineteenth-century thinkers.

Mayo's élitism

Mayo wrote that the interviews with workers at Hawthorne had shown that 'the major difficulty was no mere simple error of supervision, no easily alterable set of working conditions; it was something more intimately human, yet more remote'. 'Supervision' indeed had 'shown itself to be another word which meant so many things that it meant nothing'.[10] This discovery, even with its obvious exaggeration, represented an enormous advance in organisation theory. If it is recognised that supervision is not the simple business of total unified control and direction which Fayol implies, or the several precise classified functions of Taylor, it is then possible to start the difficult task of analysing its various and changing social or technical functions. One can examine what supervisors actually do and can do, and their place in a complex pattern of systems and relationships and attitudes. This was perhaps the greatest value of the Hawthorne studies, particularly the factual analysis of individuals' activities, attitudes and relationships.

Unfortunately it was difficult entirely to distinguish this fact-finding function of the interviews from their actual or presumed beneficial effect on the morale of those interviewed. Hence it was easy to pass to the enveloping Big Brother idea of paternalist management. This theme develops as Mayo's argument is carried forward to higher levels and to the wider sphere of society generally. 'The world over we are greatly in need of an administrative *élite* who can assess and handle the concrete difficulties of human collaboration', he wrote. 'Our administrative *élite* has become addict of a few specialist studies and has unduly discounted the human and social aspects of industrial organisation', and 'the appropriate enquiries—biological, anthropological—are so little developed that their findings are relatively unavailable for the training of an administrative *élite*'.[11]

T. N. Whitehead: democracy and cybernetics

One of Mayo's disciples and collaborators in the Hawthorne experiments was Thomas North Whitehead, Alfred North Whitehead's son. His *Leadership in a Free Society* (1937) is concerned with the problems of maintaining the cohesion of social structures, and human satisfaction, vitality and initiative, in a society when 'for the first time in history we find complex societies dedicated to the creed of continual, never-ending change controlled by relatively logical scientific thinking'.[12] He describes the Hawthorne researches and discusses the problems of small groups, formal and informal organisation, social balance and integration. Although he has traces of the naïvety of pre-war optimism about human society his approach is broader, deeper, more balanced and more democratic than Mayo's and bears many marks of the genius of his father's mind. He claims that 'in any society each member is to some degree a leader, whilst to a large extent he is directed by others or the ways of life he finds about him. For leadership consists of obtaining the permission of a group to make an individual contribution.'[13] It is interesting that a social scientist so interested in the problems of maintaining balance in social organisms (and also adaptation to environment) should four years earlier have published *The Design and Use of Instruments and Accurate Mechanism: Underlying Principles*.[14] This engineering manual contains an element of philosophy and perhaps some foreshadowing of later thought about control mechanisms and 'feedback'. It incidentally includes a warm tribute to his father as 'the main influence in determining my own standpoint'.

Chester Barnard: practical experience and theory

Chester Barnard (1886–1961) gave the systematic study of organisations, especially large organisations, a broader scope, and took it to a deeper level than it had probably ever achieved before. He also introduced a better balance between theory and practice. As President for twenty-one years of the New Jersey Bell Telephone Company and twice State Director of the New Jersey Relief Administration, he had practical experience of middle and top level management at least comparable with that of Fayol and Mooney, and probably better than any other previous writer on organisation theory. He was also President of the Rockefeller Foundation and closely associated with the academic world, notably with the Whiteheads, Mayo, and their colleagues in the Harvard Business School and also with the Harvard biologists. His writing reveals a breadth of reading and a depth of scholarship much beyond that of Mooney's and Urwick's mere citations of narrative history. He digested and synthesised his practical

experience and philosophised in a way which earned him respect in
the academic, business, Government and military worlds. It is only
unfortunate that he does not cite practical examples from this experience in much detail.

The ideas in his great work *The Functions of the Executive*[15] (1938)
were formed in the turbulent self-critical America of the Great
Depression and the New Deal—rather different from Fayol's and
Taylor's confident pre-1914 world. His vast practical experience protected him from the naïve over-optimism of Mayo, whom he greatly
admired; but he nevertheless professed a profound though sober
idealism. His major contribution to organisation theory was to apply
the ideas of Mayo and his colleagues to the middle and top levels of
management. He testified to the importance of informal organisation
and the necessity for management by consent at those levels, but also
to the importance of formal organisation (which he discussed at
length) and the interdependence and interaction of the two concepts.

Communication and consent

He preached the necessity of cooperation, but pointed out that the
more cooperation there was in an organisation the more complex it
became. Hence his great concern was communication. He emphasised
the necessity of rule by consent, of cooperation as something coming
up from below and not merely elicited from on high. He took this line
not because he was soft or sentimental, but because he frankly admitted that in large organisations, even in an army,[16] one or a few
men at the top just cannot get things done unless they can induce the
large numbers of people on whom they are dependent to be willing
to do them, and to take initiatives themselves. Nevertheless, he said,
executives, and especially top executives, had as their prime duty the
formulation of the purposes of organisations and the selection,
development and motivation of the right people to carry out these
purposes. All this was in the context of organisations which were
systems involving both purposes and people—systems regarded in
the light of the ideas of Mayo and the Whiteheads. He emphasised
the importance of the small groups of people, between two and
fifteen, which form the essential cells out of which any organisation,
however large, must be built. Complex organisations, he says, must
not be thought of, either logically or historically, as being created as
large wholes and then subdivided, but rather as built up gradually
from basic component units or cells. He cites a government, a telephone system and biological analogies.[17] An organisation was a
community of people and interests, which included management,
employees and customers. His doctrines were based on considerable
studies of jurisprudence as well as sociology, and he quotes as the

thesis of Ehrlich's *Fundamental Principles of the Sociology of Law*
'that all law arises from the formal and especially the informal understandings of people as socially organised'.[18] He protests at the way
in which formal organisation theory has been influenced by historical
analogies from authoritarian régimes of church and state.

In all this and much else which cannot be briefly summarised,
Barnard is on the side of the organisation theory revolutionaries.
Perhaps he is the leading figure among them. He protests that he cannot recognise anything to correspond with his practical experience,
or the activities of competent managers, in the theoretical literature
of his time. Professor Mackenzie says he 'played the Copernical
trick of standing classical management theory on its head'.[19] Yet he
is classical in generalising about all types of organisation, irrespective
of their purpose, and he is included among those criticised for this
reason by Burns and Stalker.[20] But what he is saying is that the feel
of things is very similar in the most diverse kinds of organisation,
rather than that structures and processes all the way down should be
similarly modelled. He was also rather classical in the amount of
space he devotes to formal organisation and he appears to accept the
Graicunas fallacy about the span of control.[21]

He concludes that the heart of the matter is in the antithesis and
the synthesis between on the one hand cooperation and absorption
of the individual in the purposes of the group and on the other hand
the necessity of free will and individual initiative. In other words the
dilemma of organisation and management theory is the eternal
dilemma of freedom and order. Barnard gives as his final declaration
of faith, 'I believe in the power of the cooperation of men of free will
to make men free to cooperate; that only as they choose to work together can they achieve the fulness of personal development.'[22]

Herbert A. Simon: behaviour within organisations

Simon published his *Administrative Behaviour* in 1945, with a preface
by Barnard, and a second edition with a long, new introduction in
1957.[23] He therefore writes against the background not only of the
New Deal but of World War II and the consequent elevation of public
sector management into a subject of greater practical importance and
more serious academic study in USA. An academic and consultant
concerned with both the private and public sectors, a substantial
amount of his personal management experience was in local government and public utility services, whence his analogies and examples
are mainly drawn. He has also written, and collaborated in writing,
more specifically about American public administration, as we shall
mention later.

Decision-making

The subtitle of his book *Administrative Behaviour* is *A study of decision-making processes in administrative organisations*, and the opening chapter almost seems to be equating all administration and management activity with decision-making. He indeed takes the starting-point of organisation theory away from the static idea of structure, which so largely preoccupied the classical writers, to the dynamics of processes—in fact from anatomy to physiology. Yet he also has important chapters dealing with the nature of organisations, notably the concepts of equilibrium and of authority. He only reaches these concepts, however, after analysis of decision-making and its related processes, and in particular the functions of individuals. Organisations for Simon are essentially groups of individuals, and environments within which individuals and groups function. They are necessary for certain types of activity, notably decision-making. Simon sees decisions not as isolated, self-contained events but links in a chain. The end-product of one decision is the raw material for the next. There are 'hierarchies' of decisions. The ideal decision-making process, the assembly and review of all data and all possible consequences of decisions, is beyond the capacity of any individual; nor is it practicable in the time, nor with the information, normally available to him. Practical decision-making is therefore dependent on group and cooperative activity and on an organisation.

It is the organisation which can provide the support and the information for the individual or group and the framework of customs and routines within which ranges of choice can be limited and controlled. Routines and customs of organisations supplement or substitute the individual memory or habit which is the basis of quick, routine, standardised decision-making—'programmed' decision-making as Burns and Stalker later called it.* Organisations also provide frameworks of both information and value-systems within which the larger, more complex, less 'programmed' decision-making processes can be made manageable. They also divide and distribute functions and spheres of responsibility among their members, so that each can concentrate on a part of what is essentially a continuum of decision-making processes. I have myself argued,[24] from practical experience before reading Simon's or any other work on decision theory, that decisions in large organisations can seldom be attributed to individuals; but that a whole series of people and organisational layers at different levels contribute to them. They indeed largely emerge from the facts of a situation, once an orderly and reasonable procedure for eliciting and evaluating these facts is established. This

* See pp. 64, below.

is just what Simon is saying. But in doing so he is developing an analysis, not only of the decision-making process, but of organisations. 'One function an organisation performs is to place the organisation members in a psychological environment that will adapt their decisions to the organisation objectives and will provide them with the information to make these decisions correctly.'[25] He adds, 'Administrative systems are systems of cooperative behaviour'.[26] In particular the organisation establishes and defines the succession of short-term and long-term goals and objectives in the light of which decisions are taken.

Here Simon is very enlightening in view of his public service experience. 'In one respect the decisions problem in private organisations is much simpler than in public agencies. The private organisation is expected to take into consideration only those consequences of the decision which affect *it*, while the public agency must weigh the decision in terms of some comprehensive system of public or community values.'[27] We will consider this point later when dealing with the multiplicity, variability and potential conflict of objectives in the public sector. This is the key to the essentially different nature of organisations in the public sector and of their structures and administrative processes compared with most of those in the private sector. Of course the distinction is not clear-cut and there are exceptions on both sides. There are small, single-purpose public bodies like Government printing works and large international conglomerate companies carrying on many activities in many countries.

Criticisms of classical theory

Simon attacks some of the 'accepted administrative principles' of classical organisation theory, notably its principles of division of functions, unity of command and span of control. Division of responsibility and specialisation can be either by function, or by process, or by objective, or by place.* Classical theory, he says, gives no clue as to which basis is preferable in any particular circumstances. Hence its principle of unity of command is also ambiguous—unity within what defined sphere? Classical organisation principles are mere 'proverbs', each paired with a contradictory proverb—for instance spans of control should be narrow, but chains of command should be short. These ambiguities and inadequacies of classical theory are due to inadequate diagnoses of situations and definitions of terms and to lack of detailed research into real situations. They are also due to lack of understanding of the purpose and functions of organisations in relation both to their members and to the processes which they

* See the discussion of these principles in relation to the Haldane Report on the *Machinery of Government* on pp. 120–1 below.

comprise. Of organisation, Simon says, 'even when it is discussed by
some of its most perceptive students—for example by Colonel Urwick
—it takes on more the aspect of a series of orderly cubicles contrived
according to an abstract architectural logic than of a house designed
to be inhabited by human beings'.[28]

He discusses the concept of authority, both the formality of defined
powers and also authority in the sense of decisions which will have
practical effect. He writes of the extent of 'zones of acceptance' of
decisions and orders, and the various factors which in practice determine whether and how far decisions get carried out. These factors
include habits and customs, the degree of respect by its employees
for the objectives of an organisation, the personalities or competence
of individuals, and so on, as well as formal or informal punitive
sanctions. 'Most organisations will', he says, 'tolerate large quantities
of insubordination—particularly if not verbalized—without dismissal.' He also discusses (not very conclusively) limited and divided
authority in particular spheres, on the lines proposed by Taylor, and
also the kind of *de facto* authority which derives from advice—even
from a subordinate—which it is impracticable or undesirable, or not
customary, to ignore. He discusses appeals to higher levels in large
organisations, sometimes on the ground that the original decisions
were unjustified on merit and sometimes that they were constitution-
ally unauthorised. He even suggests that the technique of top administrators leaving authorities inadequately defined so as to divide and
rule is 'used . . . so often that it cannot be casually dismissed as poor
administration'.[29]

Communication

He discusses communication, its instruments and its practical techniques, from rule-books and reports to gossip and the grapevine.
'Without communication', he says, 'there can be no organisation.'
Here he is wisest when he is emphasising the psychological elements
and personal relations, the 'presumption of friendliness' in a large
working unit. Perhaps he is less wise when he appears to over-
emphasise the role of formally constituted information-gathering
internal units. He does not mention the prime necessity for managers
at all levels to get out and about inside and outside their organisations and make direct contact with concrete situations.

Efficiency in the public sector

The 'criterion of efficiency', particularly in the public sector, he
defines neither in the loose, traditional sense, nor the engineering
(input/output) sense, but as the ratio of actual to standard or possible
achievement, relative to resources, policy considerations or other

limiting conditions. He leaves the problem somewhat in the air, because he is pleading for a quantitative approach to problems which, at least when he wrote, could only be very inadequately measured. He was however doing very important pioneer work in defining problems, notably the assessment of community values, which have now been more thoroughly tackled, although by no means solved, by the techniques of cost/benefit economics.

Motivation

Simon has a valuable chapter on 'Loyalties and Organisational identification'. Quoting, but not wholly following Freud, he discusses how individuals identify themselves psychologically not only with other individuals but with groups and organisations. Such identification he says 'is an important mechanism for constructing the environment of decisions',[30] yet exclusive identification with sub-groups and departments rather than the whole organisation or community is obviously bad, although very common. Here he compares the public and private sectors.

The private segment of our economy operates on the assumption that management will make its decisions in terms of profit to the individual business [though he states elsewhere that private business may have other motivations]. This institutional psychology of choice may easily be carried over to the public segment of the economy through lack of recognition of the fundamental differences in the assumptions that underlie these two segments. . . . These same attitudes may be present in persons who, while they never have had administrative responsibility in the private segment of the economy, have absorbed these notions from a predominantly private economy cultural environment.[31]

The dangers of narrow departmentalism place a special responsibility on higher administrators of harmonising the attitudes and activities of their subordinates not only with one another but with the outside world. The predominant administrative task at higher levels 'is an artistic and an inventive one. New values must be sought out and weighed; the possibilities of new administrative structures evaluated.'[32]

Summing up his review of what he calls the anatomy and physiology of organisations, he again emphasises the cooperative nature of administration, that no decisions are really made solely by individuals and that coordination, communication and review (he implies but does not use the word 'feedback') are the supreme tasks of the administrator. But he ends up by disclaiming any desire to build up higher administration as a general abstract science unrelated to the functions and purposes of organisations. Foreshadowing Joan Wood-

ward, and implicitly criticising the classical theorists, he says that
forms of organisation must depend on circumstances.[33]

Simon, Smithberg and Thompson: organisation theory and the American public sector

These were not Simon's last words on organisation theory. His
writings include a substantial work in collaboration with Smithberg
and Thompson. Although entitled *Public Administration* its importance for the British reader lies as much in its comprehensive synthesis
of classical and other contemporary schools of general organisation
theory as in its application of this theory to the American public
sector, to which its examples are almost entirely confined. With a
scholarly balance of theoretical analysis and well-digested practical
evidence, the authors demonstrate that the classical and human relations views of organisation need not be regarded as mutually exclusive. Indeed, they also introduce important ideas which would be
best classified with 'systems' theory (discussed at the end of the next
chapter). They have a lot to say about organisational structures and
the classical ideas, notably those of Gulick, of division of responsibility; but they also demonstrate the incompleteness of any such
mechanistic approach. Hence they interleave their exposition of this
approach with extended discussion of organisations as composed of
groups of people, of inter-group relations and of communication in
general. The idea of an organisation as an 'open system, emerges in
their discussion of 'organizational equilibrium' and the relationship
of an organisation with its 'participants' and its 'clients'. An organisation, they say, is 'a system of inter-related social behaviours of a
number of persons whom we call participants . . .'. These, they say,
'in a governmental organization include not only its employees, but
also . . . other organizational units with which it co-operates, legislat-
ors, members of interest groups and lobbies that are concerned with
its program, citizens who are regulated by it and those who receive
its services'.[34]

The value of the book for the student of public administration is
however limited not only by its almost exclusive concentration on the
USA but also by its focussing largely on the more modern functions
of public utility services and economic planning. It has little to say
about the original 'law and order' functions of Government. It
specifically excludes the legislative and judicial functions including
the administrative services which support them. It cites with apparent
agreement the opinion of the mid-nineteenth-century President
Andrew Jackson that in his day 'the tasks of Government were
sufficiently simple so that any person of intelligence could perform
them without preparation or training' and 'governing could and

should . . . be done by amateurs'. The fact that 'the situation is vastly different today' is attributed to the need for numerous specialists, all of whom, in the examples cited in this passage, are technologists and economists[35] and not apparently specialists in administration as such. It is surprising that as Simon and his collaborators have contributed so much to the theory of administration, decision-making and organisation building, they do not devote more space to applying this theory to the more elemental functions of Government.

In consequence they deal largely with US Federal agencies and functions of State and local government of a public utility character, which correspond mainly to the nationalised industries, local authorities and the service-providing elements of Government Departments in Britain. So they stress the similarities of public and private sector administration as much as the differences.[36] This is partly because his environment compels any sympathetic American exponent of public administration to write more defensively than his British opposite number because 'There is a widespread conviction that what governments do is inefficient and often corrupt'.[37] Points about impartial personnel administration which a British reader might regard as almost self-evident have to be argued at length. Yet it may be salutary for the British reader to be told that there was a sincere democratic argument, however weak, for a 'spoils system' based on the 'Jacksonian theory', and of American reactions to British Civil Service meritocracy as élitist.[38]

We cannot summarise all the lessons to be learnt from this work. One outstanding impression it leaves is the importance of considerations of the national environment in public administration, and how severely it sets limits to abstract generalisation. We shall return to this point in Chapter 4.

The Behavioural scientists: Argyris, McGregor and Likert— people in organisations

We must now consider some American social psychologists, who in the fifties and sixties have developed and extended the ideas about people in organisations which Mayo, Barnard, Simon and others propounded in the thirties and forties. Such writers are now usually described as behavioural scientists.

The theme of Chris Argyris is embodied in the title of one of his books, *Personality and Organization: The Conflict between the System and the Individual.* In one sense this theme is very old and is to be found in Greek tragedy, Shakespeare and much other literature. These ancient conflicts, however, were generally set between exceptional individuals and the political or religious order of society as a whole. Argyris is concerned with the peculiarly contemporary con-

flict, in an educated democratic society, between any large organisation and all or any of its employees. He starts from the psychology
of the individual and says, 'An analysis of the research literature
suggests substantial agreement on the assumption that personality
manifests some type of energy.'[39] This energy needs expression and
adjustment with its environment. Moreover 'most personality
theories state that personality becomes complete, organized and
integrated only when it interacts with other people, ideas and social
organizations'.[40]

However the formal organisation as described by Fayol, Taylor,
Urwick and other classical theorists will not meet this need.
Indeed it positively frustrates and represses the individual by imposing on him its own inflexible logic. It allows no freedom for initiative
and narrows the scope of individual responsibility by its excessive
subdivisions of function and its concentration of authority.[41] Argyris
says, 'there is a lack of congruity between the needs of the healthy
individual and the demands of the formal organization'. Hence 'the
resultants of this disturbance are frustration, failure, short time perspective and conflict. In every form of formal organization (and its
derivatives of directive leadership, management controls and pseudo-
human relations programs) lie the roots of disorganization.'[42]

Argyris's remedies for all this seem tentative—tolerant, flexible
'employee-centred leadership' and 'reality leadership', involving
both objectivity and flexibility, both sympathetic diagnosis of situations and detachment. 'Leadership behaviour depends primarily on
the situation.' Leaders should be 'self-aware, independent and self-
responsible'. They must develop 'frustration tolerance' and 'the
ability to express hostility diplomatically'.[43] Argyris also advocates
job enlargement (that is, 'the increase of the number of tasks performed by the employee along the flow of work'), so as to 'permit the
individual to use more of his personality' in contrast with the subdivision and narrowing of functions implied in classical organisation
theory.[44] Argyris does not carry these ideas to a conclusion but he
points the way to new directions of thought.

McGregor: theories 'X' and 'Y'

McGregor says much the same as Argyris but rather more confidently
and optimistically, and he has crystallised it in the form of 'Theory
X' and 'Theory Y'. By these he means not theories argued explicitly;
but the conscious or subconscious assumptions on which managers
base their activities. 'Theory X' assumes that most people have 'an
inherent dislike of work' and have to be directed and coerced into
doing it. Indeed they are glad to be directed and are mainly concerned
about security.[45] 'Theory Y' says work is natural to human beings

and a high proportion like, or can be brought to like, work, responsibility and a sense of achievement—yet under modern industrial conditions (largely he says based on 'Theory X') few are normally allowed such scope. For this, McGregor blames classical organisation theory and practice, as too much preoccupied with a type of authority of ecclesiastical and military origin.[46] The classical, hierarchical or 'scalar' principle of subdividing responsibilities and objectives frustrates initiative. To this McGregor opposes the principle of integration: 'the creation of conditions such that the members of the organisation can achieve their own goals best by directing their efforts towards the success of the enterprise'.[47] As this remedy involves a flexible, permissive attitude in management, McGregor, like Argyris, is not very precise in spelling it out.

McGregor contributes to an understanding of the confused 'line-and-staff' question by claiming that higher managements, anxious to exercise authoritarian control, but finding the normal 'line' channels inadequate instruments, turn to the ostensibly advisory 'staff' units and tend to use them (with their statistics and other monitoring material and expertise) as policemen. Hence they exacerbate relationships all round. This McGregor suggests is a natural consequence of attempts to exercise rigid detailed controls in organisations which are too big for such methods. The remedy, following 'Theory Y', is for 'staff' specialist units to be available with their advice, expertise and information services at all levels of management. Their function should be to help and support, rather than control and restrict.[48]

Likert: 'interaction/influence groups'

Likert's starting-point and general approach are similar to those of McGregor and Argyris; but he tends to be more optimistic and positive and to carry his thinking further forward into the problems of organisational patterns. He starts by quoting research results to demonstrate, not merely that authoritarian ('Theory X') managerial styles are restrictive and frustrating, but that 'Theory Y' ('supportive') management has produced positive results in terms of higher productivity. He suggests that the new style is becoming widely adopted: 'Managers with the best records in American business and government are in the process of pointing the way to an appreciably more effective system of management than now exists.'[49] Nevertheless, he thinks that for some circumstances and types of industry or function, authoritarian methods or systems may be more appropriate.

After discussing the individual relationships between managers at different levels, he goes on to the forms and mutual relationships of groups of managers and replaces the traditional straight-line organisation chart with a series of intersecting circles representing the linkages provided between different parts of an organisation—upwards, downwards and sideways—'interaction/influence groups'. Hence, anyone in a responsible position in a large organisation finds one of his main functions to be maintaining communication between his own units and those of many different groups of colleagues. He finds himself to be not merely a link in a chain, or even in several interlocking chains, but a member of a variety of different groups, formal and informal. To get and to give guidance on policy he must maintain these personal liaisons, these memberships of a series of groups. The larger the organisation and the more complex and varied its creative concern with policy, the more true this is. Likert's model has an air of realism which any member of the headquarters of a Government Department or large nationalised industry will recognise. We shall see later* how the complexity of organisational patterns and their pliability is greater the more they are concerned with policy or innovation or operate in a changing environment.

To sum up, the theme of Argyris, McGregor and Likert is that there is usually a clash of interest between, on the one hand, the individual personality and the groups into which individuals naturally form themselves, and, on the other hand, the organisation, at least as traditionally structured and managed. It is never quite clear how far any of these writers hope for a full reconciliation or synthesis of the opposing interests, and how far they are saying that the best that can be looked for is compromise in which sacrifices are made on both sides. Of the three, Likert seems to go furthest in suggesting synthesis, particularly in terms of the anatomy and physiology of organisations. Argyris and McGregor expose, analyse, and perhaps even exaggerate the problem and their somewhat tentative answers seem to be more in terms of tolerant, flexible, 'supportive' behaviour by individual managers than in that of the nature and design of organisational systems.

Maslow, Hertzberg and Gellerman: motivation

The ideas about motivation of three other American psychologists, Maslow, Hertzberg and Gellerman, have important implications for the structure and the functioning of organisations. Maslow[50] expounded the idea that men have 'a hierarchy of needs'—physiological (food, etc.), security, social ('belongingness'), ego (public esteem and self-esteem) and finally self-fulfilment. The first group of needs must be satisfied continually, but give largely negative satisfaction. Hence the latter groups, especially the last, can be the really important factors determining conduct. Hertzberg has developed somewhat similar ideas and reported various researches to substan-

* See p. 145 *et seq.* below.

tiate them. The first category of needs he calls 'hygiene factors'. These, he says, remove dissatisfaction, but do not give positive satisfaction. That can only be obtained from the other factors, which he calls 'motivators'. These arise from man's capacity and need for psychological growth—'achievement, recognition, work itself, responsibility'.[51]

Gellerman,[52] a management consultant, has developed and popularised the ideas of Hertzberg and others, including Revans (in the context of British hospitals). His main conclusions are to relegate financial reward to a subsidiary, largely negative position and to stress the importance of work itself as a motivator, provided those who do it have adequate scope, encouragement and opportunities for two-way communication. He limits the effectiveness of authoritarian management to short periods and emphasises how environment and changing treatment can enlarge the capacities and performance of managers and others.

These writers have not proved scientifically any general hypothesis concerning human motivation. The researches on which their work is based seem mainly to have involved asking various sorts of workers, professional, management and manual, how and when they felt satisfied or dissatisfied with their work. Nevertheless the researches have been replicated and have produced widespread support in management circles in America and Britain. They confirm what has been assumed about motivation in most occupations outside industry and commerce, at least in Britain. In a variety of public sector jobs, it has been accepted that the main motives were the needs of the job and its intrinsic interest and prestige. Yet outside the public sector, and sometimes within it, this has been generally ignored or explicitly denied. Professor Merrett of the London Business School in a recent book[53] on *Executive Remuneration*, while admitting the possibility of 'non-financial motivation' almost confines it to status and honours in the public services and brushes it aside in just over a page, although admitting there is undoubtedly a need for a theory about it. The rest of his book is based on the assumption that business managers and perhaps all executives have no motivation but money and fear of dismissal. If, however, the existence of a wider range of motivating factors than these is accepted, the potential consequences for organisation theory are considerable. Direction, coordination, ultimate arbitration and expert advice will still be needed. Yet organisation will no longer need to be planned on the assumption that all or even most of the drive must come from the top. Everything need not depend on rigidly channelled authority and responsibility. Many people will be largely or partly self-motivated although they will need training, guidance and direction.

Golembrewski: the 'line and staff' doctrine disputed

We must here notice a recent frontal attack on the classical 'line and staff' concept,* by Robert T. Golembrewski. He challenges a long-current 'myth' in organisation design, that 'staff' should be subsidiary and outside the chain of command.[54] He cites various writers to suggest that the concept has been crumbling for some time. For instance Brecht writes, 'The more one endeavours to scrutinise the "line-and-staff" concept analytically, the more one comes to the conclusion that it is an arbitrary and artificial notion whose implications have never been thought through'.[55] Golembrewski criticises the unreality, in sophisticated modern organisations (especially those making much use of computers), of what he calls the 'Neutral and Inferior Instrument ("NIIL") Model' of the staff function. He substitutes his own concept, the 'Colleague Model' which attempts to create an environment within which the various specialists can feel free to make their contributions to effective performance.[56] It 'implies what may be called "functional leadership" . . . a fluidity which allows leadership to pass from individual to individual at the same level of organization'. This makes possible job enlargement and job enrichment, as opposed to classical ideas of specialisation and division of labour. Hence it encourages the more complex and flexible patterns of internal relationships advocated by Likert.

Brown and Jaques: authority redefined

Although battered by Golembrewski, the line-and-staff concept is not dead, nor indeed are various other concepts of formally defined authority and responsibility. They have indeed been revived and defined in sharper and more practical terms by two writers, Brown and Jaques, who have come to their present positions from very different starting-points. Wilfred Brown (now Lord Brown of Machrihanish) was for nearly three decades the chief executive of the Glacier Metal Company; Professor Elliott Jaques, a Canadian psycho-analyst, has been his adviser and collaborator in management, research and the development of theory. Starting with problems of industrial relations in factories and ideas of participation in the human relations tradition, they have covered, jointly or separately, a very wide field of organisation theory and social and individual psychology.

The most important message now emerging from their work concerns the importance of clarity and firmness in defining formal organisation structures, the responsibilities of management and the nature of work. Work, they say, involves the exercise of degrees of

* See p. 31–3 above.

discretion, varying according to the capacity of the individual and his place in a hierarchy. People's psychological needs are best met if they have clearly defined scope to exercise the degree of responsibility of which they are capable, and if their relations with subordinates, superiors and colleagues are clearly specified. In Brown and Jaques's view freedom and mental health for the individual, for the group and for the organisation, are dependent on a firm framework. Jaques writes, '. . . formal organization can and must be discovered, organization which conforms to human nature and which is made up of roles in which individuals can be expected to work effectively and creatively while conforming to the explicit and teachable policies governing that work'. In contrast to Argyris, McGregor and Likert, Jaques questions the practicability of improving organisations by changing the personal management styles of individuals: '. . . This orientation tends to underrate the difficulties of changing personality, and fails to inquire first whether the organizational structure and policies we have are so constructed as to provide an effective setting for human endeavour.'[57] Jaques's clinical experience and research and Brown's experience of management have convinced them that although most people need reasonable freedom and scope, they are not happiest when freedom is so broad as to be undefined. They would also appear to agree with Hertzberg that they are happiest when their attention is focussed on specific jobs. Brown is sceptical of the value of informal organisation.[58] He and Jaques give much useful advice about the design of organisation structures, stressing the need to limit the number of layers and keep the effective gaps between the layers wide enough in terms of discretion, responsibility, power and remuneration. Brown expounds the practice of 'staff' specialists as having definite authority within specified spheres—that of assisting a manager in the coordination of the work of the manager's immediate subordinates in a particular field by exercising authority and issuing instructions on his behalf'. He spells this out in detail with the aid of diagrams.[59]

The Brown–Jaques doctrines and practices of management have been criticised as authoritarian[60] and much of the detail into which they enter is open to debate. Yet what they say is highly relevant to the public sector, which Jaques has been studying extensively in recent years. One of their most important notions, to which we must return in our concluding chapter, is that of initiative and personal discretion flourishing best when their scope is defined within a firm outer framework of authority.

1. Tom Burns and G. H. Stalker, 1961. *The Management of Innovation.* Tavistock. The second edition, with new long preface, Social Science Paperbacks, 1966.

2. David L. Sills (ed.) under 'A. N. Whitehead', 1968. *International Encyclopedia of Social Sciences*, p. 535. The Macmillan Co. & Free Press (USA).

3. A. N. Whitehead, 1926. *Science and the Modern World*, pp. 129, 130. Cambridge University Press.

4. e.g., by Joan Woodward in *Industrial Organisation Theory and Practice*, p. 35. O.U.P., 1965.

5. Mary Parker Follet, 1941. *Dynamic Administration.* (Eds. H. C. Metcalf and Urwick), p. 282.

6. ibid., p. 200.

7. ibid., p. 194

8. William H. Whyte, 1956. *The Organisation Man*, pp. 36–40, 45–6, Simon and Silvester, N.Y.; Penguin edition, 1960.

9. *Human Problems of Industrial Organisation*, 1933. Harvard.

10. ibid., p. 94.

11. ibid., pp. 175–7.

12. Oxford University Press, 1937.

13. ibid., p. 258.

14. Dover Publications, Inc., New York, 1933. 2nd ed., 1954.

15. Harvard University Press, 1938.

16. ibid., p. 164, quoting Major-General James C. Harbord, 1936. *The American Army in France*, p. 259. Little, Brown and Co., Boston.

17. ibid., p. 105, note.

18. ibid., Preface.

19. W. J. M. Mackenzie, 1967. *Politics and Social Science*, p. 252. Penguin.

20. Burns and Stalker, op. cit., p. 108.

21. Barnard, op. cit., pp. 106–9.

22. ibid., p. 296.

23. Quotations here are from the Free Press Inc., New York (Collier-Macmillan Ltd, London), paperback edition 1965.

24. R. J. S. Baker, Autumn 1963. 'Discussion and decision-making in the Civil Service', *Public Administration.* (See also pp. 99 *et seq.* below).

25. Simon, op. cit., p. 79. F

26. ibid., p. 72.

27. ibid., p. 69.

28. ibid., p. xvi.

29. ibid., p. 145.

30. ibid., p. 211.

31. ibid., pp. 210–11.

32. ibid., p. 217.

33. ibid., p. 240.

34. Herbert A. Simon, Donald W. Smithberg and Victor A. Thompson, 1950. *Public Administration*, pp. 381–2 *et seq.* A. A. Knopf, New York.

35. ibid., p. 15.

36. ibid., pp. 8–9 *et seq.*

37. ibid., p. 11.

38. ibid., pp. 321–3 and ch. 5.

39. Chris Argyris, 1957. *Personality and Organization*, p. 24. Harper and Row, New York.

40. ibid., pp. 47–8.

41. ibid., ch. 3, pp. 54–75.

42. ibid., pp. 232, 233.

43. ibid., pp. 205–8, 209, 214 and 215.

44. ibid., pp. 177–87.

45. Douglas McGregor, 1957. *The Human Side of Enterprise,* pp. 33–4. McGraw–Hill, New York.

46. ibid., pp. 47–9.

47. ibid., p. 16.

48. ibid., chs. 11 and 12, pp. 145–75.

49. Rensis Likert, 1961. *New Patterns of Management,* p. 3. McGraw-Hill.

50. A. H. Maslow, 1954. *Motivation and Personality.* Harper, New York.

51. Frederick Hertzberg, 1968. *Work and the Nature of Man*, pp. 72–3. Staples. This is an extension of the ideas in his earlier work (with collaborators) *Motivation to Work.* Wiley, 1959, p. 72.

52. Saul Gellerman, 1968. *Management by Motivation.* American Management Association Inc.

53. A. J. Merrett, 1968. *Executive Remuneration in the United Kingdom,* pp. 2–3. Longmans.

54. Robert T. Golembrewski, 1967. *Organization, Men and Power: Problems of Behaviour and Line Staff Models,* p. 1. Rand McNally, Chicago.

55. op. cit., p. 3, quoting E. F. L. Brecht, 1957. *Organization: The Framework of Management,* p. 52. Longmans.

56. Golembrewski, op. cit., p. 126.

57. Wilfred Brown and Elliot Jaques, 1965. *Glacier Project Papers.* Heineman. Jaques' paper, 'Psychology and Organization', pp. 184 and 186.

58. Brown's paper, 'Informal Organization', in ibid., pp. 144–62, especially p. 153.

59. Chapter on 'Analysis of Operational Work' and 'Specialist Organisation' in Wilfred Brown's *Exploration in Management*, pp. 163–94, especially p. 117. Penguin, 1960.

60. e.g., Joe Kelly, 1968. *Is Scientific Management Possible?* Faber.

ORGANIC AND SYSTEMS THEORIES

Burns and Stalker: organism and mechanism

The variation of organisation in relation to function and environment is the subject of one of the most important modern British works on organisation theory, *The Management of Innovation* by Burns and Stalker. It is based on researches in the electronics and other manufacturing industries in the mid-fifties. The authors were concerned with organisations, both as social systems and also in respect to their appropriateness for different kinds of industry, those where the technological and market conditions were changing, and those where they were stable. The results were a classification of systems of industrial organisation into 'mechanistic' and 'organic' types, or rather 'polar extremities' of the forms which such systems can take.

They arrived at this classification partly by research based on interviews with managers, and partly analytically. Following Simon and others, they distinguished between the kinds of decision-making required of management. They said there was 'programmed'decision-making, based on routines and standard frames of reference, and 'non-programmed' decision-making involving new initiatives and a flexible approach to each problem. A rigid 'institutional framework' was appropriate for managers making mainly programmed decisions. Non-programmed decision-making, however, they said, 'required a common culture of dependably shared beliefs about the common interests of the working community and about the standards and criteria used in it to judge achievement, individual contributory expertise and other matters by which a person, or a combination of people, are evaluated. A system of shared beliefs of this kind is expressed and visible in a code of conduct, a way of dealing with other people. This code of conduct is, in fact, the first sign to the outsider of the presence of a management system appropriate to changing conditions.'[1] These phrases coming from authorities on private enterprise industrial management are worth remembering in connection with the organisation and atmosphere of the policy-making elements in Government Departments and the public bodies.

Burns and Stalker's lengthy classification of characteristics of the two types of systems follows from these types of decision-making. It is well worth reading in full; but may be summarised as follows:

(A) *Mechanistic*

(i) the differentiation of functional tasks is based on specialisation and every functional role is defined in terms of the rights, duties and technical methods attaching to it.

(ii) 'hierarchic structure of control, authority and communication'; with lines of internal communication mainly vertical.

(iii) working methods prescribed in instructions from above.

(iv) emphasis on loyalty to the organisation and to superiors.

(v) assumed omniscience at the top.

(vi) internal or local knowledge and skill are valued more highly than that derived from a broader or external experience.

(B) *Organic*

(i) individuals' responsibilities to the organisation broad and not precisely defined; evasion of personal responsibility discouraged.

(ii) the presumed common interest of all employees in the survival and growth of the business is relied upon as the principal sanction for individual conduct rather than the contractual relationship between the employee and the impersonal corporation.

(iii) omniscience no longer imputed to the head of the concern. Knowledge and points of initiative may be located anywhere within the organisation.

(iv) internal communication lateral rather than vertical, ignoring differences of rank. Information, consultation and advice rather than command. Readiness to cooperate with others in promoting the purposes of the organisation.

(v) 'commitment to the concern's tasks and to the "technological ethos" of material progress and expansion is more highly valued than loyalty and obedience; . . . importance and prestige attach to affiliations and expertise external to the firm. . . .'

These two types are not the same thing as the Theory X and Theory Y of McGregor. The former are organisational systems, the latter

A.T.A.P.A.—C

styles of management adopted by individuals. Moreover, although it may have something in common with Theory Y, life in an organic system is not easy or soft. Whereas in a mechanistic system, a man's specific responsibilities are clearly defined and he need not worry about anything else, in an organic system, 'Great stress is placed on his regarding himself as fully implicated in the discharge of any task appearing over his horizon.' A manager often finds he has 'an uneasy, embarrassed or chronically anxious quest for knowledge about what he should be doing or what is expected of him and similar apprehensiveness about what others are doing'.[2]

Burns and Stalker believe that 'as production and the market have moved into fundamentally unstable relationship and as the stream of technical innovation has quickened, the legitimacy of the hierarchical pyramid of management bureaucracy has been threatened by the sheer volume of novel tasks and problems confronting industrial concerns'. One might add that it is a much less novel experience for Governments to have to confront utterly unstable and unpredictable world conditions and this has probably promoted an 'organic' atmosphere at the higher levels of many types of Government Department. However, in conditions of change and stress, people seek not only freedom and flexibility, but also reassurance and stability. Is it possible to have flexibility within a firm framework, a supple and adaptable nervous and muscular system and a solid bone structure?

Burns and Stalker are more definite even than Likert in saying that their two types are not 'good' and 'bad', but that each arises from and is appropriate to particular industries, tasks and circumstances. Nevertheless, their classification, although representing probably one of the greatest single advances ever made in organisation theory, cannot be final or exhaustive. The analogies are too simple. It is indeed surprising that two authors who have spent so long among the advanced technologies of the electronic and related industries should use a term 'mechanistic' in a sense which suggests the simple steam-engines of Watt, or rather the simpler ones of Newcomen. (Watt at least introduced a governor into his engines which gave them some characteristics of a self-adjusting system.) Modern scientific study of control-systems, biological and engineering, seems constantly to suggest bringing them closer together despite the vastly greater complexity of the former.[3] At least biological systems, which include, for instance, 'bio chemical mechanisms', are never unstructured and only the simpler types of engineering mechanism are inflexible. Burns and Stalker are fundamentally right, however, in advocating 'the study of the social world as a process instead of an anatomy frozen into structured immobility . . . the identification of the abstraction of society with the empirical fact of behaviour'.

Lawrence and Lorsch: variety and integration within the organisation

In an important recent work two Harvard professors, Paul R. Lawrence and J. W. Lorsch,[4] carry further the ideas we have so far discussed by analysing different styles and structures of management within different parts of single large organisations. They take as examples sales, production and research. They imply that there may be many further differences according to the organisation's size, extent of diversification and geographical extent. Accepting that such internal varieties of styles and structures are essential for the vitality of a large concern, they discuss the resulting problems of coordination and integration. They conclude that the successful large organisations of the future will be those which can both provide full integration, yet also ensure continual diversification and adaptability of structures, styles and methods. These will be needed to cope with the continual variations of environment within which such large organisations will have to operate, particularly if they are multi-national. Lawrence and Lorsch suggest that the result of this controlled diversification will be a humanising tendency, that the great corporations of the future need not and should not be oppressive monoliths.

This argument is built up on the findings of a comparative study of ten organisations at different levels of economic performance in three industries—food products, plastics and containers. The styles of individual managers and the structures of the organisations are analysed on the basis of quantitative studies. As a result, it is argued that each industry and, indeed, each company, has a different degree of diversification of styles and structures, and hence different and not equally successful means of achieving integration. It may be carried out largely at the top levels, or by close lateral contacts lower down, or by special departments or groups of people designated as 'integrators'. 'Procedures should be more effective in helping people to find the succession of assignments that meet their developing needs and personal abilities. The organisation will serve as a mediator or buffer between the individual and the full raw impact of technological change by providing continuing educational opportunities and various career choices.'[5]

This discussion of the problems of the integration of diverse elements in a single, large organisation is particularly interesting from the standpoint of the public sector. On the whole, we have had little contribution to the solution of such problems from general management literature deriving mainly from the private sector. When the basic patterns of our main public institutions (other than the nationalised industries) were being built up in the century ending with World War II, the private sector had few problems of size and, hence, of internal integration and diversification, at all comparable with those of the public sector. Hence it was the public sector which developed the organs of integration and employed the individuals who were largely concerned with integrating and co-ordinating—the 'generalist' function which is now denounced in some quarters as outdated and Victorian. In fact, the function of coordination and integration is very much a present-day requirement, and for some organisations in the private sector a new one, resulting from mergers and take-overs. It is strange that the Fulton Report does not say a great deal about the integrating function, although its importance, as Lawrence and Lorsch demonstrate, must surely be accentuated by the very specialisation and increased professionalism which the Report advocates.

These authors have therefore performed an important service in emphasising the increased need for integration. They have not, however, gone far in analysing the integrating function and its processes. They describe different 'modes of conflict resolution' which they classify as 'confrontation or problem solving; smoothing over differences; and forcing decisions';[6] but this analysis is not developed. Although some individual managers' brief descriptions of these processes are quoted, the authors do not enquire what actually happens when individuals and groups of people are trying to solve conflicts and differences within and between large organisations. This, however, is what a large part of the day-to-day stuff of public administration consists of. Few experienced administrators would put it all into these authors' three simple categories—which presumably involve either coldly rational argument, specious papering-over of cracks, or dictatorial arbitration. The integrating processes still await full scientific analysis.

Joan Woodward: organisation for technology and function

Professor Joan Woodward was an industrial sociologist with wide research experience ranging from dockworkers to saleswomen. Her major work was based on extensive studies in a hundred manufacturing firms in south-east Essex in the mid-fifties and later.[7] She assessed the results in the light of similar contemporary work, including that of Burns and Stalker. They imply two types of organisation appropriate to two types of industrial situation—static or dynamic, stable or changing. Joan Woodward analysed organisations not by individual industries but by types of technology and manufacturing processes: (a) small batch or unit production (the making of 'one-off' products), (b) large batch or mass production and (c) continuous process production (e.g., oil or other liquids, etc.). She concluded that at the two extremes, (a) and (c), a high pyramid organisation with narrow spans of control is most successful; but with (b) flat pyramids, wide spans of control and generally more formal structures work best. She qualified these statements to some extent and amplified them, for instance in relation to communication systems and informal organisation. She discussed the different types of firm and situation in which the production, the marketing or the research and development functions were dominant in the management structures and processes, and emphasised that formal structure and actual process and function are not necessarily the same.

The correctness or otherwise of her analysis of particular industrial situations is less important than her fundamental assertion that organisation and management processes (both formal and informal) should vary with purpose, function, technology and working methods. She pressed further than most previous writers the attack on the rigidities of line-and-staff doctrine. She said 'the line-staff organization is based not on a differentiation of skills, but on assignment of roles',[8] and 'although at a formal level joint accountability was not recognised, the power and prestige of the staff managers in some firms were so high at the informal level of organization, it was almost impossible to distinguish in practice between advice and executive instructions'.[9] Again, 'The high status conferred on operating personnel sometimes gives the impression that theirs is the line role, but the work of the maintenance and technical departments is certainly not advisory. Fortunately the higher level of sophistication of the people concerned makes it less necessary for them to rely on the line-staff convention as a mechanism of resolving conflict. They appear to understand and accept the concept of joint accountability.'

Professor Woodward did not publish any major studies of the public sector, but her work is nevertheless highly relevant to the development of public administration theory. In the past organisation theory developed from manufacturing industry, but was expounded as if it were of universal application. Joan Woodward, Burns and Stalker and others have since demonstrated that even within manufacturing industry there is no one rigid theory or single set of rules. Practice must vary according to environment, purposes, functions, technology and other circumstances. Hence, one must expect even greater variations outside manufacturing.

Sir Geoffrey Vickers: process and environment

Sir Geoffrey Vickers, in *The Art of Judgment: A Study of Policy-Making*[10] takes the study of organisations and administrative processes deeper than any other writer we have discussed so far. He is most closely comparable with Simon, to whom he acknowledges a great debt, while specifying the points on which he differs from him. The breadth of his intellectual background and of his practical experience spans various academic disciplines and a variety of organisations in the private and public sectors. He was a City solicitor, a director of a group of engineering companies, a member of the London Passenger Transport Board, the National Coal Board and the Medical Research Council, and Head of Economic Intelligence at the Ministry of Economic Warfare in World War II. Vickers has such a wealth of subtle and original ideas that he can only be inadequately summarised.

Although he clearly recognises the importance of various advanced technologies and specialisms in modern management and administration, he also demonstrates, in his own person and by description, the importance of the generalist manager and administrator. Both as a practical administrator of vast experience and as a theorist of administration he is interested in the functions of producing a synthesis from a variety of specialisms and of integrating and coordinating the different specialist functions within an organisation. He has a graphic metaphor for the value of the generalist in a world of increasing specialisation. In explaining and defending his own theoretical work as a synthesist he writes, 'Even the dogs may eat of the crumbs which fall from the rich man's table; and in these days when the rich in knowledge eat such specialized food at such separate tables, only the dogs have a chance of a balanced diet.'[11] This thought is relevant to Lawrence and Lorsch's concept (discussed above) of the integrating functions in industrial management and to what we shall have to say in Chapter 8 about generalists and specialists in Government.

The Art of Judgment spans the public and private sectors, but Vickers does not classify organisations on this basis; but rather by 'the ways in which they generate the resources needed for their survival and growth'. His first subdivision is between 'user-supported' and 'public-supported' concerns. This cuts right through the public sector. The nationalised industries (e.g., gas, electricity and coal) are user-supported, while hospitals, Government Departments, the police and state schools are 'public supported'. Among the user-supported he makes a further subdivision between profit-making and non-profit-making, and another between competitive and monopolist. Vickers is greatly interested in the administrative processes of institutions on or near the borderlands of Government, business and voluntary activity, such as the University Grants Committee, trade associations, the Medical Research Council, research associations, professional institutes, charitable institutions and Universities.

Vickers looks at all kinds of decision-making, and widens the intellectual scope and the practical basis of the concept by cutting it free of the insistence on 'goals' and 'objectives' which has bedevilled management literature since the days of Urwick's 'principle of the objective'.[12] Even later and more sophisticated writers such as Etzioni, following Talcott Parsons, continue to define organisations in such terms as 'social units devoted primarily to attainment of specific goals'.[13] The vast popular literature of 'management by objectives' is similarly narrow in outlook. 'MBO', sensibly and flexibly used, may be a valuable management tool; but it tends to exclude scope for 'the masterful administration of the unforeseen'.[14] There must be scarcely any organisation in the public sector which has a single unchanging objective or even a simple series of objectives which are generally agreed and accepted. Consider all that has been written about the purposes of schools and Universities! The purposes of Government have been debated by philosophers as well as politicians for more than 2,000 years with little sign of agreement. Even the financial and other objectives specifically enacted by law for modern public corporations may be the subject of controversy or uncertainty. What is meant by 'the public interest' or balancing income and expenditure 'taking one year with another'? Some recent American social psychology supports these doubts. 'Goal statements', writes Wieck, 'exert little control over action. . . . Much of the organization's work does not seem to be directed toward goal attainment.'[15]

In place of the simple concept of the purpose of an organisation being to pursue objectives, Vickers substitutes the alternative concepts of 'optimising' and/or 'balancing'. By this he means that administration and decision-making are only sometimes, and in some types of organisation, mainly matters of optimising (profit, output and so on). Alternatively, he argues they may be largely a matter of regulating and balancing. He says, 'I have described policy-making as the setting of governing relations or norms rather than in the more usual terms as the setting of goals, objectives or ends.'[16] Moreover, he says, the process of policy-making, even when it includes a financial or numerical 'budgeting' function, should never be confined to quantitative terms. 'The cost-counting voice of budgetary judgment should never be mistaken for the voice of policy-making, for it is concerned only with the conditions, not the criteria of success.'[17] This thought is somewhat similar to Professor Peter Self's criticism, which we shall cite in Chapter 5, of the use of cost-benefit analysis as a substitute for policy judgment rather than as its tool. In quoting these comments we are not arguing against the current trend to make administration more numerate in the assessment of its data and in measuring the results of its activities. We are, however, suggesting that the most fundamental administrative judgments, at least in the public sector, must still be made in qualitative as well as quantitative terms.

Vickers' engineering analogy which is at the basis of his concept of the policy-making, decision-making, regulatory process is worth quoting at length. It is more realistic than Burns and Stalker's mechanistic/organic model and provides a suitable introduction to the 'systems' concept of organisations.

The process of regulation in its simplest form has been conveniently modelled by system engineers. An ongoing physical process, a ship at sea, a heat treatment plant in operation or what you will, is so designed as to change its state in response to signals; and it contains a sub-system (an automatic pilot, a thermostatic control) designed to generate the signals by collecting information about the state of the main system—about the internal relations which constitute it, such as the direction of the ship's head—and comparing this with standards which have somehow been set for these variables. This disparity between the two generates a signal which triggers change in the main system, sometimes through the medium of a selective mechanism which chooses from a repertory of possible actions. In due course the effect of the action taken, along with all other changes which have happened in the meantime, is fed back to the regulator through later information about the state of the system and thus contributes to further regulative action.[18]

This analogy illustrates two points: first the importance of the management or administrative function of maintaining balance within an organisation and, second, the importance, in carrying out this function, of internal communications systems (which engineers call 'feedback') to report the results of management decision-making. Both points are of especial relevance to public organisations owing to the size of such organisations and the complexity both of their purposes and their processes. From these engineering analogies Vickers develops his concept of 'appreciation' which he defines, extending the concepts of Simon, as 'the exercise through time of mutually related judgments of reality (fact) and value'.[19] These appreciative and regulatory functions are 'diffused through the organization'. There is 'a hierarchy of sub-systems', he writes, 'each role has both a prescribed and a discretionary content'.[20] There is 'an elaborate and closely woven structure of mutual expectations and self expectations of human agents'.[21]

Perhaps one of the most interesting and original of Vickers' concepts is that of the way the processes of appreciation and decision-making themselves change the people and organisations that make them. They can enlarge the outlook and scope of activity of individuals, their mutual confidence and hence the shape and orientation—the 'setting'—of the organisation as a whole. 'Unlike experimental rats, our blundering alters not only ourselves but our maze; so we never run the same maze twice.'[22]

'Systems' theory

A large organisation may indeed appear like a maze, even to those who have worked in it for many years. Yet the impression is usually exaggerated. There is more underlying logic and pattern in most organisations than is generally perceived, and more than appears in its rules and formal organisation charts. It is, usually, a more complex pattern, of more dimensions and more subtle and changing than we can explain entirely by the concepts of classical organisation theory. Nor does the human relations school, nor any purely psychological concept, provide an adequate corrective. There are definable logical patterns of function and work as well as just those of the feelings of individuals and groups, and it is with these patterns that the 'systems' school of organisation theory is concerned.

Although it now constitutes a distinctive body of thought and writing, it has emerged only gradually from the earlier schools of organisation theory and from a variety of other academic disciplines, notably mathematics, engineering and the natural sciences. The germs of systems thinking can be found as far back as Follet and Mayo with their interest in biological analogies. There are much more than germs of it in Simon and his collaborators and in Likert and in Lawrence and Lorsch with their concepts of interaction and integration within large organisations. A large part of Vickers' ideas may be described as systems theory, but he is a writer of such profound and many-sided wisdom that he cannot be contained within the confines of any one school. It is indeed hard to find any one exponent or group of exponents of a specific school of systems theory, partly because it is continually developing and partly because the whole concept is wider than the field of organisation theory and extends over a variety of disciplines.[23] There is a fair body of American management literature of the Systems School.[24] In Britain systems thinking about organisations has been developed at the Tavistock Institute by Trist, Miller, Rice, and others, and by writers on cybernetics such as Stafford Beer.[25]

It is difficult to summarise such a complex and still developing subject, but its key ideas include:

(a) The concept of an organisation with an identity of its own which is different from, and greater than, the sum of its parts or even the sum of all the relationships between its individual parts.

(b) The concept of an organisation as a very complex multi-dimensional system where many different elements and sub-systems and patterns of organisation interact, notably where there is interaction between the technical and work organisation systems and the patterns of human relationships. (Trist, Miller and Rice use the phrase 'socio-technical system', for example, in Trist's description of the relationship between technical methods of coal-mining and the human relationships of the groups of miners involved.)

(c) The concept of systems which are built up and bound together by the common elements in the component parts or in the participating individuals—with analogies from the combination of molecules, atoms, electrons and so on.

(d) The concept of an 'open system' which interacts and links up with its environment because it has elements in common with it and is dependent upon it.

(e) From this there develops the concept of a system with an input and an output, whether of materials to be processed or cases to be adjudicated or problems to be resolved.

(f) The concept of control mechanisms, such as those for which Vickers quotes engineering analogies, to keep the input and output in balance.

(g) The closely related biological concept of homeostasis, that is the self-adjusting control mechanism which keeps an organism in balance with itself and in relation to its environment—for instance, as an animal's body temperature is automatically maintained at a certain level.

(h) The concept of 'feedback', a system of internal communication which forms a basic element in the control mechanism.

All these concepts are valuable in explaining the nature of, and the functioning of, organisations in general.

They should be of particular value in explaining the nature and functioning of public organisations, because, as we shall seek to show in Part 2, both the environments and the functions of public organisations are generally more far-reaching, more complex, various and varying than most of those in the private sector. The problems of internal coordination and coordination between different public institutions are much more difficult, not only because of the size and number of public institutions; but because of the multiplicity of their conflicting objectives. These are reflected in the variety of sub-units within many large public institutions and the importance of their integrating and coordinating elements. For many contemporary public bodies, and especially for Government Departments, the classical organisational models are too simple. Systems theory should be particularly relevant to the public sector in providing the concept of the open system, the system which is part of its environment and in which the environment itself provides an essential component element.

Recapitulation of organisation theories: their relevance to
public administration

Before we go on to look specifically at the field of public administration it will be well to sum up those concepts of the various schools of organisation theory which may be most relevant to it. From the classical school we get the idea of an orderly structure of authority and responsibility, deriving usually from either one man or a board at the top and with clear lines both of accountability and of demarcation below. Functions, in order to be adequately performed, are divided and delegated. There is a stated framework within which everyone can work. The functions of planning, organising, command and control are clearly distinguished and further subdivided as necessary. Large problems, large masses of administrative work and large organisations are thus made manageable by subdivision. All this we shall find highly relevant, at least as a framework to most kinds of public organisation we study, whether governmental or public utility.

For most public organisations and public functions, in varying degree, we shall need additional concepts and models. Most Government and public service can only be carried on effectively by consent, both of employees and of the public generally. In many public functions consultation is more important than the exercise of authority. Moreover, the human needs of the employees at all levels must be considered if they are to give the best service. The size and complexity of public bodies makes it essential to consider the human elements, internal and external. The more new and sophisticated the tasks they undertake for an increasingly sophisticated society, the less is it possible to rely on mere exercise of formal authority. There is more and more consultation and lateral and informal communication. Hence we shall expect to find situations in which the ideas of Mayo, Barnard, Simon, Likert, Burns and Stalker and others are highly relevant.

Yet it will not only be a matter of considering the human, psychological needs, and characteristics of employees, colleagues and clients, of all those people and organisations at home and abroad with whom public institutions must deal. As their functions become more complex and various their internal organisation and the systems through which they operate become more complex and less standardised. They vary not only with the nature of their work, but with the technologies which they use. So there is much to be learnt from Burns and Stalker and from Joan Woodward. Some tasks of public bodies are of a fairly standardised, repetitive, routine nature and mechanistic models of organisation largely suffice. Others are innovative and creative and need highly flexible adaptable institutions. Purposes and objectives may be various and variable and have the effect of changing the nature of the institutions which undertake them. So Sir Geoffrey Vickers may have more to teach than any other writer. His distinction between the 'optimising' and the 'balancing' functions is of fundamental importance. So is his introduction to the concept of organisations as systems, and to the subtleties of control and balancing mechanisms.

Yet we must not over-simplify the picture and equate the developing complexity and subtlety of organisation theory with that of Government and public administration. It is tempting to concentrate, like Simon, Smithberg and Thompson and like the Fulton Report, on the most modern functions of Government and ignore the continuing importance, and also the complexity, of its primary functions. We must start in our next Part with these functions and see what tasks and processes they involve. We shall find they involve very much more than the simple concepts of authority and control expounded by the classical theorists. Most Government and public service has, from its earliest days, been a much subtler subject than most kinds of business management. Conversely in the most modern and sophisticated Government functions, we shall find that the classical concepts of a firm framework of authority and responsibility are still of great value. Yet our final picture, when we come to the end of our survey of the whole public administration field, will be one of developing complexity and a diffusion of authority in a democratic society and hence a diffusion of the administrative function, so that increasing numbers of people in any organisation are actively involved in the administrative processes.

1. Tom Burns and G. M. Stalker, op. cit., pp. 114–19.

2. ibid., pp. 119–25.

3. See the close analogies drawn between the two in the symposium, H. Kalmus (Ed.), 1967. *Regulation and Control in Living Systems*. John Wiley.

4. *Organization and Environment: Managing Differentiation and Integration*, 1967. Harvard University, Boston.

5. ibid., p. 241.

6. ibid., pp. 73–8.

7. Professor Woodward's first conclusions were published as a pamphlet *Management and Technology*, HMSO, London, 1958, No. 3 in *Problems of Progress in Industry* series, but her major work is *Industrial Organization: Theory and Practice*. OUP, London, 1965.

8. *Industrial Organization*, p. 99.

9. ibid., pp. 104 and 167.

10. Chapman and Hall, London, 1965.

11. ibid., p. 11.

12. L. P. Urwick, 1947. *Elements of Administration,* pp. 26–32. Pitman, London.

13. A. Etzioni, 1961. *A Comparative Analysis of Complex Organizations,* p. 11. Glencoe, Free Press, New York.

14. Robert Bridges. *The Testament of Beauty,* p. 1.

15. Karl E. Weick, 1969. *The Social Psychology of Organising,* p. 37. Addiston-Wesley, Reading, Mass., USA.

16. Vickers, op. cit., p. 31.

17. ibid., p. 199.

18. ibid., p. 36.

19. ibid., pp. 39–41, 67–8.

20. ibid., p. 229.

21. ibid., p. 231.

22. ibid., p. 73.

23. For a good recent introduction to systems thinking in this wider variety of disciplines, see F. E. Emery (Ed.), 1969. *Systems Thinking.* Penguin.

24. e.g., Stanley Young, 1966. *Management: A Systems Analysis.* Scott, Foresman & Co., Glenview, Illinois.

25. e.g., E. L. Trist, G. W. Higgin, A. Murray and A. B. Pollock, 1963. *Organizational Choice: the capabilities of groups at the coal face under changing Technologies.* Tavistock. A. K. Rice, 1963. *The Enterprise and its environment.* Tavistock. E. J. Miller and A. K. Rice, 1967. *Systems of Organization.* Tavistock. Stafford Beer, 1959. *Cybernetics and Management.* English Universities Press.

PART TWO

The Nature of Public Administration in Britain

4

AUTHORITY, ENVIRONMENT AND FUNCTION

Authority and environment

Having set out our background of theory about organisations in general we must now look specifically at public organisations, their functions, tasks, processes, forms and structures. We must first consider their environment, what they are there for, and what they do and how they do it. This leads us to look at their authority.

In Great Britain we have a highly integrated unitary state in sharp contrast with the USA and other federal constitutions. The legal sovereignty of Parliament is absolute and has been unchallenged for two and a half centuries.* With this goes a great concentration of administrative power. In normal times parliamentary sovereignty is effectively activated, steered and implemented by the closely integrated group of men who compose the Government. They are subject to many external stimulating and moderating influences; but most of these are channelled through Parliament, the legal system or Government Departments, or at least operate on a national basis within a single national culture, and usually within well understood 'rules of the game'. The result is a great concentration of power at the apex of a closely integrated pyramid.

This legal and political predominance of Parliament is reflected throughout the structures of public administration. Local authorities are not only created and controlled, but regulated in great detail, legally and administratively, and even procedurally, by Parliament and Government Departments, from whom they generally draw a great deal of their finance—capital and revenue. It is sometimes

* Five centuries, taking England and Wales only and overlooks the Civil War and Commonwealth period—although in the whole United Kindom including Northern Ireland that is, it has hardly ever been completely unchallenged.

suggested that this central control of Local Authorities is a recent encroachment on ancient liberties; but Professor W. J. M. Mackenzie has suggested somewhat the reverse. 'The idea that local self-government was part of the ancient English constitution was somehow invented or rediscovered in the years between 1836 and 1847.'[1] Before that there were merely ancient local property rights, individual or corporate, recognised and used by the Crown for its own purposes. Indeed the very term 'local government' is said only to have been invented in 1858.[2] In the nineteenth century and after, reforming national Parliaments imposed a certain democratic pattern on local government. This has since become accepted as traditional, but it is nevertheless not so democratic, Mackenzie implies, as that of central government. He may exaggerate, but it is clearly true that local government in England is very largely subordinate to central government. Scotland and Wales may be special cases, and Northern Ireland is a very special one, but otherwise it is only on the rarest occasions that even the largest and most powerful local authorities can oppose major Government policy effectively. This concentration and centralisation of political power derives from a community which is geographically, economically, educationally and socially as compact and cohesive as any of comparable size anywhere in the world.

Public administration: functions in general

What, within this context, do public administrators do? Put briefly and crudely, they implement and embody and in some cases symbolise, the ideas and wishes of those in control of policy in the central political institutions. This applies throughout the system from the centre to the periphery of a fairly closely woven net which includes the Cabinet Secretariat, the hospital secretary and Electricity Board district engineer. The local government field is only a partial exception. It is the function of central Government Departments in particular to serve, to sustain, to inform and to advise Ministers, to help them formulate their policies and to carry them out or get them carried out by other agencies. The ranges of their objectives are far more varied than those of any other kind of concern. They are kaleidoscopic. Most Government Departments have certain functions defined by law; but no major Department is limited to these. It will often have to contribute to the making of new law or new policy. Ministers may wish, or be pressed by Parliament or by public opinion, or by forces overseas, to undertake all kinds of new commitments. Hence what most organisation theorists of any school say about the relations between organisations and their objectives is not adequate for governmental institutions. Vickers' expositions of the functions of 'optimising', 'balancing' and 'appreciation' are, however, highly relevant.

The Civil Service function

A civil servant's duty, in contrast to the business executive's, can often only be defined as dealing with anything which may arise within a certain sphere, and sometimes there may be no permanent overriding commitments to single tasks. The setting of specific targets should be valuable in most types of organisation; but in Government Departments the process has its limitations. The overriding objective of the civil servant is to do whatever his Minister, within the law, wishes him to do, even though the wishes of successive Ministers and Parliaments, and even the same Minister and the same Parliament, may often vary.* This does not mean that even higher civil servants spend most of their time supporting politically controversial policies. Much of the administrative work of Government Departments is not controversial, in any party sense; but it is still not necessarily simple nor unchanging.

Apart from changes of policy or environment or of external pressures, the complexity and subtlety of work in a Government Department derive from the fact that there is a permanent multiplicity of simultaneous objectives which are very hard to reconcile. The situation is aptly described by the Minister in Balchin's novel:[3]

You think that people . . . want democracy and justice and peace. You're right. They do. But what you forget is that they want them on their own terms. And their own terms don't add up. They want decency and justice without interference with their liberty to do as they like . . . [successful political leaders] are the chaps who've spent a life-term learning to compromise between a set of demands that are all very reasonable in themselves, but that don't add up. How to do less work and have more money. How to spend more, reduce taxation and balance the budget. . . .

A Government Department in a civilised democratic community is expected to be economical, to be fair between all classes of citizens,

---

* 'The Report of a Management Consultancy Group', annexed as vol. 2 to the Report of Lord Fulton's Committee on the Civil Service, makes similar points in its section on 'The Working Environment of the Civil Service' ('The first duty of the civil servant is to help the Minister meet his responsibilities to the electorate'—p. 9, para. 21); and in the section on 'Management and Organisation' (pp. 82–5), where a series of important contrasts are drawn between the objects, methods and environment of the work of the Civil Servant on the one hand and industry and commerce on the other (paras. 303–15); but further paragraphs (316–18) follow enumerating characteristics which Civil Service work has in common with that of industry and commerce.

to cooperate with all those interests at home and overseas with whom it is Government policy to cooperate, to support all current defence and economic policies—and so on and so forth. Not only on major issues, but also on minor cases these policy considerations constantly conflict. Whether to use compulsory powers to get a particular site, whether to allow a certain alien to stay in the country, whether to grant a concession to a trades union representing Government employees, whether to improve public services for a certain part of the country—such decisions have to be taken daily in Government Departments. They involve hard, clear thinking and the careful assembly of as much evidence as is available in time; but they seldom depend wholly on financial or mathematical calculations. There may be no single, overriding objective except the public interest as interpreted in the last report by the Minister and Parliament.

The basic functions of a State: defence, law and order, and taxation

Public administration functions in Britain fall into certain broad groups, and the varieties of task, process and form in administration cannot be fully understood without an understanding of the distinctions between these groups of functions. As soon as a full sovereign state emerges, its first concern must be to preserve its own sovereignty against any internal or external threat, and then to provide protection for its subjects against foreign powers and against each other. It must be able to settle internal disputes and provide the necessary framework for the prevailing economic system, in particular, a currency. Moreover, it must finance itself. In terms of institutions this means some provision for armed forces, a diplomatic service, a legislature and a central government executive, criminal and civil courts, a treasury, and a tax system.

As a community becomes larger and more complex, not only does the state assume new and more complex functions, but its original simple functions themselves become complex. We have criticised Simon, Smithberg and Thompson for over-concentration on the more modern functions of the American state with a relative neglect of its old basic functions. They might well have written more about the Pentagon, the State Department and the Department of Justice. Similarly a recent academic writer on the British Civil Service, Dr G. K. Fry,[4] bases his central argument on the presumed supersession of the nineteenth-century 'Regulatory State' or 'Law and Order State' by the 'Welfare State' or the 'Positive State' with functions of 'managing the economy'. He does not actually say that the former functions have ceased, but his whole theme is that it is the second category which matters. Much of the Fulton Report's thesis seems to be based on similar assumptions; but it sets out the situation more fairly than Dr Fry. Indeed in its opening chapter, and before describing the new functions of Government, it says: 'Its traditional regulatory functions have multiplied in size and greatly broadened in scope.'[5] Some of the most complex problems of British public administration today concern defence, diplomacy, law and order, and taxation. Some of the largest and most complex Government Departments are those which provide for them.

Apart from these few subdivisions of function between Departments of Government, there is the essential function in any state for some central secretariat, however small, combined with an intelligence system to serve the central executive of Government whether that is a Monarch, a Prime Minister, or a Council or Cabinet of Ministers. Any legislature also requires secretarial services. We shall discuss the administration processes of these various secretariats in Chapter 7.

The extended modern functions of public administration: regulatory and service-providing

Much of the other functions of contemporary British public administration (except 'management of the economy' which we shall mention shortly) may be classified very broadly as either regulatory or service-providing. As a society becomes more complex it requires regulation far beyond that needed merely to prevent physical violence. It needs controls of industrial processes, public health, road traffic, town and country planning, and so on, linked with such control functions as services of registration and public record and published Government statistics. In Britain some of these functions are carried out by central government and some by local government under varying degrees of central government control or coordination. There are also a vast range of activities which can all be classified in some sense as public services. Such services can again be broadly divided between, on the one hand, physical public utility networks such as roads, railways, telephones, gas, electricity, water and drainage and, on the other hand, many different services provided more by the activities of persons than by systems of physical equipment—although both are involved. In this latter category are education, police, and health services and a variety of public advisory services (e.g., for exporters, farmers and others), industrial conciliation services, employment exchanges and social insurance. Some of these services are operated on a national basis either directly by Government Departments or by public corporations or by local authorities with some degree of central government control. Some other special functions, which we cannot enumerate exhaustively here, fall into categories of their own. For instance, owing to technological or other

conditions, broadcasting, coal-mining and steel manufacture are
operated by national public corporations in Britain.

National economic planning

The acceptance by all major political parties of an obligation on any
British Government in some sense to manage the economy and make
economic plans is relatively new. During World War II the Government managed the economy in the sense that direct Government
controls—physical or financial—largely replaced market forces.
Such Government intervention is a different thing from helping to
coordinate the whole economic system in collaboration with all the
leading forces normally composing it. The wartime style of relatively
short-term emergency planning is also different from planning in the
sense of setting targets and taking long-term anticipatory action for
the future. In the sixties it came to be fairly generally accepted firstly
that Government had obligations to manage, or at least coordinate,
the economy as a whole, and secondly that, both for these general
purposes, and for the management of its own and other public sector
activities, the Government must forecast, plan and take anticipatory
action for several years ahead.

This should have been obvious from the time-scales of the development of the major new capital projects on which the economy so
largely depended (both in the basic public utility services and manufacturing industries). Indeed, by the late forties the coal and electricity supply industries had published fifteen-year plans. Yet the impression remained that these plans were visionary and impractical or
that there was something quite exceptional about power stations and
coal mines which took eight to ten years from the initial steps to full
production and that, in any case, a little hustling would eliminate
such 'delays'. In fact the time-scales of many major projects—railway
electrification, motorways, supersonic aircraft and airports—have
since got longer and longer. The reasons for this are not purely
technological, but also administrative and political—the multiplicity
of interests to be consulted and the lengthy procedures and defensive
activities intended to safeguard the numerous interests affected. The
time-scale of many types of capital project is such that five-year
planning is now insufficient and twenty-year plans are desirable.[6] The
argument, however, has not yet been universally accepted, nor has the
dilemma which it poses for democratic government been faced. Governments now commit their successors and their electorates to many of
the major features of economic policy nearly a generation ahead.

In 1961 the Chancellor of the Exchequer, Mr Selwyn Lloyd, announced the setting up of The National Economic Development
Council ('Neddy'). It is a means of collaboration in indicative plan-

ning between Ministers, Heads of privately owned and nationalised industries, trades unionists and economists. It consults, agrees, and publishes plans, forecasts, statistics and recommendations either by itself or through its subsidiary bodies. It is not quite an executive body but much more than an advisory body. Those who advise, and those in a position to act on the advice are associated together and can be stimulated to action and enquiry by one another. One economist is said to have described its activities by saying that in stimulating the economy to greater growth there are available not only the two classic methods of making a donkey run faster—the stick and the carrot—but also 'stroking behind the ears'. Other bodies of somewhat comparable composition but more specific powers have since been set up.*

These were only a few of the new types of institution set up as a result of the acceptance of a new function of Government in respect of the stimulation, coordination and forward planning of the national economy. In a variety of ways Governments have become deeply involved in what would, scarcely more than a generation ago, have been usually regarded as outside their sphere. This is illustrated by the following account of the Labour Government's activities in 1970 in the ICI–Viyella affair, by the City Editor of *The Guardian*:

. . . what sticks out is the amount the Government has felt able to do. Mr Lever has told ICI what firms it can take over, how big a shareholding it may hold in the long run, and how it must vote in the meantime. He is now at work on a code of conduct for the whole fibre industry to ensure fair marketing.

. . . There is nothing very new in this kind of proceeding. Ministers have long had the habit of fixing things with the heads of big companies. It's all quite informal, but the fact is that big companies like to keep in with the Government. Some of them have to: If they are making electrical equipment or telephone gear, or aeroplanes, the Government is their only important customer.

But even those companies which sell only to the consumer need the goodwill of the Government. They need planning permissions and industrial development certificates, investment grants and exchange control authority, and occasionally the intervention of the conciliators from the Department of Employment and Productivity.

. . . This state of affairs leaves Ministers free to indulge in all kinds of cajoling and arm-twisting. . . .[7]

The significance of this quotation for us is not the particular policies

* Among them the Prices and Incomes Board, the Industrial Reorganisation Commission, the Commission for Industrial Relations, the Monopolies Commission and the Restrictive Trade Practices Court. The first two have since been abolished.

pursued by the Wilson Government but the general phenomenon of
the involvement of Governments with industry. The more recent
Rolls-Royce affair could also be cited.

Classification of types of function: regulating

This sketch of some of the outstanding functions of Government has
not been exhaustive, but it is sufficiently representative to enable us
to summarise the kinds of function modern Governments and other
public bodies in Britain have been concerned with. We must emphasise that the original basic functions of Government have not been
superseded but remain in parallel with the new ones. Even though
Government may engage in sophisticated economic planning, it still
has to deal with elementary crime, to collect taxes, to provide the
courts of justice and their administrative supporting services, to
administer patent law, electoral procedure, public health regulations,
and so on. How much regulation any state attempts depends partly
on the prevailing philosophy and partly on the complexity of the
society, its economy and its political system. It is bound to attempt
the protection of persons and property against violence, and the
control of entry of aliens, of epidemic disease, of road traffic, and so
on. Such regulatory functions involve two very different processes,
the formulation of legislation and its application to particular cases.
The first, including delegated legislation, rule-making and issuing of
policy directives, is an innovative, to some extent a creative and
imaginative function, one which certainly ought to involve foresight,
planning and the gathering of information before decisions are made.
It also usually involves consultation with representatives of sectional
groups and the reconciliation of interests and points of view. The
application of legislation on the other hand, though requiring intelligence and flexibility, is a more circumscribed, routinised activity. It
is one to which classical management theory and Weberian bureaucracy often fit. Regulation may be highly legalistic or highly discretionary. It may be carried out by policemen, Government lawyers,
customs officers, civil servants of low rank, or by Permanent Secretaries, courts of law, or appeal tribunals. Yet it is always, in Vickers's
phrase, a 'balancing' rather than an 'optimising' function. It is difficult to apply to it the business technique of 'management by objectives' except in its quantitative aspect.

Balancing

When a Government's sphere of activity is extended very widely,
unless it is a very strong dictatorship, much of the regulation has in
effect to be done by agreement and compromise, often with a multiplicity of interests. Even very strong Governments in past ages, like

that of Elizabeth I, governed largely by consent and compromise. Compromise made directly with each of a number of interests is not very different from the bringing about of compromises between such interests. The ancient function of kings holding courts and councils to adjudicate between rival barons is the equivalent of the modern function of Governments getting the support of major interests for new legislation, adjudicating in industrial disputes, encouraging or discouraging company mergers, promoting cooperation for scientific research, exports, protection of the environment and so on. This second, conciliating or compromising function of Government can never be completely distinguished from the first, that of regulating.

Service-providing

Almost all strictly *governmental* functions fall into one of these two categories. But departments of central government perform a variety of functions which do not involve any kind of governing. They can be classified as the provision of services, personal or physical. In local government the majority of functions are service-providing and only a minority are governmental. The nationalised industries' activities are mostly service-providing; but one major nationalised industry (the British Steel Corporation) is exclusively engaged in manufacturing and another (the National Coal Board) mainly in mining. The Atomic Energy Authority does research, development and manufacture and the National Research and Development Corporation promotes the development and exploitation of inventions. Some Government Departments, mainly those of defence, do some manufacturing and, like local authorities, some construction. Various Government Departments control, or at least are involved in, the service-providing activities of local authorities and nationalised industries. The manufacturing and research functions have many close parallels in the private sector: the service-providing functions have fewer. They involve the development and deployment of large quantities of capital equipment and personnel over wide areas, sometimes over every populated area. Like the governmental functions, they involve elaborate coordinating activities and measures to ensure equality of treatment, but in other respects most of them have much in common with private sector industry and commerce. Some services are paid for by their users and hence can be judged to a limited extent by financial yardsticks. This does not, however, apply to many services, such as employment exchanges, meteorological services, public libraries, the police, the Health Service and education.

Allocating and directing

There are various other ways of classifying the function of Government but the above division into the three categories of (a) Regulatory, (b) Conciliatory, (c) Provision of services, seems the best as an introduction to the analysis, in the following five chapters, of administrative tasks, processes and structures. A sampling of the day-to-day activities of senior public servants would show many doing something which does not at first seem to fit neatly into any of the above categories, such as the allocation of resources, usually money. However, most allocation work could be classified as forming part of (c) above, provision of services. We might divide that category into (i) direct provision of service by the organisation itself: for example, the Home Office maintaining prisons or a local authority providing libraries, and (ii) regulation of the provision of services by another organisation such as a local authority or other public corporation. The Ministry of the Environment (formerly Housing and Local Government) does not provide houses, but lays down and maintains the framework of policy within which Local Authorities provide houses. The Ministry's policies in regard to grants influence the extent of the total national provision, its distribution and also the character of the dwellings.

This latter function may sometimes be described as one of optimising more than balancing, but it will nearly always have a balancing element as well. Moreover, few central government functions, and not all functions of local government, can be confined to any one of the three main categories alone. Those who regulate must sometimes keep in mind Government policies of conciliation: those who conciliate should try not to embarrass those who regulate. Those who provide services, or oversee the provision of services by other bodies, must bear in mind Government policies in other spheres. Throughout the whole area of Government and the public services there is, or ought to be, what Likert calls an 'interaction-influence system'. At all levels there should be organs such as those suggested by Lawrence and Lorsch for maintaining communication, balance and cooperation between systems of different kinds.

Symbolic functions

Public administration has a duty of maintaining the fixed landmarks in the social, political and economic system. It should therefore try to maintain a firm and coherent framework of a classical character. Along with, and closely allied to, the governing, conciliating and service-providing functions, there are also symbolic and confidence-maintaining functions. Some organs of public administration in some countries pay more attention than others to these functions but few entirely neglect them. Even when they appear comical it is usually a mistake to take them lightly. The policeman patrolling his beat symbolises law and order apart from his active role in detecting or deterring criminals. So does the very rigidity and even stodginess of a bureaucratic system, just as the Grecian façades and other minor pomposities of the banking business symbolise financial stability. British Government Departments make discreet use of the Royal Arms and exercise many of their functions formally in the name of Her Majesty. American Government officials have large and magnificent Stars and Stripes flags hung beside their desks. Whether a public administration system should symbolise stability more than dynamism, or vice versa, depends on the policy of the political régime and the needs and the climate of the community concerned; but in some measure every public administrative system will need to symbolise both active power and confidence-creating stability.

1. W. J. M. Mackenzie, 1961. *Theories of Local Government,* p. 9. London School of Economics.

2. R. C. K. Ensor, 1936. *England 1870–1914*, p. 124. OUP, London.

3. Nigel Balchin, 1949. *A Sort of Traitors*, p. 88. Collins.

4. G. K. Fry, 1969. *Statesmen in Disguise.* Macmillan.

5. *The Civil Service:* vol. 1: *Report of the Committee 1966–8*. Chairman, Lord Fulton. HMSO, Cmnd. 36.38, p. 10, para. 7.

6. R. J. S. Baker, 1963. *The Management of Capital Projects*, p. 239. Michael Shanks (Ed.), 1963. *Lessons of Public Enterprise,* pp. 46–7. Cope.

7. *The Guardian*, 31 March 1970.

5

TASKS (1): CONTROL, DECISION-MAKING

AND COORDINATION

Control: judicial

We have described the development of the main functions of Government and the public services in Britain, and how, as their variety and complexity has increased, they have ceased to be understandable solely in terms of classical organisation theory. We must now consider some of the administrative tasks these functions involve. We will do so in historical, not logical, order—at least not that of Fayol. He started with foresight and planning, put coordination in the middle and ended with control. Historically, however, as we have already seen, planning was one of the last functions to be developed by the British and many Western Governments (although some newer Governments have attempted it very soon after first achieving their independence). Control, on the other hand, was one of the earliest tasks of Government. At first much, perhaps most of it, consisted of intervention by a higher authority to right wrongs on the initiative of complainants. This is an organisational function of which little account is taken in classical organisation theory, which assumes that most initiatives in any organisation come from above.

Such control goes back to feudal times. It antedates not only audits and modern management control systems, but also parliamentary control. Judicial control of Government Departments and other public bodies in Britain derives from the character of English and Scottish law. These systems of law bind all public and private bodies and persons, including the Crown or Government Departments. The law can prescribe positively what they must do or the way they should do it and the courts, at the instance of an interested party, will enforce such provisions. The law, moreover, presumes that local authorities or other public corporations have no authority to do anything *ultra vires*, that is, outside the powers allowed them by law, and the courts can decide that any action of theirs is *ultra vires* and hence illegal. The doctrine of *ultra vires* can also apply, but not in quite the same way, to the Crown, and Government Departments. The legal position of corporations created by Royal Charter is freer in theory than that of corporations created by Act of Parliament. The latter can only do things specifically authorised or implied by statute : the former can do whatever is not specifically prohibited for them. In practice, however, the powers of chartered corporations are fairly closely determined either by their original charters or by subsequent general or special statutes. There is therefore an independent system to ensure that public bodies observe all the provisions of the law, including any law defining their functions and processes. However, this is not a regular system of checking, inspecting or monitoring. Nor is it normally a check on the merits of decisions taken by public authorities acting legally within the scope of the powers of decision and discretion given them by Parliament.

Control by the democratic process

There has been a tendency of recent years to denigrate the parliamentary processes of control of public administration—Questions in the House, letters to Ministers, the special debate, lobbying and deputations. It has even been asserted,[1] usually without evidence, that Ministerial responsibility is a 'myth' or a 'fiction' or even that 'no one believes it'. To some extent this is part of a wider contemporary tendency to lose faith in parliamentary democracy and to exalt bureaucracy and technocracy. It will, however, be argued in Chapter 7 that control of a very large organisation by an individual who cannot attend to every detail personally is a normal, practicable and fairly well understood process of management in the military, the business and the governmental spheres, provided sensible and flexible methods of delegation are followed. It does not, however, by any means always work well. There are always difficulties of size, complexity, variety of activities and functions and rate of change within the organisation. Probably one of the greatest factors is human. To some extent it is a matter of knowledge, capacity and intelligence; but above all it involves the will-power of the various individuals chiefly concerned to make the processes of delegation and control work. This subject would be almost impossible to analyse systematically by research and one is driven to the less scientific basis of personal experience—but not to this alone.

Various former Ministers[2] have described their personal control processes with generally an implication of confidence in their capacity to control the essentials of their departments. Most Ministers have taken credit for their achievements and blamed their opponents when in office for their failings. It would be hard to deny that there are Ministers, civil servants, M.P.s and people among their constituents who have the will-power not to take 'no' for an answer and to cut through a jungle of paper and fogs of half-truths and get at the real nub of a case. It can be done. Sometimes it takes much reading, but more often a knowledge of who to talk to and ask to get the whole thing looked at again in a new light. A Minister or senior civil servant may do this in a few moments. It is not so much a matter of time or administrative machinery but determination. That is why Fayol stresses the moral qualities of his ideal administrator—energy, strong-mindedness and courage, as much as intellectual qualities.[3] If determination and a sense of fair-minded responsibility are lacking no administrative machinery, no judicial processes, no paper safeguards, will prevent inefficiency, hardship or deliberate oppression. The essence of effective democratic control is the will to make it work.

This, of course, depends on the genuine acceptance of its justification and necessity by all concerned, politicians, officials and the public. It will not work in the atmosphere of cynicism which would result from the general acceptance of some of the defeatist views recently expressed about it. The mechanics are of lesser importance. A Minister or senior civil servant must use all available means to find out what is really going on—by talking to those directly responsible to him and to a sample of others all down the line, by reading reports and statistics, by using visits, particular complaints and chance meetings and then drawing the right conclusions by probing and inference from each random sample. Having assessed a situation, he then needs to make his wishes, particular and general, clear to all concerned. He must also check that this has been done by further occasional random sampling. It can be done and in well-run organisations—public and private—it is done, at every level. What is needed is the will.

Audit

All auditing includes direct examination of major documents, accounts and records, sample checks of others and, most important of all, check that there is a further more detailed system of internal auditing and other checks and safeguards. It is necessary, however, for such special controls to have the support also of all the normal management controls, statistics, visiting, reports and internal conferences, supplemented occasionally by special investigations. All these different controls complement one another. Financial auditing is of two kinds, that common to most public and private organisations and that special to Government Departments. The first is, broadly, concerned with checking the accuracy of accounts and financial statements and ensuring that they truly reflect the financial state of the organisation and that no expenditure has been incurred without proper authority. Auditing of the nationalised industries is the same as for privately owned industry except that the auditors are appointed by a Minister. Local authorities' accounts are audited by the central government's district auditors. They are particularly concerned with the legality of expenditure, and can, in cases of irregularities, personally surcharge councillors or other individuals responsible. Government Departments are audited by the Department of the Comptroller and Auditor General who is as independent as a judge. It covers all the elements of commercial audit, and local government audit—but also much more. It makes critical and very broad ranging examinations of general financial policy, financial administration and financial prudence. It ensures that money is only spent in accordance with the intentions of Parliament. The C. and A.G.'s staff have access to any Government Department's papers and their reports are the basis of the detailed investigations of the Public Accounts Committee. The Committee cross-examine Permanent Secretaries and other Government officials (not Ministers). Their reports criticise financial maladministration as well as financial impropriety, but not policy in the political sense.

The Ombudsman

Another system of detailed, expert, independent checks of administrative processes was introduced when the office of Parliamentary Commissioner for Administration was set up in 1967. It was modelled on those of the 'Ombudsman' in Denmark and Sweden. The Commissioner has a right of access to internal papers similar to that of the C. and A.G., but no general auditing or monitoring function. He can only act on specific complaints made through a Member of Parliament. His concern is anything which he considers to be 'maladministration', but he may not act as a court of appeal in respect of a Minister's or Government Department's decision on policy or exercise of discretion. His status and functions are therefore quite different from those of the French *Conseil d'Etat*. His prime function is to protect the citizen who may have suffered through some confusion or incompetence in the working of the administrative processes, such as the taking of decisions on wrong or inadequate information, undue delay or undue haste. The setting up of the Commissioner's office is a recognition of the crucial importance of administrative machinery and administrative processes in determining whether policy is translated from the sphere of mere abstract inten-

tion to concrete results for the citizen. In fact, policy in its impact on
the individual citizen, or groups of citizens or the community generally, is inseparable from the process that implements it. Sometimes
the process virtually is the policy. The fact that the earthy and
detailed processes of administration are worthy of the high level
adjudication of the Commissioner when they go wrong is a measure
of their importance on the more normal occasions when they go right.

Control of local by central government

The extent and nature of control of local government activities by
central government is a subject of great complexity and subtlety and
one on which classical organisation theory cannot give us much
guidance. It differs greatly in different states.

In Britain many services are run by the agency of elected local
authorities. Yet not only the general sovereignty of Parliament, but
the right of central government Departments to exercise much direct
detailed control, and even more, pressure and influence, is generally
accepted. How far they actually do this varies. There is a wide range
of local authority functions. At one extreme they are purely optional
or peculiar to certain authorities only, like the running of theatres.
At the other extreme the authority has an obligation to operate a
service on a standard pattern, with virtually no local discretion.
Between these extremes are the major functions such as education,
roads, housing, social services, and town and country planning.

Professor J. A. G. Griffiths says that the kind and degree of central
control varies not only with different central departments but with
parts of departments and to some extent with different local authorities.[4] There are various factors, size of authority, distance from
London and the competence and individual and collective experience of the people operating the system at both ends. However,
Griffiths concludes that the prime factor is the nature of the function,
and its importance to the nation as a whole. He describes three kinds
of relationships: 'One is basically *laissez-faire*, one is basically
regulatory, and one is basically promotional.'[5] By *laissez-faire* he
means not laxity, but a deliberate policy of leaving the maximum
scope for local discretion. By 'regulatory' he means a concern mainly
with the consistent application of rules and precedents. This process
is inclined to be legalistic and Weberian, but usually necessarily so
because it is applied to mandatory duties, such as enforcing certain
standards and safeguards. By 'promotional' Griffiths means the
active promotion by central government of certain policies on a
national basis, in recent years for instance, those for education and
roads. One cannot argue that this difference of attitudes is inevitable
except when there are urgent physical or technological needs for

national or regional coordination, as in water supply. From time to time it comes to be regarded as a matter of national concern to pursue a positive coordinated policy on some such subject. This is a matter of opinion and policy. For instance some future Government might care less about roads and more about the homeless.

When a British Government Department seeks to control local government activity, it has a variety of means at its disposal, direct and indirect, formal and informal. Specific Government approval is required by local authority borrowing, otherwise for certain sizes and types of scheme, for proportionate grants for certain capital or revenue expenditure, for certain by-laws and so on. In form, therefore, a great many of these powers are powers to permit rather than to require the local authorities to do certain things. Hence much of the power and influence of central government Departments is exercised in the form of advice or persuasion, but often with sanctions available. Griffiths indicates that the main ways in which a central department may pursue a positive or 'promotional' policy are by research, by 'the collation, analysis and dissemination of the experience of local authorities' and also through its inspectors. Of these he suggests the high prestige and acceptability of H.M. Inspectors of Schools is assisted by long tradition and that some other inspectorates may be more purely 'regulatory' in their approach. In some Government Departments he says personal contacts with Local Authorities are largely left to the inspectors while in others administrative staff actively cultivate such contacts. Lady Sharp, late Permanent Secretary, Ministry of Housing and Local Government, stresses the important, variety and wide extent of such informal contacts and from her forty years' experience, concludes: 'However tough the argument, however complete the disagreement, . . . the sense of partnership for better or for worse usually holds firm. It is this which finally governs the relationship between the Ministry and local authorities.'[6]

This close cooperation at national level—largely between officials —is no doubt excellent. Yet it is striking that Griffiths, himself formerly an elected member of two local authorities, has so little faith in any local and democratic, as distinct from national and official, control of local government. He says that what he has called the *laissez faire* attitude of certain central departments, is 'sometimes supported by the democratic argument that if they make mistakes, the remedy is with the electorate . . . it is nonsense. Local electorates do not act in this way, even if they know the facts—which would be so only if a major scandal immediately preceded the election. It is straight democratic myth.' Whether or not most other people experienced in local government would agree with this, one is

A.T.A.P.A.—D

left wondering what the main motive for efficiency in local government really is. There are no doubt great difficulties in the local democratic control of such a complex of activities. Some are highly technical, many closely bound up with national schemes and policies. Much of the central control is of a negative or even informal nature. In terms of orthodox ideas of control in business management, or classical organisation theory, or the principles and practices common within central government, it is hard to know how local government can work so well.

Anyone with experience of central government or private business must wonder how this infinitely complex tangle of legalism and informality can produce such apparently excellent public services. Could not one of the most powerful real controls and motivating factors be, not any administrative or political machinery, but simply the obviously useful and necessary character of the services concerned and the fact that they are operated mainly in full public view? The explanation may sound too simple, but why should not the ideas of Hertzberg* on the psychology of motivation be relevant in this sphere and apply collectively as well as to individuals? There is surely scope for someone to follow up Griffiths's research by applying some human relations and systems theory to the relations of central and local government in Britain. There is need for some systematic analysis of motivation and of the complex patterns of relationships.

The resolution of disputes

Resolution of disputes is another of the primary and ancient tasks of Government. We are not concerned here with the formal legal procedures of the law courts and arbitration tribunals, but with the administrative tasks of conflict-resolution which can only issue in Government policy decision and not a legal award. Examples are pressures from conflicting interests for different types of legislation, for or against the siting of major public installations in particular areas, pressures for greater control of this, or less Government interference with that, pressures for standardisation on one basis, or another or not at all. Most of these may be classed as matters of general national policy, but there can be local disputes of a similar kind. Finally there can be disputes within the public service, indeed within Government Departments. Most important, however, are those either between different groups of interest outside Government or between groups inside Government reflecting or supporting the views of opposing outside groups. The ingredients of any such dispute are normally, first, a complex situation in which more than one

* See pp. 58–9 above.

course of action is possible, secondly, parties advocating different courses of action and third, some authority within Government with a duty of deciding. Sometimes the complex situation is hard to define, the parties are hard to identify, distinguish and enumerate, and the location of the responsible point of decision in Government is itself in dispute. The doctrine of the collective responsibility of Ministers requires all Government Departments to collaborate and agree, and when they cannot do so the doctrine must be taken literally and the matter taken to the Cabinet or one of its Committees, or a special meeting of Ministers.

Decision-making in general

Just as Simon* described all administration as essentially a process of decision-making, so it would be tempting to say that all public administration is decision-making—usually involving the resolution of disputes. However this would be too sweeping. Moreover this is indeed only part of the more static side of any kind of management. It is part, as Vickers would say, of the 'balancing' as against the 'optimising' function. We have also seen† that there is a yet more static but still important one—the function of symbolising the cohesive framework of society—one could almost say the ritual function. The task of any management has indeed been analysed by Professor J. F. Morris[7] into three parts—'dramatic', 'ritual' and 'routine'. (This analysis itself is, of course, a dramatic symbolisation or simplification of what really happens.) At the bottom are the purely automatic, repetitive tasks which are like *routines*. In the middle Morris puts those which he says involve some, but not much, scope for discretion and judgment—*ritual* functions. At the highest levels there are the *dramatic* tasks, involving creativity and the resolution of conflicts, or the production of a synthesis out of opposites, a process which also, like great drama, involves the risk of tragedy. Under the older classical organisation theory such tasks would be described as respectively carried out by people at the bottom, middle and top layers of an organisational hierarchy, like the former Clerical, Executive and Administrative Classes of the Civil Service. In practice, however, people at all levels get involved to some extent in all three types of task, including decision-making and the resolution of disputes.

The special nature of decision-making in disputes

The last two phrases are not synonymous. All resolution of disputes involves decision-making, but not all decision-making involves a

* See pp. 49–51 above.
† See pp. 90–1 above.

dispute, in the sense of different solutions to a problem being advocated by different persons or interests. One may simply have a situation where a certain end-result is needed but no one is strongly advocating—perhaps not even suggesting—any particular way of bringing
it about. Hence the problem itself and the alternative means of
solving it need to be formulated explicitly and extensively and the
very process of formulation may lead to the solution. In its most
sophisticated form this process is one of operational research. In any
case if there are no pressures of advocacy from interested parties, it
can, or should be, a highly rational process. But disputes involving
separate pressures and advocacy identified with particular solutions
are a different matter, and their resolution is probably a more normal
task of management in the public than the private sector. It is easy
to think of all disputes in terms of pressure groups and interests and
it is, indeed, a basic process of administration to recognise these behind the rationalising which usually covers them.

Yet it is very easy to take this process so far as to abandon rationality altogether. For instance, if some organisation representative of
lawyers proposed that certain arbitration tribunals must always have
a full-time legally qualified Chairman it would be easy to say that
they were basically influenced only by the interests of their members
in obtaining such jobs. This of course would be a possible element of
subconscious bias that would have to be taken into account, but not
to the extent of ignoring the legitimate rational arguments for the
proposal. The ideas of Marx and Freud have so pervaded modern
thought on all kinds of subjects by all kinds of people (including
many who would abominate these two particular names) that the
presumed status of rationality in the processes of Government has
progressively declined. Nevertheless the formal processes of the state
—legislative, judicial and administrative—are all designed to institutionalise the rational processes of argument and dispute, and
isolate the elements of interest and bias. In Parliament and local
councils and the law courts personal interests must at least be
'declared' and may even then disqualify certain individuals from
taking part in the decision processes. Within the British Civil Service
rules and traditions on the subject are rightly very strict.

Institutional safeguards against bias: Royal Commissions and Committees

The presumption of bias in decision-making and the erection of safeguards against it was, however, an important concern of public
administration long before the days of Freud or even Marx. It was a
matter of great concern throughout the nineteenth century when the
idea, and the fact, of an efficient independent, regulatory state

machine superseded the eighteenth-century agglomeration of separate independent, often local, propertied interests reconciled only or mainly by the processes of Parliament itself. The slow and gradual implementation of the Northcote–Trevelyan Report on the Civil Service, and the development of expert Government inspectorates, and of Government audit, were all part of the process.

The processes of resolution of disputes by Government are too numerous and variable to describe, but we can notice the special characteristic elements of this task (which is not to be equated with all kinds of policy-making). These are not to be found in the ultimate decision-making authority (which must be the Government of the day) but rather in the administrative system and the group of administrative persons who analyse issues and give advice. These must be independent and seen to be independent of the disputing parties. They can usually be civil servants, yet when pressures are very strong and issues very controversial, there may have to be a further safeguard against the suspicion that the Civil Service may be unduly influenced either by the Ministers it serves or its own interest in the work. Hence outside advisers may be used, distinguished individuals, or Royal Commissions, committees or standing advisory bodies. The Royal Commission or Government Committee in recent years has developed far beyond the mere function of adjudicating between contending interests, or opinions and evidence produced by outside parties. It now often initiates independent investigation using research staff of its own. Nevertheless it is still usually confronted with contending interests to whom it must listen. Hence it has both a primary creative role of research-based initiation of ideas and policy, and also a secondary but related role of adjudication. Both require a high degree of independence particularly in the Chairman. (The expertise required in individual members may necessarily involve some sectionalism of outlook.) The Chairman of a Commission or Committee is usually a person whose means of livelihood makes him quite independent of the issues which are in question and also a person of high intellectual attainments and analytical powers. He will often be a judge or other distinguished lawyer or academic notable. The whole system depends on a sociological characteristic of contemporary Britain: the existence of certain people who are accepted by society and who accept themselves as fulfilling a role and an ethical duty of independent judgment in the broad interests of society as a whole. Such social groups have traditionally been partly aristocratic and partly professional with many individuals combining both characteristics. The typical member of such groups today, however, is an academic, a lawyer or a 'technocrat' (in the broad French sense of that term).

The modern Royal Commission is a nineteenth-century re-creation of a constitutional device of the Tudor and Stuart monarchies. The aristocracy, or at any rate the House of Lords, has provided a large number of Chairmen of Commissions and Government Committees. In recent decades the lordly technocrat has become rather more prominent in this field than the aristocrat (though the law lord remains equally prominent). It may not, however, be necessary to have an aristocracy, a technocracy, and perhaps not any socially distinct élite, to provide independent persons of this kind. There must simply be enough people respected for their integrity, independence and intellectual power of analysis.

Committees and Commissions are usually carefully balanced to represent a variety of interests—a big-business man, a trades union official, a member of each major political party, a Scotsman, a Welshman and so on. Even people with such obvious interests as these generally have them in spheres slightly removed from the issues in dispute. The business man and the trades unionist may come from industries not directly affected, and so on. On the whole, members are not chosen as directly or formally representing interested parties, but rather as likely to command their confidence or at least their acquiescence. Sometimes a contentious issue may be dealt with by a Select Committee of the House of Commons or of both Houses of Parliament. British Parliamentary Committees, such as the Public Accounts Committee and the Select Committee on Nationalised Industries have usually demonstrated a capacity to deal with controversial issues on non-party lines.

The initial collection and analysis of data for a Commission or Committee is usually carried out by its secretariat who are civil servants (or officials of Parliament). The primary elements in the Committee task are general public invitations for written evidence, written summarisation and analysis of such evidence, oral discussion between the whole committee and important witnesses, usually visits at home and/or abroad, the production of analytical working papers by the Chairman, Committee members, the research staff and/or the secretariat and the eventual production of a series of drafts of the report. Who takes the leading part in all this analytical work may depend on personalities and on the relative freedom of individuals from other commitments. Both the analytical and the creative work is extremely time-consuming and intellectually exhausting. In recent years Committees have increasingly employed outside expert consultants and research staff. Yet Professor Self has powerfully criticised cost benefit research commissioned by a judicial-type independent commission to solve a major clash of interests in a land-planning problem (the third London airport). 'There is no fully objective arbitration possible in matters of public policy.'[8] Most reports of Government Committees, Royal Commissions and special one-man inquiries are published unless there is some very special reason for confidentiality. Then there is further analysis, within Government Departments, of the consequences of accepting the recommendations, further consultations with the interested parties, and nearly always a parliamentary debate.

The will to decide

In all these processes there must be a constant conflict between accuracy and impartiality, on the one hand, and speed on the other. Some of this is unavoidable; but some depends on will-power and clarity of vision on the part of all concerned—Members of Parliament, Ministers, civil servants, committee members and interested parties. It is significant how many committee reports and indeed pieces of legislation which broke important new ground on major controversial issues were produced in the latter part of World War II —the (Cooper) *Report on Hydro-Electric Development in Scotland,*[9] the Reid Committee Report on Coal Mining,[10] the 'Butler' Education Act (1944), the Beveridge *Report on Social Insurance* and so on.[11] This was partly, no doubt, because contesting parties who could have obstructed progress were otherwise engaged, but a major reason was the will-power for effective post-war reconstruction which existed within the whole community at that time. At certain other times when the administrative resources available have been no less, no one has seemed able or willing to make them work quickly and effectively. The reasons for this are essentially sociological and political and cannot be found simply by analysis of administrative machinery or processes.

Liaison with outside interests: Institutional machinery— specialised administrative units

Resolution of disputes leads on to the wider question of the ways in which Government Departments and other public bodies maintain liaison with other outside interests, not only for resolving disputes but for avoiding them, and for the carrying on of a vast amount of day-to-day business. When this business consists of the provision of services, the tasks of liaison differ little except in scale from those of private industry. Both comprise dealings with contractors, customers, trades unions and so on; but when public bodies have monopoly positions as buyers or sellers or employers, particular safeguards against bias or misuse of monopoly powers may be needed. Commercial customers may be dealt with through their trade associations, the general public through consultative councils, and both groups by market research.

Of specifically governmental functions involving outside liaison, the most ancient, formal and elaborate are diplomatic relations, a special subject we cannot discuss fully. We can only note that it involves three elements—first the permanent representatives located overseas, second, within the Foreign Office, 'territorial' Departments specialising in groups of states and third, 'General' and functional Foreign Office Departments dealing with matters of policy affecting many different groups of states. The formality and elaboration derive partly from the absence of any sovereign body capable of reconciling differences between states.

At home many Government Departments have sub-departments specialising in particular industries or other interests. It is the business of the civil servants in each sub-department to understand the outlook of the interests concerned. Hence the resolution of disputes between the interests is often partly conducted by debate within the Government machinery by different groups of civil servants. They may spend only half of their time so arguing on their interests' behalf with other civil servants or Ministers, and the other half defending the Government's policy against these interests. This two-fronted process of continuing argument can be somewhat agonising. The Treasury, as a central organ of Government, often seems to be confronting all other interests in this second-hand way through other civil servants; but it also has to deal directly with some important interests. Directly or indirectly it is concerned with all those people who provide the money, whether by taxation or loan, for all kinds of Government activities. Such people may be unwilling to part with their money without expressing views as to how it is spent. Hence the Treasury acquires any reputation it may have, both within the Civil Service and outside it, for critical attitudes to public expenditure. Other Departments, under pressure from other outside interests, acquire a reputation with the Treasury as 'spending Departments'. The push and pull within the Government system is simply a reflection of conflicting pressures within the community at large.

The American writer Murray Edelman, in his chapter on 'The Administrative System as Symbol', appears to be going a stage further than the argument presented above, and suggesting that an organ of public administration designated to deal with an outside interest does so solely by transmitting the opinions and pressures of that interest group on to the Government and thence to the community—with no reaction in the other direction: 'Administrative agencies are to be understood as economic and political instruments of the parties they regulate and benefit, not of a reified "society", "general will" or "public interest" ', and again: 'The administrative system . . . mirrors, reinforces and sometimes helps realise the major interest groupings of society and by the same token mirrors the deep ambivalences in us all.'[12]

Carried to this length the argument appears excessively and unnecessarily cynical, and to be based on rather limited evidence— wholly American. However, whether or not Edelman is right is a political and not an administrative question. The answer might be different in different countries or different periods in history. We are concerned here with administrative tasks. The *administrative* lesson which Edelman's argument emphasises is that organs of Government dealing with interest groups have a legitimate administrative function in reflecting and transmitting the opinions and pressures of such groups to the Government itself. He appears, however, to deny that they have also a critical duty which they owe not only to their Government but even to the interest groups themselves.

These liaison functions of civil servants raise difficult questions of personnel policy. People need to acquire detailed knowledge of the interests they deal with and establish personal relations and confidence. Hence it may be argued they should specialise for long periods. On the other hand they could become too closely identified with the outlook of sectional interests, or alternatively develop antagonisms against them. Either tendency could be a special problem in overseas representation and hence Governments may move round their diplomatic staffs from one embassy to another every four or five years.

Sometimes the representatives of interests may be brought almost within the organisation of Government itself, as in 'Neddy'. More often, however, they remain on the periphery. In terms of classical organisation theory this is outside the Government organisation structure, the organisation charts and their lines of command and responsibility. In the light of much non-classical organisation theory, notably Barnard's and Vickers', however, it forms an essential element in an organisation. It is indeed not possible to imagine the Department of Trade and Industry without employers' associations and trades unions, the Foreign and Commonwealth Office without overseas Governments, the Ministry of the Environment without local authorities and their associations, the Treasury without the Bank of England, the City, the International Monetary Fund and so on.

Forms of external consultation

The external liaison work of Government Departments has grown greatly in volume and variety in the last half-century. H. E. Dale, writing of *The Higher Civil Service* as it was in 1939, describes such dealings as it then had with the general public. He then goes on to refer to the 'special publics' of different Departments, the special interests and their representative organisations, and how liaison was conducted with them by and through individual contacts. He felt it necessary to explain and almost apologise for the fact that the representatives of organisations dealt mainly with officials rather than Ministers.[13] Since he wrote there has been an immense increase in the dealings of representative organisations and interest groups with Government Departments. This has meant more dealings with officials because of the sheer volume of the work. Indeed it has meant a great parallel increase in the number of full-time paid officials of outside organisations as distinct from the part-time Chairmen and other leading characters. There has, however, been an increase in the extent of these latter people's dealings personally with Ministers. As Government activity becomes more important to the outside interests they became more anxious to develop and maintain contacts with successive Governments at the highest levels. Indeed at every level outside liaison has come to represent a much larger and more important task of Government.

Hanson and Walles describe the situation in 1969:

As Government activity has extended into all sectors of society, so there has developed a realization that, for effective administration, those directly affected should be consulted and, if possible, their consent and co-operation obtained. There is now a general acceptance of group representation in the administrative processes, which finds formal expression in the plethora of advisory committees that exist to provide vital links between the Government on the one hand and the various producers' groups—comprehending employers', employees', and professional associations—on the other. There are something like 500 effective central and national advisory committees on which producers' groups have representation. . . . That these contacts are regarded as a necessary part of the political process is indicated by the formal provision made for them in certain statutes, as for instance in the 1947 Agriculture Act which obliges the Ministers to 'consult with such bodies of persons as appear to them to represent the interests of producers in the Agricultural Industry' . . . The formal contacts are also supplemented by continuous interchanges of a more informal but still highly important nature . . . Governments are often in need of information from those they administer . . . as Blondel has pointed out, 'if firms and other interests were to starve the Civil Service of . . . information the administration of the country would come to a halt.[14]

Consultation thus now takes a great variety of forms, interviews and correspondence and formal deputations, and it is often institutionalised in a variety of joint committees. Many of these are formally designated 'advisory'. Indeed Sir Kenneth Wheare in his classic work on committees in Government written sixteen years ago[15] classifies them in his chapter 'Committees to Advise' and not in that on 'Committees to Negotiate', which he devotes mainly to bodies like the Burnham Committee and Whitley Councils where public bodies meet representatives of their employees. In fact, however, many a Committee, which in form is only supposed to advise, is in fact a major forum for negotiation.

Internal liaison and coordination

As much Government external relations work involves having separate units to deal with each outside group of interests, the task of reconciling the views and pressures of such interests is partly discharged as a task of internal coordination and liaison within and between Government Departments. Indeed if, as we argued in Chapter 4,* a major function of Government is reconciling conflicting policy objectives, internal liaison between administrative units responsible for pursuing these different objectives must be one of its major tasks. This has a parallel in the internal problems of 'integration' posed, and only partially and impressionistically answered, by Lawrence and Lorsch in respect of large privately owned corporations.† Lawrence and Lorsch, however, are dealing with organisations with a variety of sub-units with different management structures, management processes and management styles, indeed different groups and types of personnel, the majority of whom would not normally be interchanged as readily as administrative civil servants.

In central government the task of coordination is much more important, and probably much more complex and much more fully provided for by institutional machinery than anywhere else, even the largest corporations, companies and local authorities.[16] All sovereign Governments, however little democratic control they are under at home, can be exposed to embarrassments of inconsistency in international relations. They vary in the extent to which they seem to mind such embarrassment. The United Kingdom, however, as explained in Chapter 4, has a powerful Parliament and a powerful Cabinet and Cabinet secretariat whose influences on Government Departments constantly press them into conformity with common patterns. Ministers are personally under constant and detailed pressure from Members of Parliament (often well briefed by special interests) who will seek to break down a particular line of Govern-

* See pp. 82–4 above.
† See pp. 67–8 above.

ment policy by demonstrating its inconsistency with Government activities or policies in some other sphere.

Coordination within and between British Government Departments is not, of course, always perfect; but it is remarkably close and constant. It is achieved, first, by a great mass of interdepartmental committees. It is indeed remarkable that Wheare in his five types of committee—'to advise', 'to inquire', 'to negotiate', 'to legislate' and 'to administer'—does not include 'committees to coordinate' or 'to inform' or 'to liaise'. Committees of civil servants ('official committees') support and advise parallel 'Ministerial committees'— usually sub-committees of the Cabinet. As well as these committees there are, of course, many meetings and much correspondence.

Much coordination is less formal. Indeed, Dale, writing of the smaller and more compact Civil Service of the thirties, seemed to imply that all important policy-making and coordination was utterly informal:

. . . little business of difficulty or importance is settled by official letters from one Department to another: the real work of government and administration is done by word of mouth—sometimes by telephone, more often by interview. Official letters, sometime lengthy ones, are in fact written; but in most cases they are written 'for record'. . . . If a civil servant wants to get the assent of another Department to some novel or doubtful action in a region where both are concerned, he does not write an official letter. He may write semi-officially to his 'opposite number' in the other Department; but it is much more likely that he will telephone to ask when he may come over to discuss the point before anything is put in writing either officially or semi-officially. If they agree, well and good; if not, the question must go to higher authorities—who similarly meet and talk. The final court of appeal is the Prime Minister and the Cabinet. When a decision has been reached, then and often not till then will there be written correspondence. The idea that Government Offices do their business by long official letters to one another is now completely wrong, if it ever was right.[17]

However Dale's 'higher civil service' (broadly the old Administrative Class and a few of the highest professionals) constituted a relatively small, leisurely and genteel world. He reckoned about 550 persons in all. Although even in that day their ultimate social origins were various, they developed a great deal of intellectual and social homogeneity—'talked the same language' as they would have said, and seem to have had a lot more time to talk it than their successors of the sixties. Apart from Lord Bridges, no subsequent description of the British higher Civil Service, not even Dunnill's, has come anywhere near the standard of Dale's lucid and charming style and careful analysis, and hence his picture has remained as a legend embodying what a good many people still imagine their higher Civil Service to be. Many a higher civil servant, however, reading Dale in 1971 may feel himself by comparison a pretty crude fellow. His dealings with other Departments may all too often depend not on cosy chats in Dale's style but on letters exchanged with people he has seldom met. Hence although internal liaison in the higher Civil Service may have appeared easy, informal and little institutionalised a generation ago, does it retain any of these characteristics today?

It is hard to generalise about such a nebulous entity as liaison among so many and such varied people, but despite all the changes of the last generation the answer seems to be 'yes'. Many of the traditions built up by the élitists of the Dale period have been maintained by their somewhat different successors. Nearly all Government Departments have a large number of posts mainly concerned with 'administration' in the Civil Service sense—general coordinating functions, parliamentary work, liaison with interest groups, 'policy' (in the various meanings of that word) and so on. The day to day work, and the training of such people in all Departments, has much in common and so does the personnel work and management development policy applied to them. These characteristics have been intensified by the coordinating activities of the Civil Service Department and its predecessor the Treasury. Hence there remains a large body of administrators who, however educated and recruited, tend to work and think in similar ways. A civil servant in one Department, considering what policy to propose in dealing with certain conflicting pressure groups, consults his opposite number in another Department whose interests are also affected. This second civil servant is also a man accustomed to dealing with pressure groups and trying to reconcile conflicting requirements of Government policy. Both civil servants are accustomed to seeing that their Department's activities can stand up to parliamentary scrutiny and public criticism, to trying to reconcile long-term planning with financial restrictions and rising prices—and so on. Hence they can talk easily, informally and above all briefly—in a certain shorthand of their trade. C. P. Snow in one of his novels describes the clipped conversation of a certain couple as 'the shorthand of marriage'. There is also a shorthand of most trades and professions—just as a professional dealer at an auction will make his bids with the minutest of muscular gestures. To develop this kind of language people must spend a good many years dealing, not necessarily with the same work, but the same sort of work. There is thus kept in being a large number of people in different Departments who can all be said to be on the same wave·length.

This kind of thing is undoubtedly helped by interchanges of staff between jobs. Such interchanges are fairly common within each Government Department, probably rather less common between one Department and another except at the two top levels. The Fulton Report castigated the generalist without specialist expertise and complained bitterly of too much interchange between jobs. This complaint, however, was based on a fairly small sample of cases and it is interesting that it was made at the very time when large-scale private industry in Britain, as well as America, faced with the problems described by Lawrence and Lorsch,* was struggling with the development of more generalists and the 'broadening' of its specialists.

Moreover, in a Civil Service such as the British, it is possible, and indeed desirable, to have certain features of work organisation and personnel management common to a large number of jobs, however long individuals concerned specialise. All civil servants in the Ministry of the Environment must, for instance, need a deep understanding of the workings of local government in addition to whatever specialisation they may have in such subjects as housing, water, rating, financial control, boundary determination and so on. What is relevant to our present argument is that this degree of generalism makes internal and interdepartmental liaison easier. So does career-long service, and fairly settled career expectations. It is important for speedy and frank liaison on complex subjects that all civil servants should treat each other as colleagues, rather than as rivals from whom information must be withheld for fear it is used to advance someone else's career at the expense of their own. These traditional characteristics of the British Civil Service have their compensatory disadvantages. Yet these can be, and are mitigated without sacrificing the advantages of the element of stability and mutual confidence.

Of course such conditions do not always obtain ideally. Civil servants, like business men, academics, service officers and others are human and sometimes get across each other. They have, however, a framework, a working environment and general conditions which normally encourage and stimulate easy and informal co-operation. It does not always stick to strict hierarchical levels either within, or between Departments. There is much 'leap-frogging' of official levels and diagonal communication through whatever seems the easiest or quickest channel Wise senior civil servants—and Ministers—will often send for the man who knows most about the subject, even though he is a junior and is not in the direct line of command.

All this can be summed up by saying that in the kind of subtle and

* See pp. 67–8 above.

complex policy work which involves much liaison within and between Government Departments, the British Civil Service operates
much more (to use Burns and Stalker's Model*) on 'organic' than
'mechanistic' lines. Or rather it is a highly 'organic' nervous system
working within a highly mechanistic external framework—of law, of
the constitution and of departmental structure. All this leads us to
consider more specifically the subject of personnel management in
the Civil Service and the public services generally.

1. e.g., Andrew Shonfield, 1965. *Modern Capitalism,* p. 394; or Brian
Chapman, 1963. *British Government Observed,* p. 38. Allen and Unwin.

2. e.g., Lord (formerly Herbert) Morrison and Dr Jeremy Bray, see
pp. 133–4 below.

3. Fayol, op. cit., p. 6.

4. J. A. G. Griffiths, 1966. *Central Departments and Local Authorities.*
Allen and Unwin.

5. ibid., p. 515.

6. Evelyn Sharp, 1969. *The Ministry of Housing and Local Government,*
pp. 32–3. (New Whitehall Series.) Allen and Unwin.

7. J. F. Morris and J. Burgoyne, 1971. *Management Development
Strategies.* Institute of Personnel Management.

8. Peter Self, 1970. 'Nonsense or Stilts: cost benefit analysis and the
Roskill Commission', *Political Quarterly,* 41 no. 3, p. 260.

9. 1942 Cmd. 6406.

10. 1945 Cmd. 6610.

11. 1944 Cmd. 6404.

12. Murray Edelman, 1964. *The Symbolic Uses of Politics,* pp. 56 and 71.
University of Illinois.

13. op. cit., pp. 181–3. For the period of reference see Dale's preface,
p. v.

14. A. H. Hanson and Malcolm Walles, 1970. *Governing Britain,*
pp. 152–4. Collins.

15. K. C. Wheare, 1955. *Government by Committee,* chs. 3 and 5. OUP.

16. See T. E. Headrick, 1962. *The Town Clerk in English Local Government.* Allen and Unwin. Also, Charles Barnett, Summer 1963. 'The Town
Clerk in British Local Government', *Public Administration,* vol. 41,
pp. 157–71.

17. Dale, op. cit., pp. 162–3.

* See p. 65 above.

6

TASKS (II): PERSONNEL MANAGEMENT AND GENERAL PLANNING

Personnel management: its special position in the Civil Service
In the Civil Service personnel management has higher relative status among management functions than is usual in the private sector, or indeed in most other parts of the public sector. It is true that the status of personnel management has been rising in the private sector for some years, as labour, particularly highly qualified labour, has become more scarce. Nevertheless, throughout the private sector, personnel management tends, to use rather imprecise terms, to be a 'staff' rather than a 'line' function. In any case it must be a subsidiary function. A manufacturing company exists to manufacture commodities and not, like a Government Department, to provide the services of people.

One of the most important developments in the building up of the administration of a modern state in Britain in the last century was the provision of large and stable cadres of reliable, qualified people. They were needed to carry out the new or newly expanded Government functions, which could no longer be provided for haphazardly, or by patronage, nepotism or the sale of offices. This happened first with the tax systems and the Post Office, then with the basic regulatory and inspectorial systems, and then finally with personal services such as those of the Local Authorities and the Ministry of Labour. There was a common requirement for all these people—postmen, registrars, public health inspectors, tax assessors and collectors, Employment Exchange staffs and many others—to be honest and reliable. Many also needed expertise and some needed professional qualifications, but integrity mattered most. If anyone thinks of this as something very elementary, he should consider how it has been, and still sometimes is, lacking in so many other countries, some otherwise quite advanced. The whole basis of the finances of the contemporary British state, the whole basis of law and order and the numerous controls of public health and public safety, depend on the general confidence placed in large numbers of public employees. Some of them are eminent and relatively well paid, but most are of middling or very modest status. The elaborate and sometimes apparently bureaucratic and legalistic rules and procedures of personnel management in the Civil Service and the Local Authorities, exist largely to preserve this public confidence. The fact that the British public services today are free of major public scandals does not make these arrangements obsolete, any more than public health legislation is obsolete because we no longer have the cholera epidemics which first stimulated its introduction. Personnel management is not, however, just a matter of negative safeguards against corruption. It is a positive function of providing the numerous groups of reliable and often highly skilled and trained people, to carry out an enormous variety of essential functions, most of which have no commerical yardstick whereby they can be measured or controlled.

Government Departments differ in the extent to which personnel work preponderates among their other major functions, but it is always sufficiently important to make the Department's 'Principal Establishment Officer', the Civil Service equivalent of a Personnel Director, into a relatively important person in the top management of the Department. He and his staff have executive powers in their own right and are not simply advisers. In some very large Departments he may stand only second, third or fourth in status below the Head of the Department. The function of Civil Service personnel management must include not only negative safeguards to preserve integrity, but positive measures for career development and training. In Britain today the Civil Service Department is concerned with all this for the whole Service, but nevertheless a major responsibility after recruitment rests with individual Departments. The centralising and systematising process has been a very slow one. It involved the gradual building up of the powers of the Civil Service Commission and the Treasury (now succeeded by the CSD) during the nineteenth century and was only completed by Sir Warren Fisher during his long reign as Permanent Head of the Civil Service in the 1920s and 1930s. The Treasury/CSD has been concerned with pay and grading and conditions of service, and central personnel management policies generally. Recruitment initially into the Service, or from one 'Class' of the Service to another, has been the responsibility of the Civil Service Commission. The CSC conducts individual selections for senior grades and prescribes how Departments carry out these procedures for lower grades. Briefly, no one can be recruited to a permanent position in the Civil Service without the Commission's certificate, but once recruited his career is a matter for his own Department. Exceptionally, Permanent Heads of Departments, their Deputies, their Principal Establishment Officers and Principal Finance Officers can only be appointed with the approval of the Prime Minister—advised by the Head of the Civil Service.*

All these arrangements safeguard the impartiality and the general standards of Civil Service personnel management, while leaving a reasonable amount of discretion to Departments. Ultimately full control is of course in the hands of the Ministers, but not entirely of individual Departmental Ministers. Other Governments in the British Commonwealth and elsewhere have devised various institutional measures to safeguard the independence and integrity of their Civil Services.[1] Some have independent public service commissions with wide powers, safeguarded in written state constitutions or special laws. There is a limit, however, to the extent to which things so intangible, though so important, as standards of conduct, public confidence and moral qualities can be safeguarded by purely legal provisions, especially if this is to be done without hampering the discretion of Governments in all their other functions. On the whole it has been understandable that some states should start with rather legalistic safeguards, and build up gradually their customs, standards and traditions. In Britain, on the whole, the Civil Service customs, standards and traditions, and hence public confidence, were built up first, largely by administrative measures, and the legal safeguards, though important, never played so large a part as in most other countries.

Grading systems and unions

Perhaps the outstanding feature common to nearly all the branches of British public services, not only central and local government but also the public corporations, is that most employees are more classified into ranks or grades and hierarchies than anywhere else, except the armed forces. Grading systems may exist, of course, within the largest privately owned companies and in some other organisations (notably Universities), but in no other type of organisation are they so important, not only for people's present positions and functions, but for their career development. This is not because public bodies or their staffs are peculiarly unimaginative, but rather because of their size, what they do and how they have to do it. It may be suitable for certain kinds of private business to give managers of separate units independent 'hire and fire' powers over their employees if there are

* Formerly the Permanent Secretary of the Treasury, now the Permanent Secretary of the Civil Service Department.

obvious yardsticks of achievement and efficiency—'accountable management', 'profit centres' and so on. This sort of approach, however, cannot usually be transferred without much reservation to the public sector. The measures of efficiency are not so simple. Moreover Governmental and public utility functions generally involve doing a great many things many times in the same sorts of ways and in many places. Thus many of the methods of dealing with personnel, notably pay and other conditions of work, can be standardised. All sorts of qualifications would have to be made if one were to spell out in detail how these principles apply in any particular part of the public services, but the general pattern of large classified and graded groups of personnel persists over the greater part of the public sector, and nearly up to the top.

Hence the management can often deal most conveniently with employees in large groups, and employees in turn organise themselves in large groups in order to deal with the management. 'White collar unionism', still a rather novel development in the private sector, has been common in most of the public sector in Britain for half a century, and includes even Permanent Heads of Government Departments and Town Clerks of the largest cities. The nationalised industries have, on the whole, followed somewhat similar patterns. The Electricity and Gas Boards were formed to a large extent on a local authority foundation. The coal industry on the other hand passed in one jump from about 800 companies to one single management, and the introduction of grading systems for managerial staff brought into being new associations to represent them.

Security of employment and motivation

Those special features of Civil Service personnel policy and practice which have attracted most attention from outside—notably that of the Fulton Committee—have been security of employment and alleged lack of competition. Both are relative and it is not possible to be precise, even about their relativity, without much more information than is readily available.

The much criticised security of employment arises from a number of conditions peculiar to any Civil Service and some peculiar to that of Britain or other states with similar political conditions. First, the basic reason was to provide a stable, neutral state organisation not disturbed or biased by party political changes. In Britain the gradual separation between political and permanent officers within the Government seems to have started in the eighteenth century and only concluded after the middle of the nineteenth. It came about as a matter of mutual convenience for all concerned in Government (politicians, officials and others) and not as a result of any one

dramatic or explicit change of policy. Later in the nineteenth century
and in the earlier part of the twentieth century the permanence of the
British Civil Service was regarded as a positive advantage and contrasted favourably with that of the United States and other countries
which were said to operate a 'spoils' system. Nowadays, comments
of a somewhat opposite kind are being made. The need for a permanent and stable Civil Service arose because many functions of modern
Government involve more continuity than controversy. Even for
those which were the subject of political controversy, the major political Parties have in the past preferred to have a neutral impartial
machine which would serve them both, although recently both Parties
have brought in or proposed to bring in very small numbers of people
of their own choice from outside.

Another factor has been the monopoly character of Government
employment. Paradoxically it is arguable that the extreme legal in-
security of the civil servant has given him an exceptional security in
fact. Although there may be certain doubts about the subtleties of the
legal position, civil servants have no formal contracts of employment, and are supposed to hold their offices 'at the Queen's pleasure'.
Pensions are non-contributory and non-transferable. For many,
there is no equivalent employment outside Government service for
which they would be well qualified. Ministers who hold this ultimate
theoretical power to wreck people's lives at a mere whim are, of
course, accountable to Parliament for its use, quite apart from any
pressures of Civil Service trades unions. Hence it has come to be
accepted in Britain that permanent civil servants (there are a small
proportion of temporaries, mainly at lower levels) are only dismissed
for pretty serious offences and dismissal decisions are taken at very
high levels. Very many more are severely punished by permanent or
temporary loss of promotion expectations. Civil Service disciplinary
standards concerning even minor dishonesty, improprieties and
breaches of trust, are severe, and the consequences particularly
severe with a non-contributory pension scheme. For inefficiency not
involving dishonesty there is also the possibility of premature retirement with proportionate pension. Owing to the size and variety of
forms of Government employment it is usually possible to deal with
redundancies by redeployment and restriction of recruitment. In the
very rare cases where it is not, people may be considered for retirement with proportionate pension. The idea that in the British Civil
Service promotion comes by seniority and not by merit is largely a
myth, as many meteoric—and ruined—careers demonstrate. However, for many appointments (even at fairly high levels) in such a
very large organisation as a Government Department, there may
well be relatively little difference in the qualifications of the candi-

dates. Hence seniority, which implies experience, is bound to be a more important factor than in smaller organisations where both jobs and potential candidates for them cannot be so systematically classi-fied. The more efficient and systematic the recruitment system in any organisation the less need for dismissals or the disappointment of career expectations.

Recruitment

The British Civil Service had to undertake personnel management for very large groups of people a generation or so earlier than the private sector. It is therefore natural that it should have been simi-larly ahead of the private sector in systematising arrangements both for initial recruitment and for periodical reporting on individuals during the course of their careers. Its recruitment arrangements have for over half a century been generally well developed and fairly sophisticated, even though they may have been over-complicated in minor details. During the nineteenth century and the first three decades of the twentieth century a system of recruitment was developed on the basis of academic-style written examinations, matched to the different levels of the national education system. At the end of World War II, the Civil Service Commission took over from the armed forces a very sophisticated system of personnel selection for the Administrative Class. It includes successive inter-views by individuals and by a board, group exercises and various psychological tests. It is understood that all these test various intel-lectual aptitudes and social skills, including skills of coordinating the activities of others. Some large industrial concerns appear to have modelled their own management selections on this system. However, it is particularly suitable for a large public service based on the assumption of career-long service, an obligation to the community to give equal opportunity to the contestants, and the overriding im-portance of skills of coordination and conciliation.

Morale and motivation

The whole system of Civil Service personnel management is designed to provide for flexibility and interchangeability internally, but within a very stable and settled external framework. The most important question for public administration theory is the effect of all this on morale and motivation. The Fulton Committee commented generally unfavourably on this and wanted more specialisation, more competi-tion and less security. Although it paid tribute to some aspects of Civil Service personnel management, it was on the whole unimpressed by it. Its most positive recommendations, however, were concerned with structure rather than the human relationships of people working

individually and in groups. For all its pose of modernity its basic
thinking retained a considerably classical character. It is indeed
strange how the Fulton Report and much other comment on the
British Civil Service ignore the most important literature of personnel management and organisation theory of the last four decades
—particularly on such questions as the cohesion of working groups,
the nature of working environments and individual and group
motivation.

Much valuable information and thought on these subjects is also
conveyed, implicitly rather than explicitly, by various writers who are
or have been career civil servants themselves, such as Dale and Lord
Bridges.[2] The final chapter of a recent book by R. G. S. Brown,
another former civil servant, is outstanding. He comments on the
mass of evidence and supporting material which the Fulton
Committee assembled, but says:

The Report itself is less helpful: it is imbued with a 'business-managerial'
philosophy, but fails to make any effective contribution to the theoretical
understanding of public administration . . . .[3]

He refers to its strictures on the relative lack of 'sticks and carrots'
and its citations of evidence—or perhaps one should say inferences—
from institutions outside the Civil Service, on the assumed effects on
morale and efficiency. He comments:

It is therefore surprising to discover how well, even in the Committee's
eyes, the present system works. Thanks to the development of good staff
relations through the Whitley Council machinery, morale is high, industrial disputes are rare, and the staff have shown a cooperative and constructive attitude to changes which may work against their immediate
interests, such as the introduction of computers. The Committee commented on the integrity, the humanity, the impartiality and the devotion of
the Service, its capacity for improvisation and the ability, vision
and enthusiasm of some of its members. . . . The 'generally high
standard of morale' is largely due to the existence of uniform and well
understood procedures and the genuine desire to apply them with
fairness.

He quotes the Committee's comment:

'It is surprising that such a system has called forth the dedication, conscien-
tiousness and enthusiasm that we so often saw' [and Brown himself
concludes, 'It looks as though there may be something wrong with the
theory.'[4]]

By 'the theory' he appears to imply the Fulton Committee's critical approach to the whole existing Civil Service system and its view that it is inadequate to meet the responsibilities of modern Government.

The pre-eminent function of personnel management for any Government service is not only or mainly its institutional arrangements or rules and procedures, but the production of traditions and a work environment which provides both confidence and stimulus. Looking all round the world one could find every variety of such traditions and environments. In some of them Government service could become an ossified bureaucracy, unimaginative, oppressive and remote from the needs of the population which it ought to be serving. In other conditions it might, on the contrary, be unstable, biassed and corrupt, so pushed about by all kinds of sectional interests that it had no confidence or ability to do its job. The first kind of situation can normally only come about if the bureaucracy is protected by a powerful and harsh political dictatorship or tolerated by a sick society where no one has sufficient incentive to put things right. The second type of situation can obtain if a Government is not strong enough to protect its own servants from pressures of the wrong kind. The root trouble of either situation is that the population which the Civil Service should be serving does not understand what a system of good Government is, or does not care about it, or is prevented from expressing its care for it.

Foresight, intelligence, research and planning

Fayol, as we have seen,* put first among his five functions of administration that of *prévoyance*, by which he meant not only planning but the necessarily preceding tasks of foresight, forethought, and forecasting. These prime tasks include the equivalent of the 'intelligence' function in a military staff and that of industrial and market research. Yet in our enumeration of the tasks of public administration we have left all this till the last. This order of treatment follows from the way in which the principal functions of Government and public bodies have developed in Britain. Management of the national economy was only relatively recently accepted as a major responsibility of the United Kingdom Government. It must involve some degree of forward planning, preceded by collection of data and forecasting. There are also many possible subjects for research, forecasting and planning, other than the entire national economy. Moreover there are particular sectors of the economy, and particular public functions, which are not necessarily best described as 'economic', for instance education, national defence, crime prevention and health. Forecasting and planning for public utility services were found necessary

* See p. 24, above; Fayol, op. cit., pp. 48–9.

long before there was any overall forecast or plan for the whole national economy. Planning has always been an important task of the British nationalised industries, and of certain local authority services. Forecasting and planning can sometimes be more fully developed for certain parts of these services than for the whole. For instance for many years the Post Office planned its individual sorting offices and telephone exchanges to meet thirty- and twenty-year needs without attempting such very long-term plans on a national basis.

Long-term forecasts of the future and sophisticated scientific and economic research and statistics as tools of administration are relatively new, but systematic 'intelligence' has for centuries, probably throughout recorded history, been a very important basis of political and administrative functions. One need only cite the Domesday Book and the elaborate international correspondence and espionage systems on which Cecil and Walsingham based their powerful positions in the Privy Council of Elizabeth I.[5] Apart from secret political and military intelligence, data derived from or required for taxation activities probably constituted the earliest information systems of most Governments, and information originally connected with taxation became useful to the Government and the community generally for all sorts of other purposes. In the nineteenth century the publication of census reports, trade returns, health statistics, and so on, was greatly developed in Britain and other Western countries. All this, however, was limited. It was largely uncoordinated. It was related to past events without normally much attempt to forecast the future. Most of it cannot be dignified by the name research, in a scientific sense, as distinct from systematic collection of data.

The Haldane Committee

On the subject of *prévoyance* the Report of the Haldane Committee on the *Machinery of Government* (1918)[6] was almost as much ahead of its time as Fayol. Like Fayol, it adopted an analytical but somewhat abstract and generalised approach, whose advantages and disadvantages we shall discuss generally in Chapter 8.* Here we are only concerned with what it said relating to foresight, intelligence, research and planning. It began its remarks on this subject:

Turning next to the formulation of policy, we have come to the conclusion, after surveying what came before us, that in the sphere of civil government the duty of investigation and thought, as a preliminary to action might with great advantage be more definitely recognised. It appears to us that adequate provision has not been made in the past for the organised acquisition of facts and information, and for the systematic application

* See pp. 160–4 below.

of thought, as a preliminary to the settlement of policy, and its subsequent administration.[7]

After referring to the analogy of military intelligence, it cited a variety of special intelligence, research or information units within existing Government Departments, and concluded that something more was needed. It recommended an expansion of the various Government scientific research activities and departmental planning units, the addition of more social research and the concentration of the whole in a new 'Department of Intelligence and Research',[8] under a separate Minister. The basic philosophy behind this suggestion was, as for military staff: 'The proved impracticability of devoting the necessary time to thinking and organisation and preparation for action in the mere interstices of the time required for the transaction of business.'[9] In other words, responsibility for thought and action should be separated—not merely between different units within a Government Department, but between separate Government Departments and separate Ministers.

This suggestion was not adopted comprehensively by the Government of the day nor by any subsequent Government. The setting up of the Department of Scientific and Industrial Research can be regarded as a consequence of the Haldane proposals; but that Department, and other research organisations set up by various Governments and Government Departments since, have been concerned with research mainly in the natural and industrial sciences, and to a lesser extent in the social sciences. They have sometimes also been concerned with development, but both research and development are quite different from the 'policy formulation' to which Haldane referred. Much nearer to Haldane's idea was the Central Economic Planning Staff. A special central organ of Government concerned with policy formulation—'a small multi-disciplinary central policy review staff in the Cabinet Office'—had indeed been announced just as this book was being written.[10] It is therefore too early to assess how it will work. As, however, this staff will form an integral element in the Cabinet Office it hardly appears that the new arrangement will involve the completely separate thought and action which Haldane envisaged.

The elements of planning

Before commenting further on the merits of this concept, we must look at the other elements in the whole planning task. Research and intelligence, in the sense of inquiry into past and present events and situations, only constitutes the first stage of planning. The other stages involve:

(a) Forecasting future events and situations outside one's own immediate control;

(b) Planning action to be taken by oneself or under one's own influence and control;

(c) Forecasting the effect of such action.

There are also the necessary consequential functions of initiating and seeing through such action, of monitoring it while it is in progress and of checking its effects after completion. The resulting situation is of course the basis of further planning, and so on.

Now the practical experience of most organisations is that if any of these elements are too much separated they tend to be conducted unrealistically. Yet if responsibility for more than one of them is combined in one individual or management unit or if either the formulation or execution of new developments is given to people fully loaded with day-to-day work then, as Haldane rightly argued, it will not get done properly—or perhaps not get done at all. On the other hand, people who spend their time making plans they will never have to implement can easily become unrealistic and irresponsible. It is arguable that it is mainly the later processes in the series enumerated above which need closely associating and that initial research and intelligence can operate as well or better when detached. There is a lot, however, to be said for making forecasters live with the results of their forecasts, and for first providing them with practical experience to help them make them.

Types and philosophies of forecasting

Forecasting can be assisted by several kinds of sophisticated techniques, but one must recognise its basic elements. There can be no question of a computer or any other device with power to foretell the future with certainty, because the future does not yet exist. On the other hand, all action, or inaction, involves some assumptions, albeit tacit or even unconscious, about the future. Everyone who invests capital, even in building a house, implicitly forecasts he will be able to get sufficient return from it by use, rent, or sale. He will often be wrong. Forecasting cannot ever be exact or certain. It can scarcely be a science. Yet it should be as thorough and rational as time and circumstances permit. It consists essentially of assessing probabilities on the basis of certain assumptions.

Broadly these assumptions can be of three kinds:

(a) that certain events which have happened in the past will recur in the future, because the determining factors are likely to remain the same.

(b) that the determining factors have been changing in the past and will continue to change in the future—one cannot say exactly how or why, but certain trends or patterns of change which have been observed in the past may be presumed to be likely to continue in the future, e.g., a birth rate, or the demand for a certain commodity, will continue to rise as it has risen in the past;

(c) certain events which have already occurred or are known to be going to occur, will produce certain subsequent effects—alterations in a rate of change and so on (e.g., an increase in the birth rate will in future years produce an increase in the number of school leavers, or a synthetic material just developed or likely to be developed will reduce the demand for a natural commodity).

In fact probably most forecasting is of the (b) variety and its sophistication often lies more in its mathematical projections of trends and curves than in close examination of determining causes. (c) is the most difficult kind of forecasting. It involves preferably both practical experience of the results of past forecasts and also critical imagination—a readiness to question, for instance, the alleged inevitability of the demand for a certain commodity increasing at the same rate till the end of time—just because it has been observed to do so in the past. (There have been highly placed engineers in more than one large public organisation deeply devoted to such myths.)

The kind of planning in which forecasting is a most important element is an essential task in most public utility services, and especially electricity, gas, water, and telephones. Such services, quite unlike manufacturing industry, are faced with breakdown if supply cannot be instantly adjusted to demand.

Political problems of planning and research

As I have described in detail elsewhere[11] the major nationalised industries have had very long-term planning from their earliest days, partly because of the magnitude and the time-scale of construction of their major capital projects. Most purely Governmental units of administration find long-term planning much more difficult and until recently it has been much less practised by them. Long-term plans, however essential, are difficult to reconcile with the democratic process. They commit future Governments, Parliaments and electorates. Moreover the very process of research, enquiry and forecasting can itself be expensive and a Government not convinced of the importance of some particular activity may be unwilling even to devote resources to assess the demand for it. It may well be supported negatively by public opinion in such attitudes. There are often serious economic, social, political and international problems about which the public just do not want to know. How far their elected representatives and civil servants have a duty of forcing them to their attention is a nice point.

Even when the need for research is admitted it may be embarrassing for a Government to undertake it directly. It will be accused of over- or underestimating the need for some provision, on the grounds of policy bias. When it comes to research and forecasting in the sphere of the social sciences, particularly controversial subjects like crime-prevention, health, or education, it may be preferable to have research carried out in Universities or by independent committees manned and/or supported by distinguished academics. This is partly because of the expertise and imaginative ideas thus made available; but partly also because people will, on the whole, believe academics when they will not believe civil servants or Ministers. But the setting on foot of a powerful research effort, whether by an inside or an outside agency, is often a major, and indeed the crucial, administrative act of policy initiation. Once the need has been searchingly analysed it is hard not to go ahead and meet it. The crucial decision may be the choice of the chief individual investigator—a Beveridge, a Robbins or a Buchanan.

Interdependent planning and faith

The making of a forecast or a plan is a creative process and it often triggers off a chain of further creative processes. It can do so both by stimulating ideas and also by creating confidence. By contrast forecasts and plans which are not followed up or not fulfilled breed bitter administrative and managerial cynicism. People will not engage the creative parts of their minds actively nor deploy the creative talents of other people (often scarce administrative, professional or technical staffs), unless they have some confidence that the results will be used. Engineers will not be keen to design equipment for buildings if they have no confidence as to when, if ever, they will be available. Architects will not want to design buildings if they have no confidence that anyone will know what equipment will be put in them. Neither is it likely that they, or anyone, will plan with much enthusiasm or confidence if they have no assurance that money will be available to implement their plans. The commercial or service-providing department of a public utility concern cannot usefully do anything to stimulate, or even estimate, growth without some confidence that the resources will be available to meet it. On the other hand the provision of new technological resources giving superior service—like railway electrification or submarine telephone cabling—may itself unexpectedly stimulate demand.

This balancing and coordinating of different sides of a forecasting and planning operation is an extremely important and complex task of management, especially in the public utility services. Indeed it is so in any activities depending on huge complex capital projects which take years to plan and complete and the cooperation of a variety of sophisticated professions. It is sometimes a matter of breaking vicious circles and pulling oneself up by one's own bootlaces. There may be a reluctance to forecast or stimulate growth because resources do not appear to be available: there may be a reluctance to provide resources because there is no sufficiently firm forecast of growth. Sometimes the cold calculation of the accountant or the economist will conclude that nothing should be, or can be, done; but nevertheless the administrator, or the politician, will need to supply the dynamic and imaginative stimulus to get it done. The modern administrator or politician may be assisted by cost benefit analysis and a variety of sophisticated research and planning techniques. Yet the essential element he must supply—just like a Stephenson, a Brunel or a de Lesseps in the last century—is faith in the practicability and value of the task he has set himself.

The process of stimulation of growth by faith, coordination and imaginative planning is very similar whether it is carried out inside a single organisation—public utility or private manufacturing company—or by a Government Department or some cooperative planning body for a whole national economy or indeed an international economy. It is 'indicative planning', getting one set of people to commit themselves to growth in the faith that another set on whom they are dependent will also do so. It is essentially a cooperative process, more amenable to the organic, interactive kind of management or administration than to the mechanistic or authoritarian. In both the Government and the military spheres one has seen so many ludicrously unsuccessful attempts to make plans go ahead (or hold them back) merely by the issue of stern orders and nothing else. Whether or not people are formally subject to the orders of Government or some other management, they will seldom deploy their own or their staffs' resources fully if they do not believe they will get the support to do so effectively. The same applies to the use of economic stimuli or sanctions to independent firms whether in planning the national economy as a whole or in a public body's coordinating of specific schemes with its contractors and suppliers.

In fact major planning processes involve the incorporation of the best ideas in all the main streams of organisation theory—notably 'classical', 'human relations' and 'systems'. There must be an orderly system with clear allocations of authority and responsibility; there must be close, easy or informal collaboration between individuals and groups and there must be a sophisticated interacting system served, but not mastered, by the most effective and relevant planning and control techniques.

One further point must be made. We have referred to faith, dynamism and creativity, all implying growth and expansion. There is also a necessary, if less pleasant and exciting, negative side to this subject. Some activities can expand too much for the health of a whole organism, either because they absorb too many scarce resources or because they would put the total organism out of balance. This can apply within a local unit, an entire public corporation or Government Department, or a national economy. The danger of unbalanced growth may be more serious than that of absorbing 'scarce resources', taking too much of the 'national cake'—one of the economists' most hackneyed metaphors. However, even if it is misleading to think of total national resources as finite and static, individual managers are usually compelled to operate with limited money and resources. So selection and restrictions are usually necessary and the problem is how to carry out these processes most effectively and with least damage. If the coordinating or approving authorities cannot investigate projects or plans in detail they may have no alternative, if there is a total excess, to imposing arbitrary percentage cuts. There is always the danger, however, that the habit of doing so will become too well known. Hence estimates and forecasts will be consciously or unconsciously inflated to allow a margin for such cuts. If, as is likely, this is found out, estimates will be looked at even more critically and compared sceptically with the resources thought to be available for their realisation. They may be cut on the ground, not that they are not justified or even that there is no money, but that human and material resources are not likely to be available in time. Yet if the schemes are not authorised and money allocated the material and human resources never are made available. Designs are not drawn and designers are not recruited and trained and so the vicious circle goes on. Such arguments have made planning a highly contentious subject.

Though some conflict in the processes of planning is healthy, they ought never to be carried out as a game of rivalry. A complex forecasting and planning process can only work properly in an atmosphere of mutual understanding and confidence. This means that most of the people concerned should either have experience of doing each other's jobs or at least know something about them. They must also obviously be very well trained and experienced in their own. Hence a basic dilemma of specialism versus generalism of personnel management in the public sector and indeed in all large organisations.

1. G. E. Caider, 1964. 'The Independent Central Personnel Agency: The Experience of the Commonwealth of Australia', *Public Administration*, vol 42, pp. 133–61. Also, M. A. Muttalib, 1964. 'The Indian Union Public Service Commission', *Public Administration*, vol. 42.

2. H. E. Dale, op. cit. Sir Edward (Lord) Bridges, 1950. *Portrait of a Profession.* C.U.P.

T. A. Critchley, 1951. *The Civil Service Today.* Gollancz.

Nigel Walker, 1961. *Morale in the Civil Service.* Edinburgh University Press.

Frank Dunnill, 1950. *The Civil Service: Some Human Aspects.* Allen and Unwin.

C. H. Sisson, 1959. *The Spirit of British Administration.* Faber, 2nd ed., 1966.

The points of view of these writers differ somewhat and some have been criticised, but all have held important administrative positions as Assistant Secretary or above for a good many years and can therefore reflect feelings and attitudes which, rightly or wrongly, actually exist.

3. R. G. S. Brown, 1970. *The Administrative Process in Britain.* Methuen p. xi.

4. ibid., p. 282, citing the Fulton Report. Vol. 1, paras 22, 270, 302, 306; vol. 2, 294 and 336.

5. See e.g., J. B. Black, 1959. *England under Elizabeth I*, p. 209. OUP.

6. Ministry of Reconstruction, 1918. *Report of the Machinery of Government Committee*, Cmd 9230 HMSO. See also, Lord Bridges, Autumn, 1957. 'Haldane and the Machinery of Government', *Public Administration*, vol. XXXV, pp. 254–64.

7. Haldane Report, para. 12.

8. ibid., para. 13.

9. ibid., para. 74.

10. A White paper, 1970. *The Reorganisation of Central Government.* Cmnd. 4506. This is the subject of a critical editorial article by Nevil Johnson in *Public Administration*, Spring 1971, vol. 49.

11. R. J. S. Baker, 1963. *The Management of Capital Projects,* pp. 33–40, 130–3, 164–74, 237–42. Bell.

7

PROCESSES

We have already argued that the first things to consider about public institutions are their environments, what they are there for, their general functions, their particular tasks. We must now go still closer and study their processes. Only after that should we discuss their forms and structures, because forms and structures develop from processes. Indeed, as Vickers has said,[1] the form of an organisation may change as a process proceeds. This is in line with the approach of Joan Woodward, who argues that it is neither general principle nor particular product which determines form and structure, but type of technology and process.

The secretarial process

At the beginning of the administrative history of the modern sovereign state, the primary process of administration was a secretarial one. Monarchs had secretaries of state, and state councils and their sub-committees also had secretaries or clerks. The function of a secretary was to keep secrets, in fact all records of proceedings and correspondence. A secretary or a clerk wrote letters, at dictation, or in his own words, to communicate the decisions of the monarch or the council. Secretaries were responsible for ordering council business, and, by extensive correspondence, records and contacts for providing the monarch with all essential information and for concealing it from others. When the office of Secretary of State had evolved into that of a Minister, with powers in his own right, he was served by secretaries of his own. According to the volume and complexity of the business, and the personalities and competence of the monarch and the Secretary, the latter would have more or less discretion to act on his own initiative. As the system evolved, men such as Mr Secretary Cecil and Mr Secretary Walsingham became great powers in the land, although a determined, intelligent and hard-working monarch such as Elizabeth I could still keep control of policy.

These functions are essentially those of any modern secretariat in a Government service, only it now services elected Ministers and their appointees instead of monarchs and theirs. The basic purpose of secretariats in democratic government is to service the democratic and consultative processes. One of their most important duties is briefing, partly for parliamentary occasions, but also for meetings with international bodies, deputations, committees and all kinds of internal and external meetings. Secretariats control, alter and generate an immense flow of essential paper: they coordinate endless comings and goings.

All these may at first glance appear rather mechanical functions, or at least matters of fairly routine management. In fact, they can be and should be distinctly creative. This is not to suggest that a secretary should be an *éminence grise*, manipulating his master: secretaries, 'private offices' and secretariats should have a subordinate though creative function, in relation to their masters, whether these are individuals such as Ministers, or Permanent Secretaries, or collective masters like boards or committees. The gathering and presentation of information, the arranging of programmes of activities, the recording concisely of diffuse discussions, the writing of letters—all these contribute to the making of coherent and meaningful patterns out of a moving and often turbulent mass of events, communications, facts and ideas. And the making of meaningful patterns is the essence of creativity. The secretary's patterns must, of course, be subsidiary to the master's patterns, and his in turn to those of the Government; but the task of ensuring that they are not only subsidiary but consistent, is one which requires great skill. Some of this is true in all walks of life of all secretaries who are anything more than typists; but in the higher spheres of public administration the secretarial process is much more fully developed. It is found at its most sophisticated in Government Departments, but it is also highly developed by such people as Town Clerks and secretaries to public boards of all kinds, Royal Commissions and committees of inquiry, advisory bodies and so on. In the British Civil Service, private secretaryships to Ministers and Permanent Heads of Departments are not regarded as the apex of a purely secretarial career, but a means of grooming young administrators who may advance later to the highest levels.

The secretary becomes executive

The secretarial element in the functions and processes of Govern-

A.T.A.P.A.—E

ment Departments is enshrined in the historic but only partly an-achronistic titles of Secretary of State (for a political Minister) and Permanent Secretary (for the highest permanent civil servant). This emphasises the gradual evolution of the functions of a person who could not only know (and, where discretion allowed, speak) his master's mind, but also act positively on his master's behalf. In fact the secretarial office evolved towards becoming first the equivalent of that of a 'staff' officer (in the military sense, which is the exact oppo-site of the civilian sense*) and then a deputy. The distinctions can be so fine as to be barely perceptible. They develop with the growing complexity of the tasks and the environment of an organisation. Eventually we have officials who are not primarily secretaries at all, but executives exercising considerable powers, yet still acting on be-half of, and within the general policy of, the Minister or some other highei authority. Their activities still retain a secretarial element be-cause their powers must be exercised in the general spirit of their masters' known or inferred policies or wishes. They may even still use the old-fashioned style of correspondence, 'I am directed by the Minister'. This is not usually because the Minister has personally directed them in that specific case, but that they know how the Minister would direct them to write, or would approve of their writing, if this particular case were brought to his notice.

Delegation

From the original processes of secretaryship we thus come to one of the most crucial processes of administration—delegation. Although it can sound simple in theory, it is in practice one of the most difficult and complex functions of any form of administration and manage-ment. It is of particular importance in public administration not merely because of the size and complexity of public organisations, but because of the problem of public responsibility and accountability of Ministers and other public authorities. This problem is essentially one of how they can exercise sufficient control of activities for which they are responsible to make their responsibility real. Delegation and control are therefore two sides of a coin, two aspects of the same problem. We have quoted† Sir Geoffrey Vickers' engineering analogy to emphasise the importance of internal information systems in the process of control, for instance in steering a ship. One might elaborate this analogy to illustrate the relationship of delegation, control and responsibility. A man steering a rowing boat on a river personally operates a rudder by means of strings or a tiller and im-mediately sees the boat change direction. Moreover he can see quite

* See pp. 31–3 and 60 above, on 'line-and-staff'.
† See p. 72.

clearly where he is going. The navigating officer of a large ship at sea operates the steering gear through a complex mechanical and electrical system. He may merely direct a human helmsman or automatic equipment to keep the ship on a certain course. In doing so he delegates part of his navigating function, but does not abrogate his responsibility. He remains responsible for the course the ship takes and exercises real control because he has reliable information as to the position and course of the ship. The information is largely indirect, depending mainly on instruments rather than his naked eye. Nevertheless he can satisfy himself that his information system is reliable, and from this system he can in turn satisfy himself that his control is effective and hence his responsibility for the ship's movements is real. More indirect but equally real ultimate control and responsibility is exercised by the captain of the ship, and, again, by his admiral or the headquarters of the shipping company. In all these processes we see responsibility depending on control and control depending on the complementary processes of delegation and information.

This is delegation of the direct processes of control while retaining the powers of effective control of essentials—the latter being whatever, on the basis of the information he receives, the controlling authority decides to treat as essential. He does not abrogate control or responsibility for anything, but merely, as a matter of practical convenience or necessity, lets the bulk of the detail go, always retaining the right to intervene. It is important to distinguish this administrative or managerial delegation from delegation in the legal sense. For instance, Parliament may delegate to a local authority the power to legislate by by-laws. The statute will contain explicit limitations on the spheres within which such powers may be exercised and may attach various conditions. Sometimes by-laws are subject to Ministerial approval which may take into account whether they conform with certain requirements. Yet subject to these limits the Local Authority can do what it likes and must take responsibility. In administrative delegation by Ministers to officials, the position is quite different. Such delegation can be passed on, or re-delegated; but always the Minister retains final responsibility and power to intervene or even withdraw the delegation.

The processes of control

There is much misunderstanding of the basic principles of public accountability and responsibility. Distinguished writers[2] describe Ministerial responsibility as a 'myth' or a 'fiction' merely because a Minister obviously cannot personally supervise every detail or indeed every important activity of his Department. Yet the exercise of personal authority and responsibility over very large organisations by various devices of indirect and often remote control is well understood and accepted in the commercial, industrial and military spheres. People are quite accustomed to speaking of Lord Montgomery's victories in the Western Desert or Lord Beeching's reorganisation of British Railways, when neither of these distinguished characters could go everywhere and see everything in their vast organisations. The great man—with many assistants and collaborators—gets information, assesses the general situation, settles a plan, and sees that the people, the organisation and the resources are there to carry it out. He then gives orders for it to go ahead, calls for reports on progress, makes snap checks, visits, asks why things are not moving fast enough or why certain types of mistake keep recurring, encourages, restrains, rewards or checks his subordinates. All this is not *doing* the whole job but *seeing* that the whole job is done. Effective communication, sample checks, selective intervention—above all seeing that the right people are at work—enables the man at the top of an organisation effectively to control, direct and take responsibility for a much larger area of activity than he could hope personally to run in every detail.

If a Minister is responsible to Parliament for a certain sphere of activity, or a civil servant is responsible to a Minister or a business manager to his Board of Directors, none of them can say 'I have nothing more to do with this matter. I have delegated it to so-and-so. You must ask him. I cannot attend to every detail personally.' The answer to this in every case would be 'No, of course you cannot; but you should see to it that things are so organised that failures like this do not happen.' A reasonable rejoinder to this might, of course, be 'I am satisfied that my organisation is as good as I can make it. I have delegated work to well-chosen and well-trained subordinates. I take all reasonable steps to ensure that they know my wishes and are carrying them out effectively. I apologise for this mistake and accept responsibility for it. I will see that the trouble is put right. But I contend that it is part of that irreducible minimum percentage of error which can never be entirely eliminated in any large concern and therefore its occurrence does not reflect seriously on the quality of my administration as a whole', or alternatively, 'I took, or permitted my subordinates to take, a calculated risk which was justified by the possible advantage to be gained.' All these contentions must be open to question by the higher authority, who may still decide that the subordinate has not seen to it that things were as well organised as possible.

The control and delegation processes of Ministers

It is difficult to deal in detail with the special question of the processes by which Ministers and senior officials delegate their functions, but we must emphasise that they are inseparable from those by which they exercise control and those by which they keep themselves informed. To delegate is, among other things, to indicate to a subordinate the limits within which, and the manner in which, he can exercise his discretion. There are in fact various ways in which control is exercised over the subordinate. The control is only made effective if he reports back and if there are independent means of checking his reports. In the course of his reporting back there is discussion and further direction is given and the process of delegation is thus continued. The whole thing depends on effective communication between the Minister or senior official and his subordinate. This necessarily involves some kind of sifting and sampling system whereby the essential major facts and typical minor facts are distilled into a form which can be assimilated in the time available. Ministers and senior officials have to inform themselves and maintain control of activities for which they are responsible while delegating a large proportion of their authority and functions. The following is a brief description of these processes by the late Lord (Herbert) Morrison, successively Minister of Transport (1929–31), Home Secretary (1940–5) and Lord President of the Council (1945–51):

. . . it is necessary for there to be frequent meetings between the Minister and his advisers. Sometimes it will be the Permanent Secretary alone or an individual civil servant lower down the line or the Private Secretary; but often it will be necessary for the Minister to have a gathering of quite a number of his civil servants, especially when more than one branch of the Department is involved. . . . It is well to encourage at such meetings not only the presence of the civil servants below the top flight, but to encourage them to speak their mind even though they may not entirely agree with their superiors. This is good training and it enables them the better to get that understanding of the mind of the Minister which is very desirable in the interests of good administration. . . .
. . . The relationship between the Minister and the civil servants should be—and usually is—that of colleagues working together in a team, co-operative partners seeking to advance the public interest and the efficiency of the Department. The Minister should not be an isolated autocrat, giving orders without hearing or considering arguments for alternative courses; nor, on the other hand, should the civil servants be able to treat him as a mere cipher. The partnership should be alive and virile, rival ideas and opinions should be fairly considered, and the relationship of all should be one of mutual respect—on the understanding, of course, that the Minister's decision is final. . . .[3]

Dr Jeremy Bray, former Minister of State, Ministry of Technology, has published recently a more detailed description of his office
methods. He then comments:

Different Ministers and departments take different approaches: some like
regular meetings to provide a framework; others try to avoid formality.
There is no unique solution, but it is essential to be aware of the problem
and clearly to adopt some method of keeping the pressure of departmental
business under control, and the priorities straight. . . .

He suggests how a policy may be distorted in the course of interdepartmental, ministerial and official consultations:

. . . Avoiding and overcoming such difficulties constitutes for the Minister
the delicate matter of managing his department. A Minister cannot do all
the work and a lively Minister needs a lively staff. It is necessary to find a
method of working in government which is an adequate two-way link
between the capabilities of the Minister and the matters for which he is
responsible—people, activities, problems outside. The performance of
successive governments has not been adequate and deficiencies in the
machinery of government have often been a contributory factor. It is
wrong to blame the civil service. Ministers are responsible. But a part of
their responsibility is the reform of government administration and of
the civil service, and civil servants must accept that this is a part of the
job of Ministers. There is no reason to believe that they do not.[4]

In public administration it is important to remember that delegation from Ministers to civil servants is only a very small part of a
vast process. If a Minister cannot know of a great deal that is going
on in his Department, neither can the Permanent Secretary, who
may even be a recent newcomer from another Department. The
supremely important and difficult problem of delegation arises all
down the line. If the senior man starts by knowing little about the
organisation he takes responsibility for, he must quickly find ways
of getting the essential picture and keeping his finger on the sensitive
spots. If, on the other hand, he knows a lot about the subject his
problem is to force himself to stand back and stop breathing down
his subordinates' necks, to keep his mind clear so as to concentrate
on the things he must do personally.

General problems of delegation in the public sector
Much of the above discussion of delegation would apply to most
kinds of management process; but the problem of achieving effective
delegation without sacrificing control and responsibility is much
more complex in the public sector where the challenges to parlia-

mentary and public responsibility are direct and frequent. This applies most to specifically governmental functions, especially to regulatory functions and to a slightly lesser extent to coordinative, consultative and conciliatory functions. It applies perhaps a little less to public service-providing functions and much less to the industrial and commercial activities of public bodies. The direct accountability of Ministers to Parliament in Britain only works because Ministers, Members of Parliament and civil servants are very sophisticated in these matters. There is usually a fairly good tacit understanding of what can and cannot reasonably be expected from Parliamentary Questions and debate and the matters which it is impracticable to investigate in detail.

We find examples in the legislative sphere of subjects which Parliament has delegated because it apparently does not wish to get involved in the details. These form an interesting, although not exact parallel to cases in the administrative sphere, where the superior hopes the subordinate will deal with details without troubling him. Lord Devlin has argued, from his great judicial experience, that not only must courts often fill in the gaps that Parliament has left when making the law, but that Parliament is content to leave such gaps and expects the courts to fill them in.[5]

An administrative authority might similarly give directions in general terms and expect subordinate officers to deal with methods of application.

On a very different aspect of delegation in the sphere of local government the Mallaby Committee noted that: 'The law does not provide for delegation of decision making to officers although in practice many officers enjoy widely differing degrees of discretion.' In saying this they were recognising what one certainly finds in central government, that the power of effective decision may well rest higher or lower than the legal power to sign the relative document. Nevertheless the absence of legal delegation often inhibits administrative delegation. Hence the Mallaby Committee recommended 'that local authorities should devolve much wider administrative powers on principal officers' and also (not expressed as dependent on the former recommendation) 'we further recommend that the law should be amended to permit delegation of statutory functions and responsibilities to them'. The reasons given were 'to provide more attractive and challenging official careers and thus stimulate recruitment' and to 'enable local authorities to conduct their business more efficiently'.[6]

Despite, however, all that has been said about the need for and the existence of delegation, neither the responsibility and authority of Ministers nor that of their senior civil servants, members of Local

Authorities and other public bodies, nor that of the Directors of companies is a myth or a fiction. It is a reality and must so remain if democratic Government and the rule of law is to survive. Yet no Minister, no General, no Permanent Secretary, no board or Company Chairman, ever directs a whole concern single-handed. A great mass of people take part in the direction by their activities and by their direct and indirect influence. What is important is that one man, or a group of men at the top, should take responsibility for overall direction and decision in crucial matters. The constitutional theory of public responsibility is like the classical theory of management—an essential framework and a model for settling disputes and doubts and organising public affairs on an orderly basis. For other purposes, however, we must look at public bodies in the light of the human relations and systems theories of management, so that we can see what complex organisms they really are.

Legislation, directives and other written communication

One of the basic functions of Government is legislation and it is often followed by other documents intended to disseminate policy, e.g. proclamations, summonses, exhortations, correspondence, and so on. As the regulatory state develops into the public utility state, the welfare state and the economic planning state, the quantity and variety of its output of written material increases, in the form of directives, licences, reports of enquiries, adjudications, statements of policy, plans for new services, indicative economic plans, advisory literature, answers to protests and complaints, internal organisational documents, and so on. In all the processes of Government the written word is one of the principal tools.

The primary form of relationship between Governments and the general community is that of law. So we must look into the use of words in the process of law-making, as a preliminary to discussing their use in Government more generally. No doubt law in its most primitive forms was spoken, but it was also probably one of the first kinds of communication to be reduced to writing. And if today we want to look at the written functions of British Government in their most fundamental form, we must take an Act of Parliament, which is the ultimate written expression of the sovereign power of the State. In reality, an Act is an act of *Parliament* and not of the Civil Service. Yet practically every word of it is drafted by that special group of civil servants called Parliamentary Counsel, on the basis of a special type of formal instructions drafted by the legal branches of Government Departments, who themselves act on the instructions of administrative civil servants, who in turn are instructed by Ministers. At various stages, all these people, or some of them, meet together for oral discussion; but almost every word of a Bill is ground out with great labour in a long series of written minutes, memoranda, drafts and revisions. The whole process represents an elaborate exercise with words. Why so elaborate and with what result? The answer lies in the fact that the ultimate authority of our law is embodied in the precise words of Acts of Parliament, and British courts, unlike those of some other countries, will not go behind these words to seek the intentions of the legislature as expressed elsewhere.

The test of a good Act of Parliament is the quality of endurance, the ability to satisfy the needs of society in changing circumstances without producing uncertainty, dispute and the need for amendment. The four-page Wireless Telegraphy Act of 1904, passed before it was possible to transmit speech or vision by radio, survived virtually un-amended till 1949, and formed the constitutional basis of all British wireless activities, including sound and television broadcasting. Some Acts of Parliament contain wording of beautiful simplicity and clarity, but this is more usually in their opening sections which set out basic conditions and principles, rather than in those which con-tained the detailed definitions and imperatives. The Coal Industry Nationalisation Act 1946 starts with great ease: 'There shall be a National Coal Board charged with the duty of working and getting the coal in Great Britain', but after a few pages, when one reaches the sections on transfer of property and compensation, one gets into a thick forest of words, almost impenetrable to the layman. This, however, does not matter in an Act of Parliament. What matters is that it should be unambiguous to the lawyer, above all to the judge.

We have emphasised these points about Acts of Parliament, because they are, to a great extent, the foundations of much else that civil servants write. There is not only the mass of orders, regulations, notices and other formal documents having the full force of law. There is much else that civil servants write on behalf of their Minis-ters which later may effectively have, if not the force of law, the force of policy. It will sometimes be quoted and bandied about by outside interests—trades unions, commercial interests, local pressure groups, and so on. No one complains of the fact that judges take extreme care with the words of their judgments and spend days pre-paring them. And people are always urging civil servants to act judicially.

Yet clearly there is something more in the art of Civil Service writing than precision and economy in the use of words. Surprisingly, per-haps, one can demonstrate this by looking at a type of writing which might be thought to require only these two qualities—the compila-tion of rules and directives for internal use within Government Departments. They are drafted in order to lay down standards and practices, and in this sense they legislate. They also lay down broad limits for the exercise of discretion. They explain. Often they merely describe procedures and methods which are optional. They sometimes contain material which is persuasive, because they can hardly be implemented except as a result of cooperation and goodwill.

Letters from Departments to the public

Some letters which go from Government Departments to the outside world are almost as austere in their purposes as modern Acts of Parliament. They announce decisions. They determine disputes. They authorise expenditure. They approve the making of orders and schemes by subordinate authorities. Among the different forms of letters, circulars and other documents coming out of Government Departments, one can distinguish between those which simply decide and define, and those which explain, advise and persuade. As the functions of Government have extended and involve consultation and coordination as well as direction, the number of communications in the second category has increased.

The difficulty about writing in this way on behalf of a Government Department is that, however easy and informal a civil servant is, people will take his letter, not merely as an expression of his own view, but as that of the Government. Moreover, they are quite likely to apply it to other cases than the particular one about which he is writing. Government Departments are not invariably consistent with one another, or even within themselves, but people expect them to be. Some people, notably the secretaries of trade unions, trade associations, and similar bodies, are constantly occupied in trying to get Government Departments to adopt or change general policies as a result of activity in specific cases. This does not mean that civil servants are, or ought to be, frightened of ever putting pen to paper in case they will create a precedent; but it does mean that, when they write a letter or any other document, they must pay regard to the effect it may have beyond the immediate case in hand.

Internal correspondence and discussion

Many of the public servant's special skills of writing are exercised upon his colleagues. Of these, the form of communication which is perhaps best known to the outsider is the minute on a file. For some types of decision, formal minutes are essential. But formal minutes are not the only, and often not the main, means of communication between public servants. They write each other semi-official letters and informal notes—and, of course, they talk.

Oral communication among individuals and groups is indeed probably more important than written communication in the Civil

Service. There is a variety of literature about meetings but that concerning the formalities of public meetings is of little relevance to internal discussions in the public services. Even the literature of psychological interaction in groups does not tell the whole story. When a group of people are brought together to discuss some subject in a Government office, they are not there as individuals, but as representing certain authorities or interests. This applies whether they are all from the same department or from different Departments, or representatives of other public authorities or of independent outside concerns. Anyone conducting a Civil Service meeting should realise the functions and status of the varied group of people who will be present. Status does not necessarily mean rank. So if a man has been authorised to come to a meeting as a representative of a certain interest (inside or outside the Civil Service), he should be treated seriously as such, whatever his rank, age or personality.

Role of chairmen of meetings

The same person occupying the chair in the same room on different occasions may each time be in a different position vis-à-vis the other people in the room, and none of the formal manuals on chairmanship would be much use to him in distinguishing the different roles which he has to play. He may, for instance, be presiding at a coordinating meeting to ensure that some practical scheme is being pushed through to a satisfactory time-table. He will be in the chair because he is the senior representative of the branch or department primarily responsible for the scheme and the policy behind it. His function will then be to urge the scheme on. This may mean getting specialists from various quarters to cooperate and it will be desirable for everyone to understand the wider purposes of the scheme and how they all fit in together. His function will be to drive the scheme through and there can be no question of his taking a majority vote or sitting back and letting the group arrive at its own collective conclusions. He may have to say plainly that the time-table, unanimously recommended by everyone else present, simply will not do.

On other occasions, however, the chairman's function may be to ensure a hearing for some group of people who want to make a protest about a matter on which no decision can immediately be made. Here the chairman's function would be to listen and possibly to prevent any of his colleagues arguing too strongly. In such circumstances, the only counter-arguments or statements of fact which it might be politic to allow might be those needed to demonstrate to the protesters themselves that their case was weak. To give people a fair hearing when it is not possible to do anything at the moment to meet their requests is not merely to let them blow off steam. It may be important to have their views on record, to find out and get into an agreed record what they really want, and what are the obstacles to their getting it. This may be a preliminary to an early decision at a higher level, or with a view to doing something at a later date, or to balance against the views and pressures of other interests. There are other types of meeting where it is desirable to establish, as between different Government Departments or different branches of the same Department, that only one course of action is practicable. Some meetings are called to resolve a clash of views, and here again very often the main task of the chairman will be to get the relevant facts clearly established, after which a conclusion may emerge of its own accord. On other occasions, after strong views have been expressed, it may be desirable to adjourn and promise a decision when feelings have cooled down, or when someone at a higher level has been consulted.

Meetings for information

There is one type of meeting which is not called primarily for the purpose of reaching decisions or dealing with clashes of views, although it may do so incidentally. Such meetings are held at regular periods mainly for the purposes of exchanging information within a large organisation, for instance conferences of local managers, of regional directors, or specialists of various kinds. Most responsible civil servants (and no doubt many other people in comparable positions in other large organisations) constantly have the feeling, on the one hand, that they spend far too much time at meetings, and on the other, that they do not know what is going on. A special case is the kind of coordinating meetings which take place inside or between Government Departments when major negotiations are going on with interests outside, particularly in the international sphere. These and many other types of meetings for exchange of information, even though time-consuming, are essential for the efficient functioning of large organisations. Written communication may reduce the time spent in oral discussion, but is no complete substitute for it.

1. op. cit., p. 73; see pp. 72 above.

2. e.g., Andrew Shonfield, 1965. *Modern Capitalism*, p. 294. OUP.

3. Herbert Morrison, 1954. *Government and Parliament*, pp. 318–19. OUP.

4. Jeremy Bray, 1970. *Decision in Government*, pp. 52–6. Gollancz.

5. Patrick Devlin, 1962. *Samples of Law Making*, pp. 71–2. OUP.

6. Ministry of Housing and Local Government, 1967. *Report on staffing in Local Government*, Para. 499, pp. 159–60.

8

FORMS AND STRUCTURES OF
GOVERNMENT DEPARTMENTS

Forms logically precede structures

In contrast with some literature, this book has considered first the environment of public bodies and what they do and how they do it, and only after that their forms and structures. The forms and structures of organisations derive from environment, functions, tasks and processes, rather than the reverse, although rather than get lost in a circular, 'chicken and egg' argument, we must admit that there is much interaction. Form is a pattern of activity. Hence as its activities vary the form of an organisation is always in flux. Structure is a more static, rigid concept. Both the words form and structure are, however, abstractions, each only representing an inadequate picture of concrete reality.

Public administration may first be said to take certain forms. That means that people do certain things in certain ways. Certain patterns of activity persist. A group of the same individuals persistently meet to discuss and decide certain things. They regularly defer to one individual as chairman. One individual regularly records their proceedings as secretary. They may deal first always with things which require little argument and then go on to have much debate, but finally achieve compromise and agreement. Such a simple description of certain events may be said to cover forms which certain activities may take, or regularly do take. Perhaps the more often the types of activity persist or repeat themselves or follow an enduring pattern, the more they may be called forms, regular relationships between individuals. All the activities described above might be said to comprise forms. Not all would comprise structures. The fact that the same individuals meet regularly and have two members with the roles of chairman and secretary—all this could be called the institutional structure of a committee. So possibly might a certain order of dealing with the agenda. But the extent of agreement or disagreement, a tendency to consensus at first, then conflict and then agreement or compromise would not be an institutional structure. It would simply be a form which these activities took on certain occasions. A tendency of a few members to take a more active part than the others, even meeting beforehand to prepare the order of business, this might start as simply a form of activity. Yet it could be institutionalised as a structure, with a formal rule constituting this group as a Sub-Committee or Steering Committee with defined rights and duties.

'Formal' and 'informal' organisation in the private sector

This distinction between form and structure is similar to that in organisation theory literature between 'formal' and 'informal' organisation. The use of the word 'informal' is strictly illogical. It cannot mean what it would seem literally to say, that is 'without form'. In fact in organisation theory literature it has come to mean certain clearly discernible patterns of activity and relationships which certainly have form, often forms which come to be rigidly adhered to. The real distinction of informal organisation is not that its forms do not exist, but that they are not formally prescribed or recognised. They may be acknowledged among the participants, but not admitted to outsiders, possibly not to higher authority or management. The essentially paradoxical concept of 'informal organisation' is a creation of the human relations school. It is most appropriate to organisations where there is the sharpest distinction and conflict of interests between employer and employed. In such cases there is a special incentive to conceal certain patterns of relationships among the employed and thus a special distinction develops between formal and informal organisation. In a committee composed of persons of equal power and status and sharing common objectives it will not be very important how formally a small sub-committee is constituted. In any case its existence need not be concealed. It is very different with agreements among shop-floor workers to restrict output or to acknowledge someone other than the foreman as effective leader. Some such 'informal organisation' has an air of conspiracy and subversion. It is the creation of employees, consciously or unconsciously reacting against management's intentions and policies.

Parliament—the archetype of public forms and structures

This sort of situation can occasionally occur in public administration but the formal/informal antithesis is not the prime characteristic of the distinction between forms and structures. Rather the distinction arises from the degree of permanence and of crystallisation of certain forms, and hence of the need to define them in standing authoritative documents. In the United Kingdom all public administration is subordinate to and derives its authority, and often its impetus and pattern, from Parliament. Hence no one can properly understand British public administration, nor indeed British society, without a proper understanding of Parliament. A General in World War II, when asked what he was fighting for, replied simply and unhesitatingly 'Parliament'. Today some people would hesitate to be so specific about the ideas or institutions to which they attach most moral value, but nevertheless most British people would recognise instinctively the kinds of society they would find tolerable or those they would find intolerable. Now, whether they know it or not, the foundations of what is for many or most of them a tolerable—because tolerant—society are rooted in Parliament. Parliament, primarily the House of Commons, is ultimately the basis of many of the forms and structures of public administration. It still exhibits daily in classic manner the most sophisticated patterning of collective public activity with a constant balance and blending of what might be called the 'formal' and the 'informal'; but what are better described as forms and structures. The pattern of activity is, of course, constantly adapted to the current political situation. Its continuing forms are prescribed partly in Standing Orders, partly in resolutions of the House, partly in Mr Speaker's rulings—whether or not codified in literature—and partly by developing custom and 'the sense of the House'. Although there are immediate contrasts between stylised but meaningful ritual and apparent casualness, the real distinction is simply between those patterns of activity which have been embodied in some form or other in print and those which have not. The former may all fairly be called established structures, the latter forms which are potential structures. In other words most forms, unless they prove to be ephemeral, will eventually 'jell' into structures.

The essence of Parliament—a free consensus in a framework of order
The fundamentals which the forms and structures of the British Parliament embody and symbolise might be described as a free consensus based on mutual tolerance—controversy and conflict accepted and contained within certain limits. The firm framework of authority and order simply provides the boundary-lines and rules within which conflict takes place and consensus is arrived at. All this is symbolised in the formal ritual as well as the almost stylised informality. The ritual so often smiled at is in fact exceedingly meaningful of the historical basis of present realities. Even the Speaker's costume—full-bottomed wig, black gown and knee breeches—is all symbolic of a period at the end of the seventeenth century when a synthesis of

political and economic forces and ideologies was at last achieved in England. Parliament symbolised this balance of previously warring elements—as did the ordered symmetry of Wren's architecture. The whole procedure of the House of Commons is surrounded with ritual, formality and rigid rules. But 'surrounded' is the significant word. All this is what guards the boundaries and holds the ring. In the centre there is a very complex net of working procedures which would be quite unworkable without a general consensus—not only between the leaders of the main Parties but between the Members generally. Despite all that is said about Party discipline, Prime Ministers and Party leaders can still fall if they cannot maintain the confidence of individual Members of Parliament. The apparently rigid rules and conventions, the virtually unquestioning deference to the Speaker's rulings—all this operates only by general tacit agreement between all Members and operates, moreover, only to define areas and procedures of conflict. Even the authority of the Speaker is entirely dependent on the support of the House and a man cannot reach that office unless he commands very wide confidence unrelated to Party loyalties. The formality is only the framework within which what the organisation theorists would probably call 'informal organisation' operates and flourishes. The rigidity of the rules and customs exists simply to protect the freedom of debate from internal and external interference. We have laboured all this to emphasise that the British Parliament is in terms of modern organisation theory a highly 'organic' institution, operating within a highly 'mechanistic' or authoritarian framework. Both Houses function organically, reflecting and responding to the pressures of most of the important independent forces and trends of opinion within British society. The Government Departments which serve them must take account of, and reflect, this situation. They must be built on 'classical' models and be mechanistic and authoritarian in their outer frameworks. Yet their processes will only be authoritarian when they are dealing with matters where the clear will of Parliament has been expressed in law or settled policy, when they are implementing and enforcing law and policy rather than helping to make it. In the processes of creating and adapting law and policy they will be organic and their procedures will often be very informal. All this means that they will tend to be organic in parts of their Headquarters and mechanistic in other parts and in their regional and local office.

Types of public and administrative activity—regulatory/routine, adaptive/creative, and managerial

Public bodies do a great variety of things. Summarising the four preceding chapters, they regulate, they control, they institutionalise custom and social controls into law regulation and policy and promulgate, apply and interpret it. They attempt to maintain a pattern of consistent activity and produce and disseminate many documents in the processes of doing so. They resolve disputes, maintain liaison and internal communication among important groups and organs within their own society, and with external powers. They apply, or threaten, forceful sanctions against various parties, internal or external, who threaten these patterns of relationships. They provide various categories of public information services, physical communication services, personal and social services, indeed an economic infrastructure for society and a variety of systems of economic planning, and coordination of the national economy. All this involves three kinds of activity:

(a) The maintenance of standard, often repetitive patterns of behaviour and relationships—regulatory activities which must severely, although not completely, limit the element of discretion.

(b) Adaptive/creative activities—which adapt policies, laws, rules, regulations and standard patterns of activities to the changing needs of society and create new forms and patterns of activity—all this largely by the interaction of many individuals and groups within and outside the public administration system.

(c) The managerial activities involved in running a great variety of public services.

All these three overlap. Even the most rigid regulatory activity must involve some occasional elements of adaptation or discretion, and it is indeed from the difficulties arising in the course of applying regulatory activities that much of the creation of new policy arises. On the other hand, many of the adaptive/creative activities do not maintain a consistent level of demand for intelligence and originality. Everyone involved in them spends much time in routine or semi-routine activities. The managerial types of activity concerned with the provision of public utility services in fact involve elements of both other types of public sector activities—as well as elements closely resembling those of the private sector.

The forms taken by the three types of activity
What forms and structures are then required to accommodate all these varieties of activity? For routine and indeed nearly all regulatory activities and also for much of the conduct of standardised, interlocked, ubiquitous public utility service, where equality of treatment and reliability are of paramount importance, the classical pattern of organisation is not only very relevant but largely sufficient. Yet

wherever and whenever there has to be discretion for commonsense adaptation of rules to changing public needs, whenever and wherever large numbers of people have to work harmoniously together without the sanction of ever-present detailed supervision, then something more is needed. Forms and structures must have an element of adaptability and subtlety. Everything cannot be done along the straight vertical lines of classical organisation charts. There must be an organic element in the structure and a provision for some spontaneity and initiative from below, as suggested by the writers of the 'human relations' and the 'systems' schools of thought cited in Chapters 2 and 3.

The formal framework

Yet in almost all public sector organisations, except a few research and high-level policy-making bodies, all this must operate within a firm classical-style framework. The application of rules and regulations, the provision of public services—whether social, personal or physical—on a standardised equitable basis, the administration of systems of taxation, the collection of statistical information, the maintenance of records and accounting systems, anything concerning the enforcement of law and order or the servicing of the basic machinery of democracy, both at the level of the electorate and of Parliament and local councils—all this requires a pattern of authority and responsibility like Fayol's. The more democratic the ultimate sovereign body (Parliament) and the subordinate authorities (Ministers and local elected councils), the more necessary it is for their authority to be exercised by formal delegation, with the scope for discretion clearly limited and circumscribed. In so far as there is discretion it is discretion to interpret the will and intentions, or sometimes the acquiescence of Parliament. It is discretion to defer to or respond to interests that are represented in or can bring pressure to bear on Parliament. To a very limited extent one could substitute 'local elected council' for 'Parliament'; but local councils have hitherto delegated little except to committees and sub-committees of their own members. On the other hand Parliament, the vastly more powerful body, delegates a great deal to Ministers, and hence indirectly to their officials. It delegates little to committees of its own members. Hence a largely formal, but at some points flexible, nation-wide framework of authority is built up to embody and transmit the authority of Parliament; and many, much more rigid local networks to embody and transmit the authority of local councils. The corporations which run the nationalised industries in many ways enjoy much wider discretion than Government Departments. Indeed a major reason for their creation was to allow such discretion. Nevertheless, many of their activities are circumscribed by law or by social or technological conditions. There must be standardisation to ensure the interlocking of networks, broad equality of treatment for the public, safety precautions and so on. Most of the industries concerned—railways, mines, electricity, gas and airlines—were subject to special statutory controls for these purposes before they were nationalised.

Hence in almost all major public bodies one finds a formal institutional framework of authority like that of Fayol and Weber and limitations on discretion. Where authority is delegated it is delegated to people or groups or units of organisation suitable to interpret these delegated powers. Where it is a specifically governmental type of authority involving the understanding of Government policies and political forces and political considerations, authority is delegated to members of what has been called 'the profession of government'— Ministers, those parts of the Civil Service which used to be called the Administrative and Executive Classes, Committees of local councillors, and much more sparingly to local authority officials. Some of these central and local government officers to whom governmental functions are delegated may also have important technical qualifications and responsibility. Where it is wholly or mainly a matter of technical or professional discretion—the provision of technical services, the assessment of technical risks, the approval of technical plans—authority is likely to be delegated more freely than where general policy is involved. As the nationalised industries do not, on the whole, exercise governmental, as distinct from commercial and service-providing powers, they have relatively few officials of the 'profession of government' type.

The exercise of discretion within them

Yet all this is the framework, the institutional structure, not the forms of activity. Some of these forms, like the structures, are fairly mechanistic and bureaucratic. In the paying out or collecting of money on the basis of legal rights, in the issue of licences of all kinds, in the distribution of mail, in the control of electric current or gas or railway operations, there must, in the common interest, be severe limitations on anyone's discretion—though never a complete absence of discretion. Policemen, tax inspectors, Customs officers, air-traffic controllers, registrars,* all exercise some (however little) discretion and judgment, and none of them could be replaced by computers. But all the activities they are involved in, even up to high levels of management, are necessarily of an authoritarian nature, corresponding more to Burns and Stalker's 'mechanistic' (rather than their 'organic')

* e.g., when deciding whether to accept a doubtful death certificate.

model. But insofar as discretion and initiative are needed, they must be protected and encouraged by a suitable environment.

There is no clear line of distinction between the spheres within which very little discretion can be allowed and those where the field is very free and flexibility and originality are essential. The areas shade off from one to the other, partly as one goes up the hierarchy, but also sometimes as one goes sideways—from an operations to a planning department, from a rule-applying job to the secretaryship of a committee considering a new subject, from accounting to finance, and from finance to the negotiation with outside interests and from this to the drafting of policy documents.

It is, however, in the administrative and higher professional levels in the Headquarters of Government Departments, and to a lesser extent in the planning and policy-making Departments of nationalised industries and the larger Local Authorities, that the greatest degree of originality and new thinking is required. Yet even here new ideas are not normally clutched out of the air or born in solitary cogitation, but emerge in the clash of debate either with and between outside interests and advisers and pressure groups, or between civil servants who are mainly occupied in dealing with such interests and groups. How can one get the necessary degree of flexibility and originality in people who are and must be trained to respect a fairly rigid framework of authority?

The organic system

In fact the dilemma is not really as stark as this, as we can see by looking at the situation from another angle. Anyone who knows the inside of the policy-making part—or almost any part—of the Headquarters of a Government Department will remark on its apparent informality. This applies to vertical and to horizontal communication. Indeed, these very terms give an impression of misleading rigidity. Some communication is, in fact, diagonal and all over the place. Subject to the broad framework of organisation, which is clearly defined, it is surprising how much of the day-to-day working system is undefined or changing all the time. Of course, legal powers have to be clearly delegated to named persons or defined categories of persons. In some other matters, such as authorities to make appointments, the rules have to be pretty formal and precise. But probably in the great majority of Government administrative functions authorities and responsibilities cannot be formally and permanently fixed. This conclusion may seem surprising; but it is based on well over twenty years' varied administrative experience in the Headquarters of a Government Department—both in work of a 'Whitehall' administrative policy type and also in work of a more executive and managerial character. Only rarely can I recollect my own authority or that of my colleagues—equal, senior, or junior—being defined by formal rules. Most of the time it was not precisely defined at all. It was nevertheless implicit and well understood. One knew that at a particular time a particular type of subject was 'red-hot' and must be submitted above one's own level or possibly to the highest level. On certain other subjects, the views not only of the Minister, but of one's own immediate chief may have been made clear plenty of times before and one knew that it was right to exercise one's own initiative. One knew which of one's own staff one could leave to carry on, subject to broad direction, and which others, through lack of experience or the difficulty of the subject-matter, needed guidance. One might spend a lot of time discussing general policies with one's chief or one's subordinates, but once this was done, particular decisions could be taken without further consultation.

It is this sort of thing that produces the air of informality and sometimes casualness which visitors to Government Departments notice—whether with approval or disapproval. In either case the impression is somewhat misleading. Informality is possible because the main bedrock is firm. There is a solid basis of law and of possibly unwritten but very definite policy. It is only subject to this that surface flexibility can exist.

However, one can say generally that in Burns and Stalker's scale the Headquarters of a Government Department where the work is mainly adaptive/creative is much nearer to the 'organic' than the 'mechanistic' pole. This conclusion may surprise some organisation theorists, but it is based on experience and supported by informed comment. Yet we should look for something even more complex than Burns and Stalker's straightforward line of variation between these two poles—something more like Likert's concept of an 'interaction-influence system' with its interlocking groups[1]—a concept which must ring remarkably true to anyone with practical experience in a Government Department's Headquarters.

The stabilising elements

A Government Department has both of the functions which Sir Geoffrey Vickers[2] has defined as 'balancing' and 'optimising'. It should be constructive, creative and adaptable, but at the same time maintain the regular and systematic functioning of the social and political system. It is the guardian of many of the fixed landmarks in our society. Some of the activities of Government Departments which can very easily be characterised as stuffy are quite essential if the general population are to be able to live their lives in some confidence in the stability of their environment. Yet with our changing society, the rapidly changing scientific and technological background, a fluid and sometimes dangerous international setting, it is essential that Government Departments should be dynamic and creative as well as stable, dependable and secure.

It is very easy to imagine that in the environment of public offices public servants are subjected to influences which inhibit originality. They are indeed. Yet it is not the stability of their environment that makes them cautious but the reverse. They face conflicting, disturbing and even turbulent pressures from all quarters. Parliamentary Questions are usually cited as the prime cause of timidity and lack of delegation in Government Departments; but there are many other pressures on civil servants and perhaps even more on local government officers. The element of legal and administrative rigidity in public authority structures is probably more effective as a protection for initiative than in inhibiting it. It may protect the position of public officials by defining the fields in which they can exercise discretion. It may also protect them from arbitrary dismissal resulting from corrupt or improper outside influence or pressure. This kind of thinking may be out of line with some current notions of 'dynamic' management; but there is plenty of experience that justifies it. The most revolutionay intellectual ideas often develop in a University environment which appears traditional, stable and secure —for instance, the environment within which Rutherford and Keynes in the 1930s respectively challenged the whole foundations of classical physics and classical economics.*

As a working community a Government Department, especially its adaptive/creative parts, should have a firm basis of confidence—internal self-confidence supported by the confidence of society. A public institution cannot work properly if society simply does not want it to work and does not believe it is doing any good. It should be protected from disruptive influences, but nevertheless be fully exposed to outside criticism, stimulus and controversy. Its legal and administrative structures should be firm; but easily capable of adaptation. Internal movement and career development should be planned so as to widen and deepen, and not to inhibit, the acquisition of knowledge and experience. People inside it must know that they will have some freedom to experiment, to think and to argue, and that when they make vigorous efforts to do things, success will be

---

* It is interesting that at the conclusion of their chapter on 'Organizational Change' Katz and Kahn appear to be suggesting that one of the most effective ways of changing an organisation is to change its formal structure rather than its informal organisation or the individuals that compose it. Daniel Katz and Robert L. Kahn, 1966, *The Social Psychology of Organizations*, p. 451, John Wiley.

appreciated, and failure will be criticised at least with understanding. They must feel that the environment is a genuine organism and not a chaos of disparate individuals pursuing conflicting ambitions.

Headquarters of Government Departments: the traditional structure

Now let us see what this amounts to in terms of the organisation, staffing and functioning of the main organs of public administration in the United Kingdom. We will take first the more traditional types of Government Department office, Headquarters, regional and local, then local authorities and the major nationalised industries, and finally some special types of public organisation—old or new—with rather complex, subtle or unusual forms and structures.

At the time this is being written (early 1971) the grading structure of the British Civil Service is being remodelled more or less on the lines recommended by the Fulton Committee. However, for the sake of clarity, let us take the traditional set-up—even though it may only have operated in its full purity in limited parts of the Civil Service and only for limited periods—perhaps a few decades at most. In theory, at least, the central body of the Civil Service in the Head-quarters of a Government Department—the equivalent of the 'staff' in the *military* sense*—consisted of three 'Classes' or groups of grades—'Administrative', 'Executive' and 'Clerical'. All three were recruited by competitive selection (relying much on written examinations), at graduate level, and at ages about eighteen and sixteen respectively. The Administrative Class were supposed to advise Ministers on the making of policy, preparation of legislation and so on, the Executives to support the administrators in work requiring executive ability but not originality, and the Clericals to perform more or less mechanical functions. Of course even at its upper layers and in its heyday in the age of Dale, the Administrative Class could not spend all its time discussing Parliamentary Bills and Cabinet papers with Ministers. It always had a lot of routine not requiring much original thought. On the other hand, Executives and Clericals, even when working at Headquarters under the Administrators and not in large detached institutions, in fact found various kinds of higher responsibilities thrust on them on occasion.

Nevertheless as an abstraction the theoretical division of functions and personnel made sense. There were types of work at certain levels which required general all-round intelligence and adaptability, a degree of originality, adaptability and sensitivity to political and other forces in society. Above all the Administrative Class were

* Which is the opposite of 'staff' in the civilian management sense; see pp. 31–2 above.

trained to understand, to respect and to serve Parliament. To adapt policy to practice they had to handle much unexciting day-to-day work because it might have policy implications. But to deploy the Administrators reasonably effectively and economically they were supported and assisted by the other two Classes. So far it may be accepted that the division of groups and functions was not unreasonable, given fair opportunities for promotion from one class to another. These opportunities naturally varied, with the size and growth of Departments. In the thirties with high unemployment outside the Service and great competition to enter, and on the whole deflationary Government policies, there was probably much underemployment of talent at all levels. The war and post-war expansions of Government activity and of non-Government employment gave large numbers of people opportunities to rise much higher. Nevertheless the broad distinction of functions remained—or at least it was revived after no doubt a good deal of blurring during and just after the war.

The generalist administrators

So was another distinction which is much more controversial—that between the Administrative and Executive Grades on the one hand and the various categories of professional and technical experts on the other. This division of function arouses intense criticism, and indeed understandable emotion, among writers on the British Civil Service—above all among economists. It is sometimes suggested or urged that the whole concept of general-purpose administrators is wrong and that all Government administrators should be experts or specialists. Yet there is a case for a separate body of general administrators. Let us take a specific, but fictitious example of a type of Government problem. Suppose large deposits of uranium were discovered in North Wales. Questions would immediately arise as to what publicly or privately owned body should mine it, purchase, process and use it; what new roads, railways and port facilities would be needed and how they should be financed; what safety and national security precautions should be imposed; on what basis private property and public amenities should be interfered with, or be enabled to benefit. There would probably be international repercussions, economic or military. Now some people might say that all these questions were basically economic and that, although other experts would be needed, the whole business should be coordinated and decided by economists. Other people might argue that the essential thing was a strengthening of national military potential which must be fully exploited and protected, and therefore that everything should be firmly controlled by military (including security) experts. On the other hand large numbers of farmers, small business men, and other private property owners and people interested in the preservation of rural Wales would be very concerned. The Welsh National Party would no doubt have something to say. So would a variety of important trades unions.

As British Government is at present organised one can be certain that several Government Departments would be extensively concerned. Probably some senior Cabinet Minister would be deputed to coordinate the whole affair; but he would need a staff of coordinators, as well as all sorts of specialist advisers, and advisory and liaison committees. Who would form the central core of his staff—his secretariat? Should they be economists, generals, nuclear physicists, civil engineers, professors of economic geography, or what? No doubt all these people would be needed, but what would be the essential qualifications for coordinating the whole?

It might be argued that they would be the same as those required for coordination in the largest privately owned corporations. Coordinators in such cases may have various original academic or professional qualifications—and varied experience obtained in a more or less planned career progression and by some form of management training. This might consist of case-study exercises on the Harvard model, economics, finance, statistics and a few mathematical 'management techniques' with a greater or lesser dose of management theory and elementary industrial psychology thrown in for good measure. This sort of intellectual equipment, which is gradually being developed in the Business Schools and elsewhere, is designed for the coordination of a variety of manufacturing activities to serve a fairly simple objective or group of company objectives, usually expressed wholly, or mainly, in financial terms. These are the objectives of the board of directors acting on behalf of shareholders with financial interests in the company.

A similarly equipped and organised group of coordinators would only be suitable for the government of a state, if the State (either a dictatorship or a democracy) were primarily or exclusively interested in the financial effect of its activities. In the example we have given, the financial aspects would be of immense importance but there would be many other aspects. The defence and diplomatic experts might well advise that certain defence considerations outweighed any consideration of finance. On the other hand developments on the scale likely to be proposed would almost certainly be impossible without the extensive use of compulsory powers over private property. Even without the use of such powers the working and living conditions of numerous local communities would be enormously affected for better or worse. Major questions of natural ecology and sociology would arise. The Welsh Nationalists and many other inhabitants and lovers of Wales would be unlikely to accept that economic or military considerations were overriding. All kinds of industrial and trades union interests on the other hand might be willing and probably anxious to support some or all of the various possible developments provided they were adequately consulted. Some people would demand urgent action, cutting through all established procedures: others would be fearful of the repercussions on political events in all sorts of other places.

The case for the interchangeable generalist

It would traditionally be argued that the generalist administrator of the type normal in the former British Civil Service, Administrative Class, would be most suitable for this sort of coordination. It is not simply a question of an abstract general intelligence such as was supposed to have been cultivated by the academic study of pure mathematics, ancient Greek and Roman culture, or modern history or literature—or indeed any other academic discipline from biology to engineering not necessarily related to the subject-matter of the administrative work. The traditional Civil Service administrator was and still often is exposed to a variety of tasks sometimes on apparently completely contrasting subjects, but as Lord Bridges wrote, 'nearly every problem bears a family resemblance to something which the experienced administrator has seen and handled before'.[3] There would often be contrasting materials composing the same basic pattern —the same political requirements of Ministers in the background, the same variety of powerful interests to be balanced—employers, trades unions and so on—the same pressure for financial economy, the same need to have a consistent case which could be lucidly explained to opposing interests: 'The first time a man is told to change from work which he has mastered to a new job he may feel that the special knowledge he has acquired is being wasted. . . . But when a man has done five jobs in fifteen years and has done them all with a measure of success he is afraid of nothing and welcomes change.'[4]

The Administrative Class Civil Servants obtained their training as much by doing a variety of jobs and having endless discussions with their colleagues as by the University education which only about half or two-thirds of them had usually had. Those who had not, obtained a substitute for it by systematic reading, argument and closely supervised and criticised writing—something very similar to what Universities at their best provide. They also learnt by constant meetings and correspondence with those with whom their Departments had to deal. On the whole the greater and more varied the amount of outside dealing the better the administrator. It is not good for any civil servant to have to deal only with other civil servants.

Sensitivity to society

There is, however, a third element in the training and make-up of a good administrator which is that provided by the society in which he has moved—not merely the individuals he meets socially but the whole national climate in so far as he is able to absorb it directly or indirectly. In their sensitivity to society in general civil servants in Britain and many other countries differ greatly. Some keep in touch with and others withdraw from their social or geographical origins. Some are shy, and others manage to mix with a wide variety of social and intellectual groups. On the whole, as modern Britain is a relatively socially mobile and cohesive nation, its Civil Service probably does not compare too badly in this respect with those of many other countries.

'Relevant' education and training

Are the qualifications of an administrator which we have implied above, sufficient—intelligence, adaptability, experience of government work in general, ability to make and maintain a variety of contacts? It has often been alleged recently, notably by the Fulton Committee but also by many other critics, that they are not, that the subject-matter of modern government is so complex and so much of it economic, sociological and technical that it requires trained experts. The difficulty is, what kind of experts? In the example we have quoted should they be economists who may know nothing of nuclear physics, or physicists who know nothing of economics? Who should decide whether a hospital should be extended to meet an expected increase in the population—a statistician, a doctor, an economist, or an architect?

The Fulton Committee, by a majority, recommended that administrators should be recruited with a preference for 'relevant' academic disciplines and that those from 'irrelevant' disciplines should receive subsequent training in them. 'Relevant' disciplines they defined rather vaguely as 'the social studies, the mathematical and physical sciences, the biological sciences or in applied and engineering sciences'. However a minority, including a former Director General of the Federation of British Industries and a Professor of Sociology, dissented and the Government of the day, without protest from the Opposition, rejected the majority recommendation.[5]

Granted the multiplicity of activities of modern government and the variety and perpetual conflict of its objectives, there seems no alternative to having central organs of coordination staffed by generalist administrators. These generalist administrators must, however, (a) be of high and flexible intelligence; (b) come from a variety of academic disciplines and geographical and social backgrounds and (c) be very systematically trained.

Their training should include both varied work experience and formal instruction—in both the principles of administration, and the management techniques and tools of analysis to cope with and sift the enormous variety of problems and interested pressures they will have to confront. It is not necessary to be either a lawyer, a nuclear physicist or an economist to promote a Parliamentary Bill for the regulation of nuclear industries. It is necessary to be well enough educated and trained to understand, criticise and coordinate what all these experts are saying. But any country will have a basically inadequate Civil Service if it provides only intellectual training and allows its Civil Service to be ignorant of basic moral values and the outlook of the common man.

Local and regional offices

This chapter, like much other literature of public administration, has devoted what may seem a disproportionate space to the tasks of the Administrative Class of the Civil Service, or whatever may take its place as an organ of generalist coordination. It is, however, central to the policies of Government administration and the main element which distinguishes it from business management. Granted that there must be some such organ in any Government, the rest falls relatively easily into place. When local and regional offices are required, they can be arranged in a more or less classical hierarchy of authority linked with the central coordinating bodies, but also with outside interests. It may sometimes be easier to keep local offices so democratically linked (and prevent their becoming bureaucratic) than regional offices. Local managers cannot avoid contact with their customers and clients. To keep regional and local offices imbued with the same general approach as the central body, and indeed to enable them to contribute to this approach, it is necessary to have frequent contacts by visits and conferences (and not merely on paper and by telephone), suitable provision in training courses and considerable interchanges of staff between all three levels as part of normal career development. This is often very difficult to organise so as to get effective and equitable career progression and with reasonable regard for the fact that the staff concerned have homes and families and local communities in which they are naturally rooted. Moreover it may sometimes be desirable to give someone a temporary change of job for experience without imagining he will be as well adapted to it as to his former job.

The position of specialists and 'professionals'

Local and regional organisation, though very important in certain
Government Departments, is less a special problem of Government
than that of specialists, professionals and experts at Headquarters
level. The latter is a problem on which it is misleading to generalise.
There is first the professional or specialist adviser to administrators
carrying out a regulatory, controlling or judicial function. Some of
these advisers may be inspectors. Now inspectors are of many kinds
and of many professions, with many different kinds of functions and
powers. There are people who assess planning or construction proposals for their technical soundness, and those who inspect institutions, social service agencies, or police forces, for their efficiency,
water or food supplies and animals for hygiene, ships and mechanical
equipment for safety, and so on. In some cases there is a straightforward question of whether something does or does not involve an
unacceptable risk to safety, or whether its technical content does or
does not contravene some legally precise regulations. In such cases
inspectors may have executive powers which they can use directly
and personally, because no other considerations besides those covered by their professional assessment are involved. Hence if there is
an appeal it is to a specialist tribunal. But other types of inspector
make assessments which do not necessarily involve a clear-cut 'Yes'
or 'No' nor cover all aspects of a case. An inspector may pass plans
of a new piece of construction as technically sound but its claim on
limited financial resources (for which different types of scheme may
be competing) may be questionable. The objections to a town-plan-
ning scheme may be insufficiently strong from a professional town-
planning point of view, but the political opposition it would arouse
may be unacceptable—and so on. Where general administrators in
the name of a Minister have power to reject the advice of specialist
inspectors or other advisers it is usually because factors outside the
specialist sphere may be involved. The general administrator may be
better equipped to deal with 'policy' aspects—meaning conformity
with general Government policy and political considerations, with
an acceptable balance of the pressures of interest groups, with the
rights of the citizen and equity between citizens. Another major consideration is finance. Sometimes it may be the main consideration.
In the Defence Departments the branches staffed by the Administrative Class have sometimes been referred to as 'finance branches' in
contradistinction to the military branches staffed by military officers.
It may often be the administrator's major function to keep his
Department out of trouble with the Treasury and the Auditor
General, or to keep projects and activities in line with the Department's

general financial policies and plans. In any case he is, as in all other subjects, simply acting as the representative of Parliament, seeing that money is only spent as voted by the House of Commons and within the general policies which Parliament has approved. He must also see that it involves no treatment of individual or group interests which would not be defensible in Parliament.

However, one may well ask why the professional specialist cannot, just as easily as the administrator, be trained to take account of all these things. Occasionally an exasperated administrator will complain that specialists are narrow, soulless technocrats who never will understand these subtle and far-reaching considerations, obsessed as they are with their own specialisms. But it could be argued on the contrary that they will always be so obsessed if they are not allowed powers of decision in the wider field. In fact in the nationalised industries, in local government and in some parts of some Government Departments, professional specialists do exercise wide executive powers covering many matters of policy. Many professionally trained specialists, whether or not formally designated as general managers, understand this sort of thing as well as 'pure'(!) administrators. There are natural generalists and natural specialists within every profession, within every academic discipline and within both the public and private sectors. The better argument for the use of non-professional administrators on generalist work is not that the professionals are incapable of being trained to do it, but simply that they would be wasting their professional training and experience. Yet if, as is often alleged, really good top-level general administrators are rarer than good middle-level engineers, doctors, chemists, lawyers, etc., it is no waste to promote such a man to be a top-level administrator if he possesses the rare gifts for such work. The arguments are pretty evenly balanced and in different Government Departments and on different subjects a wide variety of practice prevails.*

Access to Ministers

The more important question is not whether to give specialists

* The best recent discussion of this subject is in 'The Fulton Report: The Role of the Professional' by W. G. (now Sir William) Harris, C.ENG., K.I.C. (Director General of Highways, Ministry of Environment, former Civil Engineer in Chief, Admiralty), published in *Public Administration*, Spring 1969, vol. 47, pp. 33–47. Sir William suggests that professionals in the Civil Service already have more scope to exercise general management and administrative responsibilities—and less desire to do so—than is often alleged. He suggests they have more natural desire to be executive managers than policy administrators. He also urges that professionals and administrators 'are in partnership and that sometimes one and sometimes the other may lead the team'—as they already do in his own Department.

general administrative powers and functions, but how to ensure that those who concentrate mainly on their specialisms should still have an effective voice in policy decisions especially at the highest levels. The crucial point is access to Ministers. Even before Fulton most top specialists in British Government Departments probably had such access. Yet practice no doubt varied with Departments and individual personalities, and specialist advice might sometimes only filter to Ministers through Permanent Secretaries and other non-specialist administrators, or even other specialists. A physicist may not like going through a Chief Scientific Adviser who is a biologist, or a civil engineer through a Chief Engineer who is an electrical specialist. Indeed a 'lay' administrator who was in fact an outstanding authority on a certain subject might well feel similarly aggrieved. In the Defence Departments, however, the former Board of the Admiralty, the Army Council and the Air Council normally gave the top service officers access to Ministers (although the Ministers alone carried responsibility to Parliament for their activities). The same administrative device was adopted in the Post Office reforms of 1935 when a number of senior officials, some specialist and some generalist, were grouped into the Post Office Board which met regularly with the Postmaster General. It must be emphasised that this was an administrative and not a constitutional device. The Post Office Board was never legally a body corporate till the office of Postmaster General was abolished in 1969. Until then he alone carried full political, parliamentary, legal and administrative responsibility. The Board was simply a meeting of his chief officials and advisers. Its membership, and its importance, fluctuated over the years. However, it was very important initially as a means of bringing two top specialists, the Engineer-in-Chief and the Accountant General, into direct contact with the Minister and into close association with discussions about general policy. In this way it set a further precedent for various somewhat comparable arrangements in other Government Departments which broke down the classical line-and-staff pattern in a way parallel to that in which it was being broken down in various private industrial organisations such as those described by Burns and Stalker.*

There were two ways in which this could happen. Firstly specialists of various kinds, notably research scientists and economic advisers, may be associated on a more or less equal basis with general administrators, possibly under the chairmanship of a Minister, in the development of policy. They may join in policy-making committees or operate within all sorts of different patterns. For instance, an economic or other academic expert permanently, temporarily or even

* See pp. 64–6 above.

occasionally imported from outside may conduct seminars to question the fundamentals of policy. All this seems to reflect Burns and Stalker's fundamental thinking. It is 'organic' administration. Somewhat on these lines were the original joint development groups for producing new ideas of building design in the Ministry of Education, the former War Office and the former Ministry of Works*—groups headed by pairs of co-equal architects and general administrators and including other specialists. They resembled to some degree the joint management units of generalists and specialists in the Highways Department of the Ministry of Transport,[6] and in the Ministry of Public Buildings and Works.* Although they have to develop policy, most of these two latter types of units are primarily executive bodies concerned respectively with constructing roads and buildings. It has often, therefore, been possible to sweep away the old administrative/ professional divisions (which had not operated fully in the roads field for many years) and group all the grades of staff—engineers, architects, estate surveyors and so on—into territorial or functional operational units. The heads of these units may by origin be members of any of the professions or general administrators.

The patterns of organisation vary greatly between and within Government Departments, depending partly on the nature of the work and partly on the initiatives and capacity for cooperation of individuals—Ministers and civil servants. There are many possible variations of the generalist/specialist pattern. Some people entitled advisers or inspectors, such as the Inspectors of Constabulary,[7] may wield considerable influence on policy-making and management. Some administrators, particularly in finance and personnel branches, may be or become virtually specialists themselves. Indeed personnel presents a contrast between the private sector where 'line management' often has personnel specialists as advisers ('staff') without executive powers, and the Civil Service where 'establishment' departments exercise executive powers and also do the specialist work of interviewing, devising selection, appointment and career development systems, and so on.

Macro-organisation: Haldane's Theory and its critics

So far we have discussed forms and structures of Government administration within Departments. This may be called micro-organisation. We must now consider macro-organisation, the distribution of functions between Government Departments and other public bodies.

The basic document, in fact almost the only British official docu-

* As the Departments were entitled when the units were formed. Now, they are all part of the Ministry of the Environment.

ment which seeks to propound theory on this subject, is the Haldane Report on the Machinery of Government of 1918. We have already referred* to its proposals on planning, intelligence and research. We must now consider its views on macro-organisation and its general approach to problems of Government administration. The Report, immediately after citing its terms of reference, opens with the words, 'We have endeavoured to define in the first place the general principles . . .'. This is typical of the whole Report and of Haldane, the philosopher-administrator. His education, entirely in Scotland and Germany, had given him a logical, philosophical, abstract cast of mind, or perhaps it would be fairer to say a clear-headed concern for basic principles. His Report has been criticised for being too theoretical; but his very similar approach to the reform of army organisation when he was Secretary of State for War at first met a similar lack of sympathy. The Army Council were unresponsive when he told them he wanted 'an Hegelian Army' (by which he presumably meant one planned on philosophic principles). Yet his reforms in the end produced such generally admired practical results as to elicit special and unstinted congratulations from the unphilosophical Field Marshal Haig at the conclusion of World War I.[8]

Haldane's first principles which he applied to legal, military and Government reform were 'specialization of function, organization of intelligence and command, and sound financial control'.[9] The Machinery of Government Report makes recommendations on four primary issues (as well as many secondary ones): (1) the size, composition and functions of the Cabinet, (2) the formulation of policy as the basis of research, (3) the distribution of functions between Government Departments, and (4) control of finance. The first is fundamentally a political rather than an administrative question. We have already discussed the second. We will here discuss only the third.

The Committee wrote: 'There appear to be only two alternatives . . . distribution according to persons or classes to be dealt with and distribution according to services to be performed.' They briefly and firmly rejected the first because they believed the fragmentation and dispersal of expertise would lead to a lowering of standards of service. They therefore recommended the second, so that 'acquisition of knowledge and the development of specialized capacity can be encouraged to the full. These results are obviously most likely to be secured when the officers of a Department are continuously engaged in the study of questions which relate to a single service and when the efforts of the Department are definitely concentrated upon the development and improvement of the particular service which the

* See pp. 120–1.

A.T.A.P.A.—F

Department exists to supervise.'[10] In other words both individual civil servants and Departments collectively should specialise. This would mean that even the more generalist administrators at the top of Departments would be able to specialise to a considerable degree, or at least concentrate their interest in certain directions. This was probably the first attempt in a major state document to apply logical principles to the distribution of Government functions.

Although the Report recognised there would be some exceptions, its recommendation on this subject has been criticised both as over-simple and as over-theoretical.

Yet since it was produced, more than half a century ago, no other general principle, or greater elaboration of the Haldane principle, concerning the allocation of Government functions has been publicly invoked or actually followed. Particular governmental reorganisations involving the distribution or redistribution of functions between Departments have, from time to time, been criticised as lacking in a logical basis of principle. Others have been made for special reasons. Yet it is probably true to say that in most cases the distribution of new functions or the reorganisation of existing functions has followed Haldane's general doctrine without public acknowledgment. For instance, the White Paper on *The Reorganization of Central Government, 1970*, makes a notably theoretical and analytical approach to the problem of distribution of functions between Departments and evidently accepts the Haldane principle even though it does not mention the celebrated Report of 1918. The principle has been criticised on two grounds—that it oversimplifies the administrative alternatives and that it ignores the political basis of Government administration. The first criticism is advanced in Nevil Johnson's article on the 1970 White Paper. He criticises the 'functional principle' (a phrase the Haldane Report did not use) as 'shadowy' and one which 'may imply a hierarchy of objectives or it may refer to the common characteristics of a group of tasks'. He gives examples such as 'the awkward problem of deciding whether aviation is a function of transport or industry'.[11] Johnson says that the alternative the Haldane Report described and rejected, which he calls 'the client principle', cannot be entirely ruled out. 'The Ministry of Agriculture clearly owes something to the convenience of serving a readily identifiable clientele.' Moreover, Johnson says there are two other possible principles not mentioned by Haldane—'the area principle' (e.g., the Scottish and Welsh Offices) and 'the process principle'. On the latter his examples are not very convincing. He cites education, which he admits can be defined in terms of a function, a process or as having a single clientele; and the Office of Parliamentary Counsel[12] (surely a small and very special case). Perhaps the former Ministry of Works would be a clearer example of 'the process principle'.

Fifteen years earlier, Charles H. Wilson, although profoundly admiring Haldane's deep-thinking approach to administration, criticised what he regarded as a shortcoming of the whole Report and of Haldane personally, 'the sense of comprehending things at a deeper level . . . blinded him to certain aspects of the real and concrete situation . . . led him into describing that situation in terms which tended to leave out its random and disorderly elements', that is, he repeats, 'the volatile and disorderly elements in the picture, the play of political power, the shift of parties, the ebb and flow of consent'.[13] In other words he suggests the Haldane Committee treated the distribution of functions between Departments too much as an administrative problem and gave insufficient weight to its political aspects. This is perhaps unfair to the Committee, as it is arguable they were simply making a report on the administrative aspects of certain problems to the Government of the day, whose province it then was to consider their political aspects. In fact Prime Ministers when they redistribute Ministerial and Departmental functions must be perfectly well aware that they sometimes create administrative problems. Yet they must quite properly have regard primarily to political considerations—using that word not in a pejorative sense, but signifying the highest policy considerations which arise in a parliamentary democracy. Prime Ministers assume that the Civil Service will cope with the administrative problems somehow.

A somewhat similar line of argument is taken by R. G. S. Brown, in discussing contemporary problems of macro-organisation in the public sector, although he is dealing with a wider subject than the distribution of functions between Government Departments:

It is tempting to suggest that all this ferment calls for a new Haldane enquiry into the purposes of government and the most appropriate instruments for carrying them out. But the issues have not become any simpler over the last fifty years. It seems very doubtful whether an enquiry of the Royal Commission type would be able to survey such a vast field as the public sector today, even with the support of research, and produce useful conclusions. Opinions about the best division of responsibility between the public and private sectors, or between central and local government departments and public boards for whose activities the Minister is only broadly accountable, reflect broad political choices about the kind of society we want to live in, and cannot be resolved by an 'impartial' enquiry. But political choices could be much better informed than they are now.[14]

That is one of the purposes of public administration—to *inform* choices which are basically political. The great value of the Haldane

Report was that it posed, as fundamental issues, the questions of how certain major political choices should be informed. It did not provide full or completely satisfactory answers, but even if it had done so for its own day, the problem would remain to be answered afresh in each succeeding generation.

1. Rensis Likert, op cit., pp. 178–91; see pp. 57–8 above.
2. op. cit., pp. 38, 111–12.
3. In A. Dunsire (Ed.), 1956. *The Making of an Administrator,* p. 15. Quoted with other similar comments of Lord Bridges by G. F. Fry, 1969, in *Statesmen in Disguise,* p. 59. Macmillan.
4. Sir Edward (later Lord) Bridges, 1950. *Portrait of a Profession,* pp. 22–3. Cambridge University Press.
5. Fulton Report, op. cit., paras. 7–80, pp. 27–30, and Appendix, paras. 24–6, p. 162.
6. See Harris, op. cit., and D. E. Regan, Summer 1966. 'The Expert and the Administrator: Recent Changes at the Ministry of Transport', *Public Administration,* vol. 44.
7. R. G. S. Brown, 1970. *The Administrative Process in Britain,* pp. 80–92. Methuen.
8. Charles H. Wilson, 1956. *Haldane and the Machinery of Government* (Haldane Memorial Lecture), p. 8. Birkbeck College, University of London. See also Lord Bridges, Autumn 1957. 'Haldane and the Machinery of Government', *Public Administration,* vol XXXV, pp. 254–64.
9. ibid., p. 12.
10. Haldane Report, op. cit., paras. 18, 19, pp. 7–8.
11. Nevil Johnson, Spring, 1971. Editorial: 'The Reorganizing Action of Central Government', *Public Administration,* vol. 149, pp. 5, 6.
12. ibid., pp. 3–4.
13. Wilson, op. cit., pp. 12–13, 15.
14. R. G. S. Brown, op. cit., ch. 8, especially pp. 194–5.

9

FORMS AND STRUCTURES OF SOME OTHER
PUBLIC BODIES

Special types of policy-making and consultative organisation
In their activities connected directly and indirectly with national
economic planning since 1960, successive Governments have experimented with various new types of organisation,* part Government
Department, part independent corporation or commission—partly
executive, partly consultative, partly judicial. Some of these organisations have expanded or contracted their activities in recent years.
Some have been completely abolished as the economic policies of
Governments have changed. Governments have differed as to the
extent they wished to be closely involved in the economy; but all
have had some policies for the economy. Most of the economic
planning has been of the 'indicative' variety, that is not a matter of
simple or direct Government control; but rather of consultation,
collaboration and persuasion. Hence it has been a field for experiment with forms of organisation and processes not suitable for many
of the older functions of Government. What concerns us here is not
the changing economic policies, but the administrative organs which
implemented them.

It should be well known that the best way to persuade people to
do new things is to bring it about that they suggest doing them themselves. Hence we have had 'Neddy', the National Economic Development Council, which includes Ministers, individual employers and
trades unionists, with a strong staff, mainly recruited on a temporary
basis from industry; the former Prices and Incomes Board, the

* There may well be more experiments and changes in the organisations, mentioned in this chapter and the next, before this book is published.

Restrictive Practice Court (where lay members outnumber judges); the former Industrial Reorganisation Commission and the Commission on Industrial Relations. The PIB was made up of people from outside Government, supported by both civil servants and management consultants. The IRC drew its members and staff from outside the public sector, and, unlike Neddy, was given executive powers to use large sums of public money. It persuaded, brought people and companies together, reorganised and invested selectively. It collaborated both with Government Departments and private industrial and commercial interests. Its own members and staff were drawn from the groups and interests—finance, industry and so on—whom it aimed to work with and influence.

The common characteristics of Neddy, IRC, PIB, and CIR have been the flexibility of their organisation structures, the absence of formal internal lines of authority or the exercise of formal authority externally, the varied and fluctuating membership of the boards and their staffs, and use of persuasion, discussion, enquiry and research, dissemination of information, involvement and negotiation as means of achieving results. They represent the most 'organic' types among the great variety of organs and agencies which British central government has used and experimented with in recent years.

The idea of 'independent' authorities

Throughout most of the field of central and local government, however, there are clear classic lines of authority and responsibility, at least in legal, and usually in administrative, terms. They run from Parliament at the top right down to the humblest employees at the bottom. This is the overall *structure*. It does not follow that all *forms* of activity, all working processes, are necessarily purely classical and authoritarian. We have shown that some are not. Yet however 'organic' their processes, most of the organisations concerned work within a fairly clear framework of authority. At various quite separate points in the public sector, however, we come across apparent exceptions to this principle. They are both older and more independent than the organisations mentioned above. There are people and institutions who are not fully subject to any authority, and others which seem to be subject to more than one. Moreover, there are sometimes demands for more people or institutions to be freed from direct control by any authority, demands for difficult political, economic or administrative problems to be turned over to 'independent' authorities, commissions, tribunals and so on. We must consider what some such existing or proposed arrangements can mean.

Parliament, the Attorney General and the DPP

Let us look at this matter fundamentally and ask if there are any limitations on the sovereignty of Parliament. It is sometimes said that Parliament cannot debate certain subjects such as the conduct of royal persons or judges or the secret service. Both Houses of Parliament can in fact debate anything they wish. They merely refrain by custom or their own standing orders from doing certain things. Then it is said that judges are not subject to any control. Again this is wrong. Apart from the normal system of appeals they can be dismissed on petition from both Houses of Parliament and their judgments reversed by Act of Parliament—if necessary retrospectively, as in the Burmah Oil case. It is simply that Parliament normally refrains and requires everyone else to refrain from interfering with and, beyond certain limits, criticising the judges, because it considers that that is the best possible way to get judicial work done. Then it is sometimes said or implied that the Attorney General has no responsibility except to his own conscience. Sir John (later Lord) Simon in 1929 said he 'should receive orders from no one'. In fact, as Professor Edwards' authoritative work demonstrates, he is, like other Ministers, responsible to Parliament, which has on occasion debated his actions[1]—and of course he is removable by the Prime Minister. It is only that Prime Ministers and Cabinets nowadays make a practice of not directing him in certain matters. Similarly the Director of Public Prosecutions, also sometimes thought to be 'independent', is, in the words of a recent distinguished holder of that office, 'the servant of the public through Parliament which represents them and of the Executive which, through Parliament, is responsible to them and is in no sense the master of either'.[2]

The police

No one in the United Kingdom is independent of Parliament and no public office of any kind is, in the last resort, absolutely 'independent'. It is only that some are afforded greater discretion and relative independence than others, and it may sometimes be convenient for all concerned to treat them as if they were totally independent. They may indeed appear to behave as if they were. Nevertheless, they are consciously or unconsciously aware of limits they cannot overstep. Some of the major contemporary problems of public administration concern the reality and meaning of such terms as 'independent', 'responsible' and 'control', when applied to certain exceptionally important types of public work—judicial, police, medical, and so on.

Chief Constables have sometimes been regarded as subject to the orders of no higher authority of any kind. This view was thought

to have been justified by the medieval origins of the police and con-
firmed by the judgment of Mr Justice McCardie in 1930 in *Fisher v.
the Oldham Corporation*.[3] He quoted an earlier Australian judicial
opinion[4] (which subsequently received some support from the Privy
Council in another Australian case) that 'The powers of a constable
are exercised by him by virtue of his office and cannot be exercised
in the responsibility of any person but himself. . . . The constable
therefore . . . is not exercising a delegated but an original authority'.[5]
There has been much dispute as to what this case implied as to the
relationship between Chief Constables and local police authorities,*
the former contending it meant their total independence, the latter
that they could issue general instructions although not interfere with
the handling of particular cases. In the years 1917, 1936 and 1958
statements suggesting full control by the local police authorities
have been made by a Home Secretary, two different Speakers and a
Deputy Chairman[6] in the House of Commons. *The Royal Commission on the Police: Final Report* in 1962 concluded that a Chief Constable 'is accountable to no one and subject to no one's orders for
the way in which, for example, he settles his general policies in regard to law enforcement . . .'.[7] But the dissenting member of the
Commission, Dr A. L. Goodhart, argued that the judgments in
Fisher's and the Australian cases could not possibly justify such a
situation.[8] While he recognised the position of *de facto* independence
which provincial Chief Constables had acquired, he deplored it. It
contrasted with both that of the Metropolitan Police Commissioner
and the spirit of the nineteenth-century legislation which established
modern police forces. (He brushed aside the earlier history as
irrelevant.) He concluded his argument:

It has been suggested that the recent dictatorships on the Continent
ought to be a warning against the establishment of a strong centrally-
controlled police force here. I believe that the lesson is the exact opposite.
The danger to democracy does not lie in a central police that is too
strong but in local police forces that are too weak. It was the private gangs
of Fascists and of the Nazis that enabled Mussolini and Hitler to establish
their dictatorships when the legitimate police proved impotent.[9]

He contended that independence is not a guarantee of impartiality
but the reverse. 'The primary guarantee of impartiality is that the
person who acts should be held responsible directly and immediately
to his superior officers; if the chain of command ends with him there
is no adequate control.' He wanted an integrated national force for

---

* These consist of local councillors and, in English counties, partly also of
magistrates.

which the Home Secretary would be responsible to Parliament. Control, delegation and responsibility should operate through all the formal and informal means available in any large integrated organisation. They should not need to depend on a few legally specified and rather drastic powers, such as dismissal of Chief Constables. He said 'the step of dismissal is so extreme that it will be taken only with the greatest reluctance'. 'There is a fundamental difference between a Chief Constable who is inefficient and one who is not as efficient as he ought to be.' 'No private organisation'—he might also have said no Government Department—'could function efficiently if the only method of control lay in a threat of dismissal.'[10] On a variety of points Dr. Goodhart regarded the then existing position of the police and the limited changes proposed by his colleagues as illogical and therefore unacceptable. Somewhat similar views have since been expressed in Marshall's scholarly analysis.[11] This, however, was not the conclusion reached by Parliament. The Police Act, 1964, did not create a national police force, though it embodied many of the Commission's recommendations, including increasing the powers of the Home Secretary, enabling him to call for reports, to retire Chief Constables and to amalgamate local forces. Can we make any choice between the logical views of Goodhart and Marshall, or what we may call the practical political/administrative view which has in fact prevailed? The British police services continue to function. It does not seem to be alleged that they function less satisfactorily than those of any other countries. Occasional complaints can be investigated either by the normal processes of the civil and criminal courts or special inquiries or any new procedures that might be devised. What may be more important, innumerable day-to-day unpleasant and difficult decisions are taken by processes which most of those concerned can regard as more or less neutral and automatic. Political and administrative authorities are hence relieved of much direct responsibility for making moral choices. The general public can, on the whole, feel that 'the law takes its course' and they do not have to worry. Can it be that most people feel about the police as Lord Devlin said that Parliament felt about defining the law of criminal intention* that, in the popular phrase, 'they do not want to know'.

Of course, there are all kinds of ways in which the police, like other members of public services, must be open to influence. There need be nothing improper in this. Police work depends on the co-operation of the public and on many kinds of information, advice, coordination and support. It depends on witnesses, on recruits, on equipment and on finance. The powerful position of the Inspectors of Constabulary has often been referred to. Local Authorities and

* See p. 135.

other public bodies and Government Departments, besides the Home Office, must have considerable influence on the police, quite apart from any question of legal powers. Most non-classical organisation theorists, notably such different writers as Follet, Barnard, Likert, Vickers, and Burns and Stalker, indeed most psychologists and sociologists, would probably rate informal influence as highly as formal authority, and often draw no hard and fast line between the two.

Yet there remains the practical management problem of how the cost-effectiveness of a police force can be measured and controlled. It is indeed susceptible to quantitative study.[12] The Home Office now has an Economic Adviser who assists in the application of techniques of 'programme budgeting' to the local control of police finance and manpower. It is apparently possible to conceptualise and quantify the results of certain important elements such as 'ground cover'. Yet all the end products of police activity cannot be quantified. In the background is the ultimate authority of Parliament and the system works within a framework of formal legality. To this extent classical ideas of organisation are highly relevant to it. Yet its day to day working and its interaction with the rest of the community can only be fully understood in the light of an organic or a systems theory of organisation.

Nationalised industries

Having, we hope, disposed of the notion that there can be any such thing—legally or otherwise—as a completely 'independent' authority below the level of a sovereign state—or at least not in the United Kingdom—we are in a better position to look at the public corporations in perspective. There is a considerable literature concerning their independence—but all that this means is the extent to which successive Parliaments and Governments have been willing, by statute or by administrative action, or by default, to delegate certain functions to them, and how far and by what means they have sought to control or influence or monitor or check their performance of these delegated functions. These questions caused some trouble and confusion in the early years of nationalisation but the whole subject was largely dealt with and put in perspective in Chapters 6, 7 and 8 of Professor Robson's definitive work.[13] Here we must confine ourselves to a brief explanation of what public corporations are and to some points about their internal structures.

Juridical constitutions of corporations (public and private)

Juridically, corporations in England are of medieval origin. A corporation of any kind, public or private, is a group of persons author-

ised by law to act and be the subject of action as if they were a
person. The authorisation may be a charter granted under the royal
prerogative, or by Act of Parliament. The earliest corporations were
monasteries, Universities, guilds and boroughs. The Greater London
Council, the BBC, Universities, cathedral Chapters, are all corporations. So are commercial and industrial companies, but they are subject to special statutory provisions under the Companies Acts.
Government Departments are not corporations. In law, they are
only agencies of the Crown or its Ministers. A corporation is an independent entity over which the Government does not necessarily
have any special control or special responsibility, except that which
is specifically provided for on its incorporation or otherwise. In
medieval times the granting of incorporation to any institution—the
distinction between public and private was scarcely drawn then—
meant the granting of a certain degree of independence. This sort of
institutional independence can be an advantage to the modern public
corporation, and also to the modern Government, if it does not wish
to assume too direct and detailed responsibility for some activity
which it nevertheless wishes to see carried out.

Public corporations

English law, unlike that of continental countries, makes no fundamental distinction between public and other corporations. Indeed it
is a little hard to say what a public corporation is. The modern public
corporation may perhaps be defined simply as any corporation
created for the purpose of carrying out some function in which the
general public, locally or nationally, has some interest and which it
is desirable to bring into 'the public domain' without the Government being involved in all the details of its management. Some of the
first modern public corporations were created in the late eighteenth
and early nineteenth centuries for certain basic 'infrastructure' purposes, normally local, such as canals, turnpike roads, town paving
and draining. The modern twentieth-century, national, public corporation is sometimes described as 'the Morrisonian Corporation'
because of Herbert Morrison's creation of the London Passenger
Transport Board in 1933[14] and the major part he took in the creation
of the corporations of the nationalised industries in the period
1946–8. However other people, notably Professor Robson[15], were at
least as creative as Morrison in developing the idea, and the LPTB
had a prototype in the Port of London Authority set up in 1908. The
first modern, national corporations, the BBC and the Central
Electricity Board, were created by Stanley Baldwin's Conservative
Government in 1926. The BBC's independence owes much to the
powerful creative personality of Lord Reith, its first Director General,

but also to the generally recognised need for a body to handle the presentation of news and matters of controversy, and also matters of art, independently of the political parties. The CEB had more simple, more clear-cut, but nevertheless vital functions—to act as national wholesaler of electricity and to construct and maintain the national electricity grid. For the purposes which all these modern corporations had to fulfil it was considered desirable to have a kind of management with defined objectives, but independent of day-to-day responsibilities by Ministers to Parliament. A comprehensive 'theory of the public corporation' has been formulated by Robson:

... The starting point of such a theory is the proposition that the nationalised industries or services, like all publicly owned undertakings, form part of the public domain. The object of bringing them into the public sector of the economy is to ensure that they are subject to political control by the Legislature and the Executive in their respective spheres.

The public corporations are organs of public administration. As such they are instruments of public policy just as much as the older departments exercising conventional functions. They are distinct from the regular departments under the control of Ministers; but they are subordinate to Parliament and the Executive.

The organisation, assets, functions and powers of the public corporations spring from the creative act of the legislature; their purposes and property are given to them by Parliament. The public corporation cannot by its own authority modify these purposes; nor sell, terminate, liquidate, or pledge the undertaking with which it is entrusted.

To foster initiative and enterprise in the conduct of the nationalised industries the public corporation has had conferred upon it a substantially greater degree of independence in its daily working than is possessed by departments in charge of a Minister. In matters of finance and personnel budgeting and accounting, production, distribution and development, it enjoys a large measure of freedom. The public corporation is, however, not an autonomous institution and was never intended to be.

The public corporation is based on the theory that a full measure of accountability can be imposed on a public authority without requiring it to be subject to ministerial control in respect of its managerial decisions and multitudinous routine activities, or liable to comprehensive parliamentary scrutiny of its day-to-day working. The theory assumes that policy, in major matters at least, can be distinguished from management or administration; and that a successful combination of political control and managerial freedom can be achieved by reserving certain powers of decision in matters of major importance to Ministers answerable to Parliament and leaving everything else to the discretion of the public corporation acting within its legal competence. The Government are further endowed with residual powers of direction and appointment which mark their unquestionable authority.

The theory leaves out of account the all-pervading influence which

Ministers can exert over the activities of public corporations if they are so disposed. Where this occurs there is a danger of blurring the distinction between policy and management on which the theory rests; and a no-man's land emerges in which nominal responsibility does not coincide with the real power of decision-making. A clear allocation, recognition, and public acknowledgment of the respective spheres of Ministers, Parliament, and the public corporation is necessary; and an assurance that they will be respected.

The allocation of powers need not be static but may be altered if and when conditions change. But a re-allocation should be publicly announced in a formal manner. . . .[16]

Internal structures

The major public corporations include those which operate the nationalised industries—coal, steel, railways, airlines, electricity and gas—and also the BBC, the Atomic Energy Authority, the British Airports Authority and the Post Office (the last three formerly run by Government Departments). All these provide a huge, varied and fascinating field for the organisation theorist. Apart from the classic works of Robson and Morrison and a few penetrating essays, most of the serious detailed discussion on the subject is in public docu-ments—the Reports of the House of Commons Select Committee on Nationalised Industries, and the various committee reports—notably Fleck on Coal and Herbert on electricity. More of the literature con-cerns external than internal relationships. There is still scope for several books on general and particular aspects of internal organisa-tion structure in the public corporation and we will deal only briefly with some aspects of it here. Much of what could be said is not peculiar to public administration. Indeed, in the last two decades, there has been a progressive tendency among all parties—including the major political Parties—to play down any special characteristics or purposes of the nationalised industries and for them to be assimi-lated more and more closely to the great privately owned corpora-tions which have been increasing in size, number and influence during the period. This tendency has been encouraged by the man-agement consultants and management training institutions.

There has been much discussion in Britain and America about centralisation and decentralisation in large corporations. Indeed there is much double-talk. Some people in large organisations claim to make enormously generous delegations of authority while they nevertheless find means of keeping their subordinates on a pretty tight string. Others claim to exercise far more centralising authority than they really do. This sort of issue was discussed at length in the Fleck and Herbert Reports and by commentators on them, mostly in the abstract terms used by Fayol and Weber. Yet for industries and services with such varied and special characteristics, an approach more like that of Joan Woodward is needed. Much depends on the processes they operate. Central control is required, partly because (except for coal and steel) they operate interconnected and hence, technically standardised public utility networks, and partly because they all have specific statutory obligations. On the other hand, their constitutional form derives from the fact that it was intended to free them from detailed parliamentary control and therefore in theory there should be much more delegation than obtains in a Government Department. Without a great deal of detailed research, however, it would not be possible to say whether this is really so.

The need for technical standardisation in an interconnected network may be as powerful a centralising factor as public pressure. Yet we must be very cautious about assuming that such standardisation necessarily means authoritarian control. In fact, some of the most striking achievements of technical standardisation have been in the international sphere—radio communication, air-traffic control, sea navigation and so on—where standardisation agreements have been made and maintained voluntarily between independent sovereign states, sometimes not on good political terms with one another. Similarly, the centralised control of distribution of electricity throughout Great Britain is maintained on an hour to hour basis, even though there are separate public boards involved and two of them (in Scotland) enjoy a special degree of independence from the others and are dealt with by a different Government Department. Even within very large organisations standardisation and integration are in practice often achieved largely by negotiation and agreement rather than the forcible imposition of authority. They follow Likert rather than Fayol, Taylor or Weber, and internal lateral communication may be more important than vertical. Indeed, very large organisations find the imposition of authority so difficult that individualists and non-conformists may, on occasion, get away with much more than in theory they are supposed to. Having said all this, however, about the qualifications and exceptions, the need to provide more or less standardised and universal public services is one of the prime reasons for the creation and continuation of integrated national or regional public corporations.

Organisation for capital development

Another prime reason for the creation of the major public corporations was the need to undertake massive capital development on a national or regional scale—a scale too large for the organisations they superseded. This was the case with the Central Electricity Board in 1926 and the London Passenger Transport Board in 1933, the

North of Scotland Hydro-Electric Board in 1944, the National Coal Board in 1946, the British Transport Commission in 1947, the Central Electricity Generating Board in 1956, as I sought to demonstrate in my book on *The Management of Capital Projects*[17]—also with the Steel Corporation in 1967. This factor has greatly affected the internal organisational structures of these and other corporations. In the private sector, by contrast, except in the very largest concerns, capital development, especially if it involves constructional work, is usually an occasional, rather than a continuing function. Often when it is very large its management will be farmed out to contractors and/or consultants.

The 'optimising' and the 'balancing' functions are different ones and require different organisation and different skills. All public service corporations therefore have special units of some kind for planning. They must all struggle with the dilemma of separation of function and of coordination—which Lawrence and Lorsch discussed. Planning which is too remote from day-to-day operations is unrealistic. Yet if those responsible for it are also too closely involved with day-to-day work it never gets done at all, as Haldane pointed out.

When capital development is a major continuing responsibility, as it was in the first decade and a half in the Coal Board's history, and still is in electricity generating, it justifies separate organs of management—planning departments, design and construction departments, 'project groups' (which can be major permanent departments) and so on. For some years, for instance, the National Coal Board had a Reconstruction Department at its Headquarters which seemed to be co-equal with its Production Department, and there was an equivalent unit at the subordinate Division and Area levels. For the Central Electricity Generating Board new construction has always been a bigger responsibility of top management than operating, and hence a Planning Department, a Design and Construction Department and three large Project Groups have been wholly, and a Finance Department and a Contracts Department largely, concerned with it.

Some aspects of the Hospital Service

The National Health Service has hitherto been run largely by special purpose public corporations; but in almost all its parts it defies classification with any other type of organisation in the public sector. Professor Kogan describes hospitals as 'far more complex than any other social service institution'.[18] The paragraphs which follow are intended to illustrate some of the unsolved problems of organisation, control and motivation in a very vital, very complex and very specialised public service They cannot draw a clear picture of any particular organisational model, because no such model has so far been produced for the Hospital Service and the concrete situation is one of great variety and complexity. Yet it is with such complexities, and not only with the simple types of organisation, that public administration theory must sooner or later contend.

The major framework of the National Health Service, its macroorganisation, was, at the time of writing, under fundamental review. We can therefore only here touch on certain features of the Hospital Service which are of special interest for their wider implications. These are mainly matters of micro-organisation which are likely to remain serious problems however the larger framework is reorganised. We will not discuss the public health (preventative) services and the general practitioners' and dental services.

The Hospital Service was built from a variety of elements, including the old charitable hospitals and related voluntary associations, the university medical departments, the local authority hospital services, and the dedicated, hierarchical, fiercely independent medical and nursing professions. Its creation represented a political and administrative compromise between what Aneurin Bevan referred to as 'realities' and 'abstract principles'.[19] The Hospital Service is at present controlled by the Regional Hospital Boards and the Governors of the teaching hospitals, all appointed by the Minister.* They are public corporations in law, but also agents of the Minister, who accepts parliamentary responsibility for them.

Below the Regional Hospital Boards are the Hospital Management Committees which are responsible for the nursing, 'paramedical'† and all administrative (that is, all non-medical) work and staff in Groups of hospitals. They are not responsible for the doctors or their work. In individual hospitals the division of control is even greater. There is a Secretary or House Governor and sometimes a House Committee (a sub-committee of the HMC) controlling administrative work, but not usually nursing, and certainly not paramedical services. The consultants, who themselves exercise firm control over the other doctors, are appointed and employed by the Regional Hospital Boards, not the Hospital Management Committees. Yet how far the consultants are, or should be, or could be fully responsible to or controlled by the Boards, or any other authority, seems to be a major unresolved question. The activities of consultants and other hospital doctors are coordinated, or at least jointly discussed, by committees of doctors. These committees are on three

* Originally in England, the Minister of Health, now the Secretary of State for Health and Social Security and in Scotland, the Secretary of State for Scotland.
† That is the work of a variety of professional and scientific staff in physiotherapy, chemistry, hospital social work, and so on.

levels; for Groups of hospitals, for individual hospitals, and for 'divisions' within hospitals; and their chairmanships may rotate annually or biennially. The committees seem to have varied in character and function and have been the subject of much debate.

This is by no means the only debatable subject in hospitals nor must they be thought of as places operated wholly or even mainly by doctors. They are very large, very complex, social organisms which feed, and house, large numbers of people as well as giving them specifically medical, surgical and nursing treatment and advice. Yet it is obvious to any layman that the doctors and all the other groups of professional and non-professional workers, however organisationally separate, are in fact dependent on one another. In this peculiar administrative situation, with so many specialists and independent experts and no single overall authority, the layman may wonder how anything can possibly work. That it apparently does work with such a considerable though greatly varying degree of success, can perhaps only be attributed to the vital need that it should work, and not to any administrative system. Dr Revans has written: 'There is no perfection to be brought about by administrative decree or departmental order alone; those who serve the hospital must perceive their own problems by their own lights and work out their own solutions in their own ways.' Of his own extensive and fundamental researches into the organisation and internal sociology of hospitals he says: 'Whether or not we can suggest any action by which any particular social organism may become more self-aware and whether having made these suggestions we can engineer improvements remains to be seen.'[20] If one accepts Dr Revans' approach (which is controversial) one will question Professor Kogan's view that 'the main problems of hospital organisation are accountability'.[21] Various aspects of hospital organisation have been in recent years, and still are, the subject of many official investigations and academic research efforts, including those of Dr Revans, Professor Jaques, Professor Kogan and of the First Report of the Ministry of Health Working Party on the Organization of Medical Work in Hospitals (1967).[22]

The 'Cogwheel' Report on hospital medical organisation

This became known as the 'Cogwheel' Report after the design on its cover of interlocking wheels within a wheel, symbolising the interconnections of all elements within the Health Service and in particular within hospitals. It was a complex, although fairly brief, report on a complex subject, and its recommendations were cautious, at some points even imprecise. It stressed the need for coordination both within the Health Service generally and within hospitals, and complained of 'far too vague' organisations, notably the 'ill-defined medical advisory committees' associated with Hospital Management Committees. It said:

27. Since 1948 hospital medical committees have tended to drift away from the mainstream of management which at group level is largely non-medical. Thus 'clinical management' tends to be regarded as remote from the general management of a hospital, medical care being thought to have little administrative content. In fact, practically every clinical decision affects the administrative running of the hospital. It is not too soon to redefine the problem of the administration of medical care services, and to design a system that will produce a better solution of the management problems involved.

Yet the Report did not suggest a fully defined system of all-embracing, delegated authority. It said the management problems of hospitals 'require a corporate approach which precludes the reintroduction of the erstwhile medical superintendent'. It did, however, head its recommendations 'towards a more sharply defined organisation of medical staff'. It proposed a system of grouping together of various related medical activities, within hospitals or groups of hospitals, into 'divisions', though not on any rigidly uniform pattern. The number and size of 'divisions' would be influenced to a great extent by the size and pattern of the existing group hospital services. Divisions might be formed from the medical specialities, the surgical specialities, the laboratory services, radiology and radiotherapy, psychiatry, obstetrics and gynaecology or some combination of specialities deriving from a specific development at a particular hospital. The division could include all the consultants and their junior staff and would meet regularly to review its work (para. 56) 'The divisions would each require a chairman who should be appointed . . . by Regional Boards in consultation with Hospital Management Committees and consultant staff' (para. 60).

In view of this divisionalisation, the former medical advisory committees, with their combined general functions for whole hospitals, should disappear. Instead hospitals should have Executive Committees, with different powers and functions from the former medical advisory committees. Each Executive Committee would consist of representatives from the divisions and a chairman, 'appointed in the same way as the chairman of a division, who would occupy the position preferably for a period of five or more years, who might return to wholly clinical practice' (para. 62).

As far as one can gather from its somewhat brief statements the Report did not envisage that Executive Committees or the divisions or their chairmen should have merely advisory or consultative functions, nor yet on the other hand that they should exercise all the functions of administration such as those defined by Fayol. It seems rather that they were to be mainly occupied with the two very important but not all-embracing functions Fayol described as *prévoyance* and *controle*, foresight, planning, reviewing and monitoring— also coordination, but not command or organisation (the two other of his five administrative functions). Nevertheless Executive Committee chairmen were to have some 'executive powers' (not defined— para. 62). The summary of recommendations says: 'Each Division should carry out constant reappraisal of the services it provides, deploy clinical resources and cope with the problems of management that arise in the clinical field.' The body of the Report (para. 58) gives examples, but para. 61 says, 'it is not easy to lay down a single pattern for each division and its chairman'. The Executive Committee should 'receive and consider reports put to them by the divisions, review major issues of policy and planning and coordinate the medical activities of the hospital as a whole'. Para. 63 says 'the Executive Committee is seen as a source of authority behind the Chairman'—an interesting use of the word 'authority', obviously not in the legal sense. (Clearly all this can be, and indeed has been, ininterpreted differently in different hospitals.) The Report certainly points the way to better coordination and to a classification and rationalisation of functions; but it does not lay down a complete system of management authority such as organisation theorists of the classical school, and indeed most managers in industry, would approve.

Nevertheless some thoughtful doctors seem to consider it goes too far. Dr James Stewart, a consultant at the West Middlesex Hospital (where much research into hospital administration has been conducted by collaboration between sociologists, doctors and nurses), comments: 'The argument concerns one of the great current dilemmas of western civilization—efficiency and cost effectiveness through professional management versus the personal involvement and job satisfaction of participating democracy.'[23] Dr Stewart is cautiously critical of the 'Cogwheel' approach which he suggests favours 'more streamlined efficiency', because he fears it will sacrifice the 'direct involvement' of many medical staff, permanent and temporary, in major decision-taking. Dr N. F. Coghill, a consultant at the same hospital, has written: 'In industry management courses such as doctors are now beginning to attend, often make little difference to attitudes and methods, perhaps because of hierarchical rigidities. It seems that institutions and organizations need to be trained as well as individuals.' He adds: 'The concept that administration is something which an administrator does to the administered is out of date.'[24] Both Stewart and Coghill quote Hunter's work on mental hospitals where it is stated that hospital administration 'is located not on the apex of a pyramid power-structure but at the focal point of an arena, or locale, where different professionals work together, or at least side by side on a give-and-take basis'.[25] In another article Revans, Coghill and others argue: 'Improved hospital management must aim at involving the consultant in the management of all who work with him; not until he knows who they are, what they do and, particularly, what are their problems, can he properly be thought of as a manager.'[26]

Stewart's and Coghill's brief but penetrating articles, like Revan' more extensive work, raise various subtle questions concerning the relationships of people at work and about administration generally. They deserve to be read outside as well as inside the medical world. Permissive organisation and self-motivation do not remove, but intensify, the need for good administration. Stewart therefore writes: 'Whatever the pattern the need for high quality administrative staff remains.' No doubt; but there is surely also a need for high quality administrative work by people other than administrators. Administration should not necessarily only be specialised, but also diffused. The more people in other occupations become as devoted as are doctors and nurses to both the objectives and the processes of their work, the more they will need not only to have the services of good administrators, but to become good administrators themselves. And we can observe that many people—postmen and engine drivers and auditors, as well as headmasters and architects and probation officers, are much more devoted to their work than the conventions of our society allow them to admit.

The administration of law courts

This notion of non-hierarchical self-motivated administration, however, has its limitations. As most of its wisest exponents, McGregor, Likert and so on, have stressed, it is not suitable for every purpose. It usually needs to be balanced and supported by 'classical' institutional frameworks. If one special group of people in an organisation can, or must, operate with almost complete independence in respect of their prime functions, it does not follow that they should exist in an organisational vacuum, nor that all other parts of the organisation should be unorganised. Moreover, absence of hierarchical control does not necessarily produce a vital, creative and 'organic' community. It can produce sluggish inertia or chaos.

One might expect to find a legal system strictly hierarchical and authoritarian; but in fact the Report of Lord Beeching's Commission[27] found the administrative aspects of the English higher court system failing in almost every respect. Its proposals may be summed up as the introduction of largely unified control. The independence of judges in their judicial work, and their freedom from direction even by other judges, is one of the fundamentals of British justice. This appears however to have been accompanied, quite illogically and unnecessarily, by a situation of almost total independence for court administration and court officials; and a division of responsibility, or lack of responsibility, for providing staff, accommodation and other facilities. Hence according to the Beeching analysis there have been gross delays and waste of manpower, and above all 'judge power'. The main Beeching proposals which have been generally accepted and implemented by the Courts Act 1971, involve a hierarchy of Circuit (Regional) Administrators and local court administrators, responsible to the Lord Chancellor 'for the efficient running of the circuit in all respects, but to achieve this' the Circuit Administrator 'will have to work in close conjunction with the Presiding Judge'.[28] The latter should 'have a general responsibility for the orderly running of the lists' and 'see to the convenient and efficient disposition of judges'; but not 'assume any greater burden of administration than is necessary'.[29] Hence a system with completely unified authority at all levels does not appear to be envisaged. Authority is to be divided between, on the one hand, people who are responsible to the Lord Chancellor, and on the other hand Presiding Judges who are not. A good deal must depend on voluntary agreement and cooperation.

Arrangements for the lower ('stipendiary' and lay magistrates') courts remain somewhat different. They have in the past been made by general meetings of magistrates in Quarter Sessions or Committees thereof. For Inner London there is a statutory committee of magistrates (the lay members elected from their own number, the stipendiaries appointed by the Chief Magistrate), with formal responsibility for 'division of work between metropolitan stipendiary magistrates and lay justices', the appointment of the Clerks of the Courts[30] and other matters. However, with certain variations between London and the provinces, other staffing, accommodation and miscellaneous responsibilities are shared by the Home Office, the police and the Local Authorities. The magistrates' courts seem, as yet, to have had no Beeching.*

We thus end this chapter leaving a somewhat complex picture. British public administration has a great variety of contrasting patterns of structure, some firmly classical, some flexible and organic even to the point of vagueness. Some are no doubt better suited to

* However in 1971 the Government were consulting with the interests concerned about alternative possible forms of reorganisation.

their purposes than others. Sometimes public institutions may be
made to work by highly motivated individuals despite inappropriate
organisation. Yet the extent of variation suggests for public administration a conclusion similar to that which Joan Woodward reached
for industry. Organisational forms and structures must vary at least
partly in relation to purpose and function and the application of
completely general principles must be limited. Furthermore variation
of forms and structures can be found not only between but within
particular public bodies. Some parts may be organic, some 'mechanistic'. Sometimes the basic framework may appear to be built on
broadly classical or mechanistic principles, while internally there is
much organic flexibility.

1. J. Ll-J. Edwards, 1951. *The Law Officers of the Crown,* pp. 215,
223–5. Sweet and Maxwell.

2. ibid., p. 390, quoting Sir Theobald Mathew, *The Department of the
Director of Public Prosecutions,* pp. 13–14. 1952. Law Society.

3. (1930) 2 K.B. 364.

4. *Enever v. The King* [*1906*] 3 Commonwealth, L.R., 969.

5. *Report of Royal Commission on the Police* (Sir Henry Willink),
para. 72, pp. 23–6, and para. 76, p. 27.

6. ibid., pp. 26–7, para. 74 citing: 93 H.C. Deb. 5s c 1613 (1917);
314 H.C. Deb. 1625 (1936); 314 H.C. Deb. 1554 (1936) and 586 H.C.
Deb. 5s 1294 (1958).

7. Royal Commission on the Police, para. 89, p. 31.

8. ibid., para. 25, p. 164.

9. ibid., para. 29, p. 165.

10. ibid., para. 230, p. 169–70.

11. Geoffrey Marshall, 1965. *Police and Government: The Status and
Accountability of the English Constable,* p. 72. Methuen; Unwin's paperback
edition 1967.

12. Anthony Thorncroft in 'The Cost of a police dog', *Financial Times,*
12 December 1970. See also J. P. Martin and Gail Wilson, 1969. *The
Police: A Study in Manpower.* Heinemann.

13. W. A. Robson, 1960. *Nationalized Industry and Public Ownership.*
Allen and Unwin (2nd ed. 1962, pp. 138–211, with new long preface).

14. Described and discussed in his book *Socialisation and Transport,*
1933. Constable.

15. See W. A. Robson (Ed.), 1937. *Public Enterprise.* Allen and Unwin.

16. W. A. Robson, 1962. op. cit., pp. 74, 76–7.

17. R. J. S. Baker, op. cit., pp. 19–21, 33–40, 103, 230–2.

18. See valuable discussions of the whole situation in Peter Draper,
Maurice Kogan and J. N. Morris, 1970. *The N.H.S.: Three Views.*
Fabian Society (Research Series no. 287).

19. Arthur J. Willocks, 1967. *The Creation of the NHS*, pp. 111–13. Routledge and Kegan Paul.

20. R. W. Revans, 1964. *Standards for Morale: Cause and Effect in Hospitals*. OUP, for Nuffield Provincial Hospitals Trust.

21. Draper, Kogan and Morris, op. cit., p. 11.

22. HMSO, 1967. See especially pp. 6–10 (paras. 23–41) and 15–18 (paras. 55–67).

23. James A. Stewart, 'Cogwheel: a Physician's view of a local version', *British Medical Journal,* 18 November 1969. pp. 420–32.

24. N. F. Coghill, 15 November 1969. 'Change and Growth in Hospitals', *The Lancet*, pp. 1058–61.

25. Stewart, op. cit., quoting T. D. Hunter in H. Freeman and J. Farndale (Eds.), 1967. *New Aspects of the Mental Health Services*, p. 64. Pergamon.

26. N. F. Coghill, R. W. Revans, F. M. Ulyatt, K. W. Ulyatt, 8 August, 1970. 'A Study of Consultants', *The Lancet*. The major study (now in the press) is R. W. Revans (Ed.), *Changing Hospitals*, vol. 2: *The Hospital Internal Communications Project seen from within*. Tavistock.

27. *Report of Royal Commission on Assizes and Quarter Sessions,* 1969. Cmnd. 4153.

28. ibid., para. 312.

29. ibid., paras. 258, 261, 262.

30. Administration of Justice Act, 1964, secs. 13(a) and 15(1).

CONCLUSIONS:

TOWARDS A THEORY OF

PUBLIC ADMINISTRATION

Recapitulation—the development of administration and of theory

This book does not claim to present a definitive and comprehensive theory of public administration, nor even such a theory of public administration in Britain. A number of books will need to be written by different authors, a number of approaches must be made from different angles, before such a comprehensive theory can be produced. This is only one of the approaches towards this objective.

What I have done is to attempt to summarise the most significant elements in organisation theory as that subject stands today and then look at the salient facts of British public administration in the light of it. I have not so far attempted to arrange the facts to fit the theory, although I have kept noting particular points of relevance. At other points the concrete historical development of public administration, its environment, its functions, its tasks and its processes, has not seemed to correspond very closely, or at all, to any particular organisation theory. I must now try to draw the threads together and see if there is more relevance of fact to theory than we have as yet suggested and how far there are gaps where no general organisation theory accounts adequately for administrative facts.

Organisation theory itself is still developing as society develops, and will certainly continue to evolve. The divergent approaches of the 'classical', 'human relations' and 'systems' schools have not yet been adequately synthesised. In Britain we have had rather less either of abstract thinking or practical research on organisations than in the USA, and the valuable work we have had in recent years, such as that of Burns and Stalker and Woodward has not comprehended the public sector. There are various distinguished exceptions in works which have been cited; but the field is still inadequately covered.

The situation is much better in the USA as regards both organisation
theory in general and its application to the public sector. Yet the
American political environment is so different from the British that
American public administration theory is not at all adequate for the
British situation.

The relevance of classical organisation theory

With all these reservations let us look again at what emerges from
general organisation theory which may be relevant to British public
administration. From the classical school we learn the value of
definitions of function, authority and responsibility, clear lines of
command and control and orderly administrative structures. We
learn to isolate administration as a function in its own right. We
learn to break down this function, like other functions, into its component parts and to distinguish planning from command, as a doctor
distinguishes diagnosis from treatment. All this is important to all
organisations but of special relevance in those public organisations
whose most elemental functions are regulatory, arbitral and legal—
the maintenance of order, the enforcement of rights and obligations.
In describing the historical development of public administration
functions in Britain we saw that those of 'law and order' came first
and next those of providing basic services of information, registration, protection and communication. In all these spheres—legislative,
military, political, police, hygiene control and so on—logical frameworks of authority, orderly bureaucracies were and still are necessary
and relevant. So are the classical concepts of subdivision of function
and delegation of authority. If the original personal authority of a
monarch is to be developed into the impersonal stable authority of a
modern state with a large, varied and relatively sophisticated population, then the extension of that authority must be subdivided and
delegated. Yet if stability is to be maintained the exercise of that
authority must be controlled and kept fundamentally unified and
consistent. Hence the continuing value of classical organisation
theory deriving from Fayol and Weber and expounded by Urwick
and many others.

It has been criticised by such writers as Joan Woodward and
Burns and Stalker for trying to force different kinds of organisation,
with different methods and purposes, into a common pattern. Yet in
the public sector this is one of its merits. In a unitary sovereign state
such as the United Kingdom it is as important that all public institutions should be subject to the overriding authority of a democratic
Parliament and conform to the policies of the elected Government,
as it is that they should have administrative machinery appropriate
to their own peculiar detailed processes. In particular it is important

that all Departments of central government are organised with some basically common patterns, despite all their necessary variations, so as to give consistent service to a group of collectively responsible Ministers. It is therefore good for all public servants, but especially civil servants, to be educated to think in terms of the abstract general notions of authority and responsibility of Fayol and Weber.

The parallel development of organisation theory and public administration

Hence as we start to trace them through from their fundamentals, organisation theory and British public administration have much in common. There is some similarity, too, in the way they develop from these fundamentals. In each we have traced a history of developing complexity and subtlety. Organisation theory of the human relations school looked inside the broad outer frameworks of the classical writers to the human elements and found complex patterns of informal relationships, psychological forces, and involved decision-making processes. Later theory also looked to the interdependence of organisations and their environments and to the fundamental differences of structures according to processes and of processes according to purposes. Vickers and others have shown that organisations do not always exist to pursue the same continuing single or even multiple objectives and that sometimes their most important functions may be those of balancing objectives. From these sorts of ideas, 'systems' theory is building up more complex and sophisticated pictures of organisations. These pictures take more account than the classical writers of the varieties of human material from which organisations are formed, but they also make increasing use of concepts derived from mathematics and the natural sciences. They indeed replace the classical straight-line diagrams with models of a variety of interlocking and interacting systems, always in flux.

When we recapitulate our history of the development of British public administration we also find complexity arising from a diversity of functions—first the law and order or regulative state, then the public utility state, then the Welfare State and finally the contemporary state deeply involved in the great variety of the social and economic developments of the nation and with a complex and science-based defence system. It would make a neat and tidy conclusion to this book to argue that these two historical developments—of organisation theory and of public administration activities—precisely parallel one another and hence that both the students and the practitioners of public administration should now occupy themselves principally with systems theory applied to such sophisticated subjects as economic planning and anti-missile projects.

The divergence of administration and theory

There is much truth in this argument, but it is too simple and too neat. It is not merely that research usually shows the concrete facts of history as providing innumerable exceptions to every grand design. This does not matter when the grand design is basically right. In our example it is only partially right. As an exercise of analysis it is useful to trace ideas and institutions developing from simplicity to complexity. Yet in fact the original simple ideas of organisation theory are not irrelevant to the present complexities of public administration, and the earlier activities of public administration were not so simple that they could be explained sufficiently by the dogmas of the industrialist Fayol or the abstract generalisations of Weber. Moreover, the original basic functions of public administration—the basic social controls, relations with foreign powers, taxation and registration—have not been superseded, but only supplemented, by the innovations of the present century. A more fundamental consideration still is that British public administration has, since the days of Elizabeth I, or earlier, always had a character of complexity and subtlety, not so often found in business management and certainly not adequately catered for in organisation theory, at least until Barnard.

The integrative function

Public administration, whether in our modern parliamentary democracy or under the Tudor and subsequent oligarchies, has always been concerned with the balancing of interests and the synthesis of conflicting ideas, as well as with the exercise of authority. We have the tasks of conciliation, the production of policy from situations of conflict, the processes of creative secretaryship, various types of discussion process and the processes of producing of documents to deal with a variety of existing and only partially foreseen future situations. All these situations and others I have described or hinted at arise early in the history of the British State and many other states, but they also continue and multiply in number and complexity with the increasing complexity of our society. Classical organisation theory is inadequate to deal with them and the public administrator is well advised to turn to Barnard, Simon or Vickers for guidance.

It is true, however, that the administrative integration of very large organisations with a variety of contrasting components is relatively modern. The public sector had to deal with it earliest in practice; but it is in relation to the private sector that most systematic thought has probably been devoted to it so far. Likert, Lawrence and Lorsch, Burns and Stalker, Joan Woodward, Vickers, Miller and Rice have all approached it from their different angles; but it clearly needs much further investigation and creative thinking. The systems theorists can help, especially those who draw their analogies from the natural sciences rather than engineering. Administration in a democratic society is not simply a matter of obtaining, digesting and communicating information and exercising authority. It is an organic and creative as well as a mechanical process. It derives from the humanities as well as the sciences.

Balance and stability

One might almost say that coordination, integration, reconciliation, and the production of creative ideas out of conflict are the very fundamentals of public administration, yet creativity, freedom and material growth require, in any human organisation, or natural organism, an environment of some stability and order. We have referred in discussing systems theory to the biological concept of homeostasis—a living organism's self-regulatory mechanism for maintaining some kind of internal stability, such as body temperature.

Basic internal stability in an organism is a precondition of creative activity, as Dr Grey Walter argues in his account of the evolution of nervous systems. He quotes the physiologist Claude Bernard—'*La fixité de milieu interieur est la condition de la vie libre*'—and Sir Joseph Barcroft, describing the importance of homeostasis: 'How often have I watched the ripples on the surface of a still lake made by a passing boat, noted their regularity and admired the patterns formed when two such ripple-systems meet . . . *but the lake must be perfectly calm* . . . to look for high intellectual development in a milieu whose properties have not become established is to seek . . . ripple patterns on the surface of the stormy Atlantic.'[1] This might be taken as a reasonable analogy for any form of institution whose members have sufficient security of tenure and mutual confidence in one another and the institution itself to be able to think and act creatively, to produce ideas and discuss them freely with their colleagues, knowing that even if they are not eventually accepted they will not get into trouble simply through having ideas, nor feel they are giving away secrets to competitors ready to stab them in the back.

Yet neither the biological homeostasis analogy, nor Vickers' engineering control analogy, is sufficient to explain the maintenance of essential stability in organisations, especially public organisations. One does not have to be a biologist to understand that a human being needs not only a nervous system but a bone structure. One does not have to be an engineer to know that a ship needs not only navigation instruments and steering gear but a hull. Anyone discussing how public bodies are set up, kept together and kept working effectively, can much be helped by these biological and engineering control analogies; but he will also need to consider formal structures and legal constitutions. Although one outstanding feature of the House of Commons is its unspoken understandings, compromises and friendly traditions—the 'sense of the House'—they all function within a firm framework of accepted law, the unquestioned authority of the Speaker, a whole series of rules of great rigidity, and the symbolism of formalised ritual. In any effective organisation there must be elements of stability as well as adaptibility. The subtleties of systems theory need a great deal of development and exposition, and there is much work to be done in applying them to various aspects of organisation theory and to the forms and processes of organisation —both public and private. But common sense will insist that in all this we cannot afford to neglect the simpler and more obvious realities of formal structures and elementary guide lines of classical organisation theory, while avoiding its excesses.

The framework of society

Without some framework there is self-frustrating, self-destructive formless chaos. Biological analogies are misleadingly inadequate unless we remember that the most highly developed organisms are vertebrates, not soft jelly-fish. They have rigid bone structures containing, supporting and protecting their subtle and flexible nervous systems. Great men as well as sycophants, often with recent experience of political anarchy, have extolled the virtues of authority in government—the Roman Empire, the Tudors, Napoleon and so on. Shakespeare is perhaps the supreme example of this, notably when he took a story from ancient Greece to illustrate the problems of his own and the preceding century. The following is an extract from Ulysses' famous speech in *Troilus and Cressida* (I.ii), attributing the success of the Trojans to the anarchy in the higher command of the Greek confederation:

> Take but degree away, untune that string,
> And hark what discord follows: each thing meets
> In mere oppugnancy. The bounded waters,
> Should lift their bosoms higher than the shores,
> And make a sop of all this solid Globe:
> Strength should be Lord of imbecility,
> And the rude son should strike his father dead:
> Force should be right, or rather, right and wrong,
> (Between whose endless jar, justice resides)
> Should lose their names, and so should justice too.
> Then every thing includes itself in power,

Power into will, will into appetite,
And appetite (an universal wolf,
So doubly seconded with will, and power)
Must make perforce an universal prey,
And last, eat up himself.
Great Agamemnon:
This chaos, when degree is suffocate,
Follows the choking.

Shakespeare is here, as implicitly in nearly all his plays, the philosopher and propagandist of the Tudor régime, extolling a specifically
hierarchical, élitist society. The above passage, however, is of wider
application and expresses the case for almost any ordered political,
social and administrative framework—holding it up as the only
alternative to self-destructive chaos. Parallels and analogies could
probably be produced from biological systems where self-destructive
chaos might follow the disturbance of the various internal balances.

Yet arguments for ordered administrative frameworks and balance
and symmetry are not the same as arguments for authoritarianism
and repression. They can so easily be so distorted. There is a danger
in applying very inexact historical and biological analogies to present-day administrative and Government systems and in this danger
we may need the help of the psychologists. Some of us can easily be
attracted to authoritarian systems by weaknesses in our own personalities, just as others of us, for similar reasons, may develop biases
against nearly all forms of organisation as repressive. The concept
of admittedly necessary social controls being crudely repressive of the
individual personality is essentially Freudian, and the layman is left
with the impression that there must be some flaw or weakness in what
often seems an extraordinary pessimism in Freudian ideas on this
subject. Possibly a clue to the escape from this pessimism may be
found in the ideas of Herbert Marcuse, often regarded as an extreme
advocate of permissiveness and even anarchism. Marcuse uses the
phrase 'surplus repression', thereby implying that while much social
repression is unnecessary and neurotic, there are some kinds which
are legitimate and healthy. He argues:

Mature civilization depends for its functioning on a multitude of coordinated arrangements. These arrangements in turn must carry recognized
and recognizable authority. Hierarchical relationships are not unfree *per
se*: civilization relies to a greater extent on rational authority, based on
knowledge and necessity, and aiming at the protection and preservation
of life. Such is the authority of the engineer, of the traffic policeman, of
the airplane pilot in flight. Once again, the distinction between repression
and surplus-repression must be recalled. If a child feels the 'need' to

cross the street any time at its will, repression of this 'need' is not repressive of human potentialities. It may be the opposite.[2]

It is not, however, easy for the reader who is not both a philosopher and psychologist to follow where Marcuse's rather obscure argument leads on from this point.

In such a book as this we need not make the attempt; but merely note that in any human organisation there are not only legitimate utilitarian arguments for an element of authority and an element of freedom, but also strong psychological forces likely to operate in and among many of the people concerned (both inside and outside the organisation) to press either of these arguments to excess. Most of those of us who live and work within large organisations are bound to become somewhat mixed-up—or as the psychologists say, ambivalent—about the whole business.

The engineering of cooperation

Yet this is not the end. We need not leave this philosophical basis of public administration in an insoluble dilemma. I have noted the need for order and form, the value of institutions, structures, rules and even rituals. I have emphasised the need for both internal balance (homeostasis) and for enclosing frameworks, and paid full tribute to the authoritarian side of public administration. In the end, however, public administration is not only a process of order, certainly not only, or mainly, of the imposition of authority. It is profoundly, essentially and basically concerned with integration, and indeed interaction, never resulting in complete reconciliation, though always tending towards it—reconciliation of a rich diversity of forces and groups and ideas and the varied and multi-coloured pattern of society. In this, one of the most supremely important of human activities, the public administrator should have a crucial, but subservient role. Public administration is not the same as management. Its most important element is not the exercise of authority—even delegated authority. It is the engineering of cooperation—and indeed of coexistence. The ideal motto of the administrator might be a free translation—but perhaps a more accurate one than the traditional—of a famous saying: 'Happy are those who are cooperative with others, for thereby will they be able to realize the full potential of the natural resources of this Earth.'[3]

The diffusion of administration

This will not satisfy all those to whom 'administration' means something dull, negative, lifeless, frustrating and restrictive. These include many sensitive people—some of them artists and some of them scientists, who still try, in this complex interdependent world, to be individualists (and among them many doctors, who must be both scientists and artists, often provide outstanding examples). It may be doubted, however, if they include the less articulate mass of the general population. Ordinary people who are constantly complaining about the way 'they' influence and frustrate their lives, are not really asking that 'they' should do nothing, or that no one should try to organise anything. It is rather that 'they' cannot organise things properly: 'we' could organise it better ourselves. Something ought to be done about it. No doubt some things ought to be stopped, but other things ought to be started. These are the kinds of phrases which millions of ordinary people are using about administrators.

The kind of good administration which the less articulate mass of the population subconsciously have in mind is a matter of practical, constructive, tidy-minded commonsense. It is a matter of eliciting loyalty and organising cooperation. It is a misconception to treat administration as something which can be sold to the individualists as a very rarefied art or as a very abstruse science. Administration can never be accepted by individualists as long as they remain such, because it is in its very essence the opposite of individualism. It has elements of both art and science; but the best administration is essentially something which large numbers of people can and must grasp and be involved in. Otherwise the life goes out of it and it becomes sterile and life-hating—bureaucracy. It is a short step from Weber to Ludendorff and from Ludendorff to Hitler. But Weber was right in a great deal of what he said about the systematic, fair and orderly breaking down of large-scale activity into its component elements, the delegation of duties and functions, and the equitable treatment of like cases in a like manner. Administration truly conceived can never be a matter simply for Fayol's *grand chefs*. Such ideas have repeatedly been tried both in theory and practice in France and always in the end the best French minds and great masses of the French people have rejected them. René Clair's film *A Nous la liberté* was the eventual French answer to Fayol, as Chaplin's film *Modern Times* was the American answer to F. W. Taylor. Nevertheless Fayol was right in saying administration at any level and in any sphere involves foresight, planning, organisation, direction and monitoring. It is not a matter solely for the organisation men of the great American corporations. Yet practical Americans like Taylor and Drucker were right in saying that it involves looking systematically at the job to be done and concentrating on essentials.* In Britain it should not only be a matter for élitists, whether the old

* These last three words probably sum up the essential wisdom in all Drucker's voluminous pages.

Administrative Class or more modern cliques of economists and technologists. Yet it is a matter of systematic planning and cooperation—as both these exalted people and also many small town councillors, postmasters, secretaries of voluntary societies and other such people have repeatedly demonstrated. It is above all something everyone should try to understand as they have to understand reading, writing and arithmetic. The protesters and demonstrators who—very understandably—fear the dehumanising influence of large organisations ought not to be trying to destroy administration. Administration needs not to be destroyed, but to be diffused.

Summing-up: organic flexibility within a framework of order

The day-to-day concrete realities of administration are so complex that a writer whose approach to the subject has started with experience and only moved slowly into theory is tempted to leave the subject on this note of the diffuse and indefinite. It is not true, however, that as we draw away from our subject, no clear pattern emerges in the perspective view—as we defined theory originally.* There is a general pattern embracing the immense variety of particular patterns.

Any public administration system, and especially that of the United Kingdom, must operate within a firm framework of law, with rights, functions and duties defined and all lines of authority and responsibility, however long or indefinite, leading to and from a sovereign body—in our case Parliament. This framework right down to its detailed application within public bodies, closely accords with the principles of classical organisation theory. It is however only the framework, the skeleton, not the whole body; the hull of the ship not the engine, the rudder or the navigating equipment. Within this total national framework, and within the particular frameworks of particular public institutions, and indeed individual local offices, there is always a much less rigid complex of human relationships of individuals and groups. Creative ideas, adaptations to changing conditions, motivations to work depend on these interactions between people, work and environment. To try to understand these conditions and relationships, however, even human relations theory is not a sufficient guide. We need that of Vickers and the 'Systems Theorists', who think in terms of interaction between 'inputs', 'outputs' and environment, of control and information systems, who try to make ordered pictures of these complex relationships while taking into account that all the elements and the systems themselves are in a constant state of flux.

We must also note that different parts of these theories are relevant to different kinds of public administration. We have considered those

* See p.14.

functions of a routine or regulatory kind and also the managerial functions for providing standard public services. To both these kinds of function classical theory is particularly relevant. By contrast, in the various adaptive/creative, conciliatory, liaison, compromising, policy-making, planning functions, an 'organic' flexible informal pattern of organisation is wanted. However, in much public administration in the first two categories there is, as we have seen, some adaptive and often creative element. On the other hand even in the third category, creativity and adaptability can only function within a firm basis, or within a firm framework of order. Flexible 'organic' systems within an ordered 'classical' frame seem therefore to be the abiding patterns of public administration—the overall view of theory we end up with as we leave our subject.

1. W. Grey Walter, 1953. *The Living Brain*. Pelican ed. p. 41.

2. Herbert Marcuse, 1955. *Eros and Civilisation*. Beacon Press, USA. (British edition, 1969, Sphere Books, p. 180).

3. Matthew v. 5. See Stanley C. Evans, 1965. *The Social Hope of the Christian Church*, p. 47. Hodder and Stoughton.

SELECT READING LIST

The following list of works has been selected as likely to be useful to students wishing to pursue further some of the topics raised in this book. It does not purport to cover all aspects of organisation theory, or British public administration.

The books marked 'A' may be easier to read and, therefore, best for a student to start with, either owing to their length, their style, or their subject-matter, in comparison with those marked 'B'. However, the distinction is not made with any suggestion as to the quality of the writings or of the ideas in the books concerned. Those marked 'X' are of outstanding importance and are recommended to the serious student despite the fact that some of them may not be easy reading. The list is not confined to literature cited in the text, and it does not include all the works so cited.

Particular attention should be paid to the dates of the less recent publications and of the particular editions cited, and due allowance made for subsequent changes in organisation or environment since the books were written or revised.

PART I
GENERAL THEORIES OF ORGANISATION

Chapter 1: Classical organisation theory

B   Brecht, E. F. L., 1957. *Organization: The framework of Management*. Longmans.

B X Fayol, H., 1962 ed. *Administration, Industrielle et Génèrale*. Dunod, Paris.

A   Fayol, H., 1949. *General and Industrial Management* (Trans. Constance Storrs). Pitman.

B X Gerth, H. H., and Wright Mills, C. (Trans. and Eds.), 1948. *From Max Weber*. Routledge and Kegan Paul.

A   Urwick, L. F., 1943. *The Elements of Administration*. Pitman.

Chapter 2: Human relations and related theories

B   Argyris, C., 1957. *Personality and Organisation*. Harper and Row.
B   X   Barnard, C., 1938. *The Functions of the Executive*. Harvard University Press.
A   X   Likert, R., 1961. *New Patterns of Management*. McGraw–Hill.
A   Mayo, E., 1949. *Social Problems of an Industrial Civilization*. Routledge and Kegan Paul.
A   X   McGregor, D., 1960. *The Human Side of Enterprise*. McGraw–Hill.
A   X   Simon, H., 1957 (2nd ed.). *Administrative Behaviour*. Collier–Macmillan.

Chapter 3: Organic and systems theory

B   X   Burns, T., and Stalker, G. H., 1961. *The Management of Innovation*. Tavistock.
B   Child, J., 1969. *British Management Thought*. Allen and Unwin.
B   Emery, F. E. (Ed.), 1969. *Systems Thinking*. Penguin.
B   Lawrence, P. R., and Lorsch, J. W., 1967. *Organisation and Environment*. Harvard University Press.
B   Miller, E. J., and Rice, A. K., 1967. *Systems of Organisation*. Tavistock.
B   X   Vickers, Sir Geoffrey, 1965. *The Art of Judgement*. Chapman and Hall.
B   Woodward, Joan, 1965. *Industrial Organisation Theory and Practice*. O.U.P.

PART II
PUBLIC ADMINISTRATION IN BRITAIN

(The literature cited below is relevant to Part II generally, and is arranged in functional groupings.)

(a) *General*

A   X   Bray, J., 1970. *Decision in Government*. Gollancz.
B   Chapman, Richard A., and Dunsire, H. (Eds.), 1971. *Style in Administration: Readings in British Public Administration*. Allen and Unwin.
B   Chester, D. N., (Ed.), and Wilson, F. R. G., 1958. (2nd ed.)˙ *The Organisation of British Central Government 1914–1956*. Allen and Unwin.
B   Coombes, D., 1966. *The Member of Parliament and the Administration: the Case of the Select Committee on the Nationalised Industries*. Allen and Unwin.
A   Cross, J. H., 1970. *British Public Administration*. Universal Tutorial Press Ltd.

B X Griffith, J. A. G., 1966. *Central Departments and Local Authorities.*
       Allen and Unwin.
A   Hanson, A. H., and Walles, Malcolm, 1970. *Governing Britain: A
        Guide to Political Institutions.* Fontana.
A   Morrison, H., 1954. *Government and Parliament.* O.U.P.
B   Pariss, H. M., 1969. *Constitutional Bureaucracy.* Allen and Unwin.
A   Popham, G. T., 1969. *Government in Britain.* Pergamon.
B X Robson, W. A., 1951 (3rd ed.). *Justice and Administrative Law.*
        Stevens.
B   Stankiewicz, W. J. (Ed.), 1967. *Crisis in British Government: The
        Need for Reform.* Collier–Macmillan.
A X Wheare, Sir Kenneth, 1955. *Government by Committee.* O.U.P.
        The New Whitehall Series (generally by past or present Permanent
        Heads of Departments), Allen and Unwin. Especially:
B   Bridges, Lord, 1964. *The Treasury.*
B   Crombie, Sir James, 1962. *H.M. Customs and Excise.*
B   Sharp (Baroness), Evelyn, 1969. *The Ministry of Housing and
          Local Government.*

                        (b) *The Civil Service*

A X Bridges, Lord, 1950. *Portrait of a Profession.* C.U.P.
B X Brown, R. G. S., 1970. *The Administrative Process in Britain.*
        Methuen.
A   Critchley, T. A., 1951. *The Civil Service To-day.* Gollancz.
B   Dale, H. E., 1941. *The Higher Civil Service of Great Britain.* O.U.P.
B   Fry, H. K., 1969. *Statesmen in Disguise: The Changing Role of the
        Administrative Class in the British Home Civil Service 1953–66.*
        Macmillan.
A X Robson, W. A. (Ed.), 1950. *The Civil Service in Britain and France.*
        Hogarth.

                        (c) *The Health Service*

B   Lindsey, A., 1962. *Socialized Medicine in England and Wales.*
        University of North Carolina Press (London, O.U.P.).
B   Spencer, J. A., 1967. *Management in Hospitals.* Faber.
A   Willocks, A. J., 1967. *The Creation of the National Health Service.*
        Routledge and Kegan Paul.

                        (d) *Nationalised Industries*

B   Hanson, A. H. (Ed.), 1963. *Nationalisation: A Book of Readings.*
        Allen and Unwin.
A X Robson, W. A., 1962 (2nd ed.). *Nationalized Industries and Public
        Ownership.* Allen and Unwin.
B   Shanks, M. (Ed.), 1963. *Lessons of Public Enterprise.* Cape.

(e) *Local Government*

B   Headrick, T. E., 1962. *The Town Clerk in English Local Government.* Allen and Unwin.

B   Jackson, W. Eric, 1966 (5th ed.). *Structure of Local Government in England and Wales.* Macmillan.

B   Marshall, A. H., 1966. *The Financial Administration of Local Government.* Allen and Unwin.

A   Richards, Peter S., 1970 (2nd ed.). *The New Local Government System.* Allen and Unwin.

A   Robson, W. A., 1968 (2nd ed.). *Local Government in Crisis.* Allen and Unwin.

(f) *Police*

B   Marshall, G., 1965. *Police and Government.* Methuen.

B   Martin, J. P., and Wilson, G., 1969. *The Police: A Study in Manpower.* Heinemann.

British Public Reports

A X *Report of the Machinery of Government Committee* (Lord Haldane), 1918. Cd. 9230.

A X *Report of the Committee on the Civil Service 1966–68* (Lord Fulton). Cmnd. 3638.

B   *Report of Royal Commission on Assizes and Quarter Sessions* (Lord Beeching), 1969. Cd. 4153.

B   Ministry of Housing and Local Government: *Report of Committee on Management in Local Government* (Sir John Maud, now Lord Redcliff-Maud), 1967.

B   Ministry of Housing and Local Government: *Report of Committee on Staffing of Local Government* (Sir George Mallaby), 1969.

B   *Report of Royal Commission on Local Government in England 1966–69* (Lord Redcliff-Maud). Cmnd. 4040.

A X House of Commons: *Report on the Select Committee on Nationalised Industries (Ministerial Control of the Nationalised Industries),* 1968. HC 371–I.

B   Also Reports of Select Committees on particular industries, notably: Coal (1958); Gas (1961); Electricity Supply (1963); London Transport (1965); The Post Office (1967); Bank of England (1970).

A   National Coal Board: *Report of the Advisory Committee on Organisation.* (Dr—later Lord—Fleck), 1955.

A   People and Planning: *Report of the Committee on Public Participation in Planning* (Chairman: Arthur S. Skeffington), HMSO. 1969.

Two recent Government Policy Papers

A   *Local Government in England: Government Proposals for Reorgani-*
     sation, February 1971. Cmnd. 4584.
A   Department of Health and Social Security: *National Health Service*
     Reorganisation: Consultative Document, May 1971.

INDEX

ACTS OF PARLIAMENT, 135, 136–7
Adaptive/creative functions of
  government, 144–5, 149
'Administration', definition of, 12–14
Administrative Behaviour, 49–53
Administrative Class of Civil Service,
  99, 108–9, 117, 136, 147
Admiralty, 159
Advisory Committees, 106–7
Agriculture, Ministry of, 162
Air Council, 159
Albrow, Martin, 40
America USA:
  classical organisation theory in,
    30, 185–6
  industrial environment, 28, 43, 44,
    48
  legal tradition, 22, 37
  public administration and
    Government, 54–5, 81, 84
Anomie, 45
Argyris, Chris, 55–6, 58, 61
Army Council, 159, 161
Art of Judgment, The, 69–72
Atomic Energy Authority, 89, 173
Attorney General, 167
Audit, 94–5, 101
Authority:
  Brown and Jaques on, 60–1
  classical doctrine, 76, 186
  Fayol on, 24–8
  in mechanistic organisations, 65
  in public administration, 75, 76,
    143, 144, 146, 147, 166 seq.,
    178, 179, 181, 186, 192
  line and staff, 32–3
  Marcuse on, 191
  military, 32, 38–9
  Roman concept of, 21, 31

Simon on, 52
Weber on, 36

BALANCING, FUNCTION OF
  ADMINISTRATION, 17, 71, 76,
  88–90, 189–90
Balchin, Nigel, 83
Baldwin, Stanley (Lord), 171
Barcroft, Sir Joseph, 189
Barnard, Chester, 47–8, 49, 55, 105,
  188
Barnett, Charles, 111
BBC, 171, 173
Beeching, Lord, 132, 180–1
Beer, Stafford, 73
Behavioural Scientists, 55 seq.
Bernard, Claude, 15, 189
Beveridge, Sir William (Lord), *Report
  on Social Insurance*, 103
Biological analogies of organisations,
  26, 30–1, 42, 66, 73, 189, 190,
  191
Bismarck, 35
Bray, Dr Jeremy, 134
Brecht, E. F. L., 40, 60
Bridges, Sir Edward (Lord), 108, 118,
  154
British Airports Authority, 173
British Steel Corporation, 175
British Transport Commission, 175
Brodie, M. B., 10, 39
Brown, R. G. S., 118–19, 163–4
Brown, Wilfred (Lord Brown of
  Machrihanish), 60–1
Buchanan, Prof. Sir Colin, 124
Bureaucracy, 34–8, 40, 188
Burnham, James, 38
Burns, Tom, 29, 41, 49, 50, 64–6,
  68–72, 111, 149, 159, 160, 186, 188

Butler, R. A. (Lord), Education Act 1944, 103

CABINET, 85, 107, 108, 161
Cabinet office, 121
Capital development, 123, 174–5
Cecil, William, Lord Burleigh, 120, 128–9
Central Economic Planning Staff, 121
Central Electricity Board, 171, 172, 174
Central Electricity Generating Board, 175
Chairmen, role in meetings, 139
Chairmen of Committees and Royal Commissions, 101–2
Child, J., 198
Churches, 21, 22, 49
Circuit Administrators, 181
Civil Service, 38, 55, 83–4, 99, 100, 108–11
 grading systems and unions, 114–15
 morale and motivation in, 117–19
 personnel management in, 112–19
 recruitment, 117
 relations with Ministers, 133–5, 158–60
 security, employment and motivation, 115–17
 structure, 151–60
 writing by, 137–9
Civil Service Commission, 113, 117
Civil Service Department, 109, 113–17
Classical organisation theory, 16–17, 21–40, 43, 49, 51–2, 54, 56, 75, 76, 88, 146, 186, 188, 194–5
Clerical Class of Civil Service, 99, 151
Clerks of Courts, 181
Coal Board, *see* National Coal Board
Coal industry, 115
Coal Industry Nationalisation Act 1946, 137
Coghill, Dr N. F., 10, 179–80
'Cogwheel' Report, 177–9
Commission for Industrial Relations, 166
Commissions, Royal, 100–3, 129, 163
 on Assizes (Beeching) 1969, 180–1
 on Police (Willink) 1962, 168–9
Committees:
 Advisory, 106–7
 examples of form and structure, 141–2
 for research, 124
 Hospital Management, 176, 178
 in hospitals, 176, 178–9
 Local Government, 146, 147
 medical, in hospitals, 176, 177–9
 of enquiry, 100–3

of magistrates, 181
on Machinery of Government (Haldane) 1918, 120–1, 160–3
on Staffing of Local Government (Mallaby) 1966, 135
Parliamentary, 102, 146, 173
Public Accounts, 95
various functions of, 108
Wheare on, 107–8
Common Law, English, 22
Communication, 48, 52
Comptroller and Auditor General, 95
Conciliation functions of Government, 88–90
Conseil d'Etat, 95
Control systems, 72, 130–1
 by audit, 94–5
 by democratic process, 93–4, 97–8, 134–6
 by Ministers, 93–4, 131–4
 by the Ombudsman, 95–6
 Fayol's concept of, 24–5
 Judicial, 92–3
 of Local by Central Government, 96–9
Cooper (Lord), *Report on Hydro-Electric Development in Scotland* 1942, 103
Corporations:
 chartered, 93
 general, 170–1
 private, 67
 public, 85–6, 171–5
Correspondence, official and semi-official, 108, 138–9
Cost-benefit analysis, 71, 102–3
Courts Act 1971, 181
Courts of law:
 administration of, 180–1
 control of Government, 92–3
 delegation of discretion to, 135
 interpretation of statutes, 137
Crown, the, as legal entity, 92, 93
Cybernetics, 47, 73

DALE, H. E., 105–6, 108–9, 118, 151
Decision-making, 50–1, 64, 70–2, 99–103, 135, 139–40
Defence Departments, 157
Delegation, 93–4, 130–6, 146–7, 150
Devlin, Patrick (Lord), 135, 169
Diplomatic relations, 84, 104
Director of Public Prosecutions, 167
Discipline in Civil Service, 116
Disputes, resolution of, 98–9
District auditors, 95
Doctors, 176–80, 193
Domesday Book, 120
Drucker, Peter, 193
Durkheim, Emile, 45–6

ECONOMIC ADVISORS:
   general, 159
   to the Home Office, 170
Economic planning, 86–8, 119, 121
Edelman, Murray, 104–5
Education, Ministry of, 160
Edwards, Prof. J. ll. J., 167
Electricity Boards, 115, 171, 172,
   174–5
Electronics industry, 64, 66
Elizabeth I, Queen, 89, 129, 188
Emet, Dorothy, 42
Employment Exchanges, 114
Engineering analogies of organisation,
   26, 30–1, 66, 72
Environment:
   American, 55
   British, political and social, 81–2
   Ministry of, 90, 105, 110
Etzioni, A., 71
Executive Class of Civil Service, 151,
   152
Experts, *see* Specialists

FAITH, ELEMENT IN PLANNING,
   124
Fascists, 168
Fatigue, 45
Fayol, Henri, 22, 23–7, 28, 29, 30, 46,
   47, 48, 50, 72, 74, 119, 186, 187,
   188, 193
Feedback, 53, 72, 74
Finance, 81, 95, 113
Fisher, Sir Warren, 113
Fisher v. Oldham Corporation (1930),
   168
Fleck, Lord, Report on National
   Coal Board, 173
Follet, Mary Parker, 30, 43–4, 73
Forecasting and planning, 119–26
Foreign and Commonwealth Office,
   104, 105
Forestry Commission, 12
Formal organisation, 142
Forms of organisations:
   consultative bodies, etc., 165–6
   Government Departments, 141–63
   Health Service, 175–80
   Law Courts, 180–2
   Nationalised industries, 170, 173–5
   Police, 167–70
France, 22, 26, 193
Freud, Sigmund, and Freudian ideas,
   45, 53, 100, 191
Fry, Dr G. K., 84–5
Fulton (Lord), Committee Report on
   Civil Service 1968, 68, 76, 84–5
Functional foremanship, management,
   F. W. Taylor on, 28–9
Functions of the Executive, The, 48

GAS BOARDS, 115
Gellerman, Saul, 58, 59
General Motors, 30
Generalists, 68, 70, 152–6, 157, 158
Gestalt psychology, 43
Glacier Metal Co., 60
Golembrewski, Robert T., 60
Goodhart, Dr A. L., 168–9
Government Departments, 30, 55, 65,
   66, 74
   correspondence, 138–9
   distribution of functions between,
      160–3, 186–7
   internal organisation, 148–60
   legal status and audit of, 92–3, 95,
      171
   liaison and co-ordination, 103–11
   main types of function, 81, 82, 83
   meetings, 140
   Ombudsman, and local
      authorities, 89, 96–8
   personnel management, 112–19
   research and planning, 120–1, 123,
      126
   resolution of disputes, 98
Graicunas, 33, 49
Griffiths, Prof. J. A. G., 96–8
Guardian, The, 87
Gulick, Luther, 30, 39, 40, 54

HALDANE, LORD, COMMITTEE
   ON MACHINERY OF GOVERN-
   MENT, 27, 120–1, 160–4
Hallbwachs, 45
Hamilton, General Sir Ian, 33
Hanson, Prof. A. H., 106
Harris, Sir William, 10, 158
Harvard University and Business
   School, 42, 43, 44, 47
Hawthorne researches, 44, 45, 46, 47
Head of the Civil Service, 113, 114
Health, Ministry of, 176
Herbert, Sir Edwin, Report on
   Electricity Supply, 173
Hertzberg, 58–9, 61, 98
Highways Department, 158, 160
Hitler, Adolf, 14, 168, 193
Home Office, Economic Adviser, 170
Home Secretary, 168, 169
Homeostasis, 45, 74, 189, 192
Hospital Boards, Regional, 176, 178
Hospital Management Committees,
   176, 178
House of Commons, 143, 144; *see also*
   Parliament
*Human Problems of an Industrial
   Civilization*, 44
Human relations theory, 42–63, 146,
   187
Hunter, Dr T. D., 180

ICI, 87
'Independent' authorities, 166–70
Industrial Reorganisation Commission, 160
'Informal organisation', 44, 47, 48, 63, 142, 143, 144
Inspectors, 97, 114, 157
  of constabulary, 160
  of schools, 97
Integration within organisations, 67–8, 188
Intelligence and Research, Haldane's proposed Department of, 121
'Interaction/influence groups', 57–8

JACKSON, PRESIDENT ANDREW, 54, 55
Jaques, Prof. Elliott, 60–1
Johnson, Nevil, 162
Judges, 167, 181
Judicial functions, 92–3
Jurisprudence, 48–9

KAHN, ROBERT N., 150
Kalmus, H., 76 n
Katz, Daniel, 150
Kelly, Joe, 63
Keynes, J. M. (Lord), 43, 150
Kogan, Prof. Maurice, 10, 175, 177

LABOUR, DIVISION OF, 25, 45
Law, 48–9, 88, 194
  American, 22
  English, 22, 37, 92–3
  Roman, 21–2, 37
  Scottish, 92–3
Law and order, 54, 84–5, 146, 181
Law courts, administration of, 180–1
Lawrence, Paul R., 67–8, 70, 73, 107, 110, 175
Leadership, 24, 30, 35, 43–4, 46, 47, 56–7, 60, 130–6, 139, 158–9, 179
Legislation, 88, 135, 136–7
Lever, Harold, 87
Liaison:
  between Government and outside interests, 103–7
  within Government, 107–11
Likert, Rensis, 57–8, 60, 66, 73, 75, 90, 149, 174, 188
Line-and-staff doctrine, 30, 31–3, 60, 69, 114, 159, 160
Lloyd, Selwyn, 86
Local Authorities, councils, Local Government, 12, 14, 100
  American, 49, 55
  audit, 95
  delegation in, 135
  history, 82

relations with central government, 81–2, 96–8
service providing function, 85, 89, 90, 181
Local offices of central Government, 150
London Passenger Transport Board, 70, 171, 174
Lord Chancellor, 181
Lords, as Chairmen of Committees and Commissions, 102
Lorsch, J. W., 67–8, 70, 73, 107, 110, 175
Ludendorff, General, 35, 193

MCCARDIE, MR JUSTICE, 168
McGregor, Douglas, 55, 56–7, 58, 60, 65
McKenzie, Prof. J. M., 49, 82
Magistrates' courts, 181
Mallaby Committee, 135
Management, by Objectives ('MBO'), 71
Management, definitions of, 12, 13, 28
Management by exception, 29–30
Management of Innovation, The, 64–6
Managerial Revolution, The, 138
Marcuse, Herbert, 191–2
Marshall, Geoffrey, 169
Marx, Karl, 100
Maslow, A. H., 58
Matthew, Sir Theobald, 182
Mayo, Elton, 42, 44–6, 47, 48, 55, 73, 75
'Mechanistic' organisation, 16, 25, 64–6, 144, 149
Medawar, Sir Peter, 14–15
Medical Research Council, 70
Meetings, 139–40
Merrett, Prof. A. J., 59
Metropolitan Police Commissioner, 168
Military staff organisation, 31–3
Mill, J. S., 34
Miller, E. J., 73, 74, 188
Mills, C. Wright, 35, 40
Ministers, 13, 14, 24, 26, 36, 38, 82, 83, 84, 85, 87, 101, 103, 128, 146, 151, 154, 157
  access of specialists to, 158
  and Civil Service, 114
  and delegation, 131–6
  and National Health Service, 176
  and nationalised industries, 172, 173
  control by, 93–4
  coordination by, 153
  Fayol on, 24, 26, 27
  in 'Neddy', 165
  liaison with outside bodies, 106
  responsibility of, 107–8, 187

Monarchs, 85, 89, 91, 128–9
Monopolies Commission, 87
Montgomery, Lord, 132
Mooney, James, 30, 37, 48
Morris, Prof. J. F., 10, 99
Morrison, Herbert (Lord), 133, 171, 173
Motivation, 44, 48, 53, 58–9
Myers, C. S., 45

NATIONAL COAL BOARD, 70, 89, 137
National Economic Development Council ('Neddy'), 12, 86, 105, 165–6
National Health Service, 89, 175–80
National Institute of Industrial Psychology, 45
National Research and Development Corporation, 89
Nationalised industries, 12, 70, 85, 89, 95, 115, 146–7, 170–5
    select Committee on, 173
Nazis, 168
New Deal, 49
New Oxford Dictionary, 12, 34
New York Institute of Public Administration, 30
Newcomen, Thomas, 60
Nelson, J. R., 40
North of Scotland Hydro-Electric Board, 175
Northcote-Trevelyan Report, 101
Northern Ireland, 81, 82

OBJECTIVES, 70–1
Ombudsman, 95–6
'Optimising' function, 17, 71, 76, 88, 99
'Organic' management and organisation, 16, 25, 26, 64–72, 144, 149, 180, 195
Organisation Man, The, 44
Organisms, 30, 42, 43, 45

PARLIAMENT, 38, 81, 83, 84, 100, 107, 123, 142–4, 146, 167
    attitude to nationalised industries 170, 172
    committees, 95, 102
    control by, 93
    delegation by, 131, 135
    questions, 135, 150
    sovereignty, 86, 96
Parliamentary Commissioner for Administration ('Ombudsman'), 95–6
Parliamentary Counsel, 136, 162
Parsons, Talcott, 71
Paternalism, 40

Permanent Head of Government Departments, Permanent Secretaries, 88, 95, 97, 113, 114, 115, 129, 130, 133, 134, 136, 159, 241
Personnel management, 112–19
    morale and motivation, 117–19
    recruitment, 117, 160
    security of employment, 115–17
Philosophy, 42–3
Piaget, 45
Planning and forecasting, 24, 86, 119–26
Police, 89, 90–1, 147, 167–70
Police Act 1964, 169
'Policy', definition of, 13–14
Politics, definition of, 12–13
Post Office, 9, 22, 27, 112, 114, 120, 159, 173
    French ('P.T.T.'), 27
Postmaster General, 159
Power:
    bureaucratic, 34–5
    legal, 93
    police, 168–9
    political, 81, 82, 91, 190–1
Power stations, 86
Prévoyance (Fayol's concept), 24, 119, 120
Prices and Incomes Board, 87, 165–6
Prime Minister, 85, 108, 114, 163, 167
Prime Minister, French, 26
Principal Establishment Officers, 113, 114
Privy Council, 120, 168
Processes of administration, 128–40
Professionals, *see* Specialists
Promotion, 116–17
Psychology, psychologists, 16, 43, 44–5, 52, 53, 55, 58, 60–1, 71, 117, 191
'Public', definition of, 12
Public Accounts Committee, 95
Public administration, academic status, 15–16
Public corporations, 12, 27, 85, 89, 92–3, 170–5, 176
Public utility services, 54–5, 85–6, 89–90

REGIONAL HOSPITAL BOARDS, 176, 178
Regional offices of central Government, 150, 156
Regulatory functions of public bodies, 84–5, 88, 144–5
Reid Committee Report on Coal Mining 1944, 103
Reith, Lord, 171

Research, 15, 17–18
    by Committees and Commissions, 68, 89, 101
    by Government, 119–21, 159, 166, 185
    Hawthorne, 44
    on hospitals, 177, 179
    social and psychological, 45, 57, 58, 60, 64, 67, 68–9
Restrictive Practices Court, 87, 166
Revans, Dr R. W., 59, 177, 180
Rice, A. K., 73, 74, 188
Robbins, Lord, 124
Robson, Prof. W. A., 9, 170, 171, 172, 173
Rolls-Royce affair, 88
Rome, Romans, 9, 21–2, 37, 190
Roskill Commission, 111
Royal Commissions, see Commissions Royal
Rubner, Alex, 38
Rules and directives, 137–8
Rutherford, Lord, 150

SCIENCE, ADMINISTRATION AND MANAGEMENT AS, 17–18, 28, 193
Scientific and Industrial Research, Department of, 121
Scotland, 82, 176
Scottish Office, 162
Secretaries, Secretarial, function, 85, 102, 124–30
Secretaries of State, 124, 130
Self, Prof. Peter, 71, 102
Sharp, Dame Evelyn (Baroness), 97
Simon, Herbert A., 49–55, 64, 69, 72, 75, 84, 99, 188
Simon, Sir John (Lord), 167
Smithberg, Donald, W., 54–5, 76
Sociology, 16, 42, 44, 48
Sovereignty, 81, 96, 185, 194
Span of control, 33–4, 49
Speaker of House of Commons, 143, 144, 168, 190
Specialists in Government Departments, 157–160
Staff, military, 31–2, 130
Stalker, G. M., 29, 41, 49, 50, 64–6, 68–72, 111, 149, 159, 160, 186, 188
Standardisation, 174
Statutes, see Acts of Parliament
Stewart, Dr James, 179, 180
Stewart, Rosemary, 34
Structures, 141–63
    Health Service, 175–80
    nationalised industries, 173–5
    Police, 167–70
    special types of organisation, 165
Symbolic functions, 90–1

Systems theories, 41, 73–5, 76, 87, 146, 194

TAVISTOCK INSTITUTE, 73
Taxation, 83, 84, 85, 88, 114
Taylor, F. W., 28–30, 44, 46, 56, 193
Technology, effect on organisational studies, 60, 64, 68–9
Theories 'X' and 'Y', 56–7, 65, 66
'Theory', definition of, 14–15
Thompson, Victor A., 54–5, 76
Town clerks, 115, 129
Trade and Industry, Department of, 105
Treasury, 104, 105, 109, 113
Trist, E. L., 73, 74, 77
Tudor regime, 188, 190, 191

Ultra vires, 93
Universities, 12, 22, 70, 71, 114, 171
University education, 154
University Grants Committee, 17
Urwick, Col. L. W., 30–1, 33, 56, 70, 186
USA, see America

VICKERS, SIR GEOFFREY, 17, 69–72, 73, 82, 88, 99, 105, 128, 130, 149, 187–8, 194
Viyella, 87

WALES, 82, 151, 152
Walles, 106
Walsingham, Sir Francis, 120, 129
Walter, Dr Grey, 189
Watt, James, 66
Weber, Max, 35–8, 45, 186, 187, 188, 193
    attitude to bureaucracy, 35–6, 37–8
    legal philosophy, 36–7
    personal background, 35
Welsh Office, 162
Wheare, Sir Kenneth, 107, 108
Whitehead, Alfred North, 42, 43, 47, 48
Whitehead, Thomas North, 42, 47, 48
Whitley Councils, 118
Whyte, William H., 44
Weick, Karl E., 71
William II, Kaiser, 35, 37
Will-power, 93–4, 103
Wilson, Charles H., 162
Wireless Telegraphy Act 1904, 137
Woodward, Prof. Joan, 53–4, 68–9, 75, 128, 174, 182, 186, 188
Works, Ministry of, 160